1

D1321076

Reading Humanitarian Intervention
Human Rights and the Use of Force in International Law

During the 1990s, humanitarian intervention seemed to promise a
world in which democracy, self-determination and human rights
would be privileged over national interests or imperial ambitions.
Orford provides critical readings of the narratives that accompanied
such interventions and shaped legal justifications for the use of force
by the international community. Through a close reading of legal
texts and institutional practice, she argues that a far more
circumscribed, exploitative and conservative interpretation of the
ends of intervention was adopted during this period. The book draws
on a wide range of sources, including critical legal theory, feminist
and postcolonial theory, psychoanalytic theory and critical geography,
to develop ways of reading directed at thinking through the cultural
and economic effects of militarised humanitarianism. The book
concludes by asking what, if anything, has been lost in the move from
the era of humanitarian intervention to an international relations
dominated by wars on terror.

ANNE ORFORD is Associate Professor in the Law School at the
University of Melbourne. She researches and teaches in the areas of
international human rights law, international economic law,
psychoanalysis and law, postcolonial theory and feminist theory.

CAMBRIDGE STUDIES IN INTERNATIONAL AND COMPARATIVE LAW

Established in 1946, this series produces high quality scholarship in the fields of public and private international law and comparative law. Although these are distinct legal subdisciplines, developments since 1946 confirm their interrelation.

Comparative law is increasingly used as a tool in the making of law at national, regional and international levels. Private international law is now often affected by international conventions, and the issues faced by classical conflicts rules are frequently dealt with by substantive harmonisation of law under international auspices. Mixed international arbitrations, especially those involving state economic activity, raise mixed questions of public and private international law, while in many fields (such as the protection of human rights and democratic standards, investment guarantees and international criminal law) international and national systems interact. National constitutional arrangements relating to 'foreign affairs', and to the implementation of international norms, are a focus of attention.

Professor Sir Robert Jennings edited the series from 1981. Following his retirement as General Editor, an editorial board has been created and Cambridge University Press has recommitted itself to the series, affirming its broad scope.

The Board welcomes works of a theoretical or interdisciplinary character, and those focusing on new approaches to international or comparative law or conflicts of law. Studies of particular institutions or problems are equally welcome, as are translations of the best work published in other languages.

General Editors James Crawford SC FBA
Whewell Professor of International Law, Faculty of Law and Director, Lauterpacht Research Centre for International Law, University of Cambridge
John S. Bell FBA
Professor of Law, Faculty of Law, University of Cambridge

Editorial Board Professor Hilary Charlesworth *University of Adelaide*
Professor Lori Damrosch *Columbia University Law School*
Professor John Dugard *Universiteit Leiden*
Professor Mary-Ann Glendon *Harvard Law School*
Professor Christopher Greenwood *London School of Economics*
Professor David Johnston *University of Edinburgh*
Professor Hein Kötz *Max-Planck-Institut, Hamburg*
Professor Donald McRae *University of Ottawa*
Professor Onuma Yasuaki *University of Tokyo*
Professor Reinhard Zimmermann *Universität Regensburg*

Advisory Committee Professor D. W. Bowett QC
Judge Rosalyn Higgins QC
Professor Sir Robert Jennings QC
Professor J. A. Jolowicz QC
Professor Sir Elihu Lauterpacht CBE QC
Professor Kurt Lipstein QC
Judge Stephen Schwebel

A list of books in the series can be found at the end of this volume

Reading Humanitarian Intervention

Human Rights and the Use of Force in International Law

Anne Orford
University of Melbourne

CAMBRIDGE
UNIVERSITY PRESS

CAMBRIDGE UNIVERSITY PRESS
Cambridge, New York, Melbourne, Madrid, Cape Town, Singapore, São Paulo

Cambridge University Press
The Edinburgh Building, Cambridge CB2 2RU, UK

Published in the United States of America by Cambridge University Press, New York

www.cambridge.org
Information on this title: www.cambridge.org/9780521804646

First published 2003
Reprinted 2004

A catalogue record for this publication is available from the British Library

ISBN-13 978-0-521-80464-6 hardback
ISBN-10 0-521-80464-7 hardback

Transferred to digital printing 2005

Contents

Preface

I have been blessed with the support of many family, friends, colleagues and students during the writing of this book. The shape and direction of my thinking about humanitarian intervention owe a great deal to my good fortune in being offered my first academic position at the School of Law and Legal Studies at La Trobe University in 1993. At that time, La Trobe was home to a community of many of the most exciting and creative critical and feminist legal scholars in Australia. My inspiring colleagues, in particular Greta Bird, Sue Davies, Ian Duncanson, Judith Grbich, Adrian Howe, Rob McQueen, Andrea Rhodes-Little and Margaret Thornton, provided me with a constant source of friendship, and taught me the great pleasures and responsibilities of critical scholarship and of engaged and innovative teaching. I was encouraged and stimulated in the later stages of the work on this project by my friends, students and colleagues at the Australian National University and the University of Melbourne, particularly Philip Alston, Jenny Beard, Jennie Clarke, Belinda Fehlberg, Krysti Guest, David Kinley, Ian Malkin, Jenny Morgan, Dianne Otto, Sundhya Pahuja, Jindy Pettman, Martin Phillipson, Kim Rubenstein, Peter Rush, Gerry Simpson and Maureen Tehan. Michael Bryan and Michael Crommelin at the University of Melbourne have been supportive of the project in many ways, and have made it possible for me to combine academic life with the pleasurable demands of caring for young children. My thanks also to Dimity Kingsford-Smith, David Kinley and Stephen Parker for allowing me to spend a research semester finishing the book at the Castan Centre for Human Rights Law, Monash University. My thoughts on the future of human rights and economic globalisation have been profoundly influenced by the experience of teaching and engaging with students at the University of Melbourne, the Australian National University, La Trobe University and the 1998 Academy of European Law at the European University Institute.

The book has also been shaped by ongoing conversations and careful readings that have informed my ideas about law, fantasy, human rights, feminism, economics, internationalism, bodies, the imaginary, militarism, colonialism, masculinity, and much more. My heartfelt thanks to: Judy Grbich for her insightful comments on draft chapters, for always asking the right question and for the example of her scholarship; Andrea Rhodes-Little who has helped me to make many of the connections in this book and to find 'the words to say it'; Ian Duncanson for being such a generous and thoughtful reader; Greta Bird and Adrian Howe, who reminded me at an important moment that it is possible to make meanings of human rights outside those deemed legitimate by the officials of the new world order; Peter Rush for coffee sessions and 'bibliographic digressions'; Karen Knop for her responses to earlier versions of this text and her assurances that one day I would submit the manuscript; Christine Chinkin and David Kennedy, for their helpful comments on an earlier version of this manuscript and their encouragement for the project; Philip Alston for his engagement with my ideas and support for my work over many years; Krysti Guest for her steady focus on the economic and our many Canberra conversations; Jenny Beard for her insightful comments on this text in its varied forms and the journeys we have taken together, and Ian Malkin for his friendship and generosity.

The ideas in this book have been presented at numerous conferences and workshops over the years, but those people involved in two such events in particular shaped my thinking and this text – I am grateful to the organisers and participants at the United Nations University Legitimacy Project Workshop held in Tokyo in 2002, and the Academic Council on the United Nations System/American Society of International Law Workshop on Global Governance held at Brown University, Rhode Island in 1996. My thanks also to Jenny Beard, Megan Donaldson, Simon Ellis, Jyoti Larke and Rowan McCrae for their invaluable research assistance and editorial skills. My commissioning editor at Cambridge, Finola O'Sullivan, has been a patient, steady and much-needed source of encouragement, while the comments of the anonymous referees and of the series editor, James Crawford, have contributed a great deal to clarifying and sharpening the connections and arguments made in these pages.

Parts of this book develop work that I have published elsewhere. Chapters 3 and 5 are substantially revised versions of articles published as 'Locating the International: Military and Monetary Interventions after the Cold War' (1997) 38 *Harvard International Law Journal* 443 and 'Muscular Humanitarianism: Reading the Narratives of the New Interventionism' (1999) 10 *European Journal of International Law* 679. Chapter 2 contains material included in 'Feminism, Imperialism and the Mission of International Law' (2002) *Nordic Journal of International Law* (forthcoming) and in 'Positivism and the Power of International Law' (2000) 24 *Melbourne University Law Review* 502.

I owe an enormous debt to the many people who have helped to care for my children during the period in which this book was written. In particular, my thanks to my parents Rolene and William Orford for all the many forms of support with which they provide me, not least being the intensive hours of baby-sitting they provided at key moments in the emergence of this text. The staff at the Queensberry Children's Centre at the University of Melbourne have made the work on this project possible. The extraordinary warmth, generosity, skill and dedication with which they have cared for my two young children during my working hours have allowed me to feel safe about taking the space and time necessary to complete this book. In particular, I would like to express my deep gratitude to Heidi Artmann, Gayle Babore, Georgina Coy, Amber Dwyer, Halayne Ford, Wendy Grace, Maria Hannah, Harmony Miller, Georgina Mitropoulos, Liz O'Brien, Effie Saganas, Cathy Simpson, Donna Taranto, Nancy Thewma, Averil Tweed, Remziye Urak and Emma Witham.

Finally, two people deserve particular thanks. I am extremely grateful to Hilary Charlesworth for her generous supervision of my doctoral thesis and her guidance and support while turning that thesis into a book. Her enthusiasm for the project from the outset and the gift of her friendship made the experience of writing this manuscript a wonderful and rewarding one. Her detailed and insightful comments on draft chapters were of enormous assistance in shaping my arguments, while the example of her scholarship guided and inspired my approach to writing about international law.

The constant encouragement and support of my dear friend and partner Andrew Robertson have helped make this book possible. My work has benefited enormously from our ongoing conversation about law, politics, life and critique, while his companionship and gentle faith in my ideas and aspirations have made all the difference. The book has been shaped by his close reading and valuable comments on many drafts over the years. The sweet company and small bodies of our beloved sons Hamish and Felix are a daily reminder to me of the wonder and fragility of life, and of all that is risked by careless power and wanton violence. This book, with its dreams of the future of human rights, is for them.

1   Watching East Timor

The era of humanitarian intervention

As I began writing this book during the early days of September 1999, hundreds of thousands of Australians were taking to the streets, marching under banners proclaiming 'Indonesia out, peacekeepers in'. These protesters were calling for the introduction of an international peace-keeping force into East Timor to protect the East Timorese from the Indonesian army-backed militia who were rampaging through Dili and the countryside – killing, wounding, raping and implementing a scorched-earth policy. These acts of destruction and violence were a response to the announcement on 4 September that an overwhelming majority of East Timorese people had voted for independence from Indonesia in a United Nations (UN) sponsored referendum held on 30 August. The Australian Opposition Leader, Kim Beazley, was to call the swell of community protests the strangest and most inspiring event he had witnessed in Australian political life.

The voices of the protestors joined with the chorus pleading for an armed UN intervention in East Timor. Timorese leaders such as Xanana Gusmao and Jose Ramos Horta were calling for such action. Australian international lawyers were speaking on the radio and television, arguing that such intervention could be legally justified – as a measure for restoring international peace and security if authorised by a UN Security Council resolution, or as an act of humanitarian intervention by a 'coalition of the willing' if no such resolution was forthcoming. As Australians watched images of Dili burning on their television screens, and read of women and children seeking protection from likely slaughter in the sanctuary of the UN compound in Dili, it felt like a strange time to be writing a reflexive and theoretical piece about the power effects of the post-Cold War enthusiasm for humanitarian intervention.

This new interventionism, or willingness to use force in the name of humanitarian values, played a major role in shaping international relations during the 1990s. As a result of actions such as that undertaken by NATO in response to the Kosovo crisis, or the authorisation of the use of force in East Timor by the Security Council, issues about the legality and morality of humanitarian intervention again began to dominate the international legal and political agenda. One of the most significant changes in international politics to emerge during that period was the growth of support, within mainstream international law and international relations circles, for the idea that force can legitimately be used as a response to humanitarian challenges such as those facing the people of East Timor. The justifications for these actions are illustrative of the transformation undergone by the narratives that underpin the discipline of international law with the ending of the Cold War.[1] A new kind of international law and internationalist spirit seemed to have been made possible in the changed conditions of a world no longer structured around the old certainties of a struggle between communism and capitalism.

This shift in support for the notion of humanitarian intervention resulted in part from the post-Cold War revitalisation of the Security Council and the corresponding expansion of its role in maintaining international peace and security.[2] Under Article 24 of the UN Charter, the Security Council is the organ of the UN charged with the authority to maintain peace and security. Unlike most other international bodies or organs, the Security Council is invested with coercive power. Under Chapters VI and VII of the UN Charter, the Security Council is granted powers to facilitate the pacific settlement of disputes, and to decide what means should be taken to maintain or restore international peace and security. For many years the coercive powers vested by the UN Charter in the Security Council seemed irrelevant. During the Cold War, the Security Council was effectively paralysed by reciprocal use of the veto exercisable

---

[1] For the argument that international law is subject to serial rewritings and attempts to reinvent the international community, see David Kennedy, 'When Renewal Repeats: Thinking against the Box' (2000) 32 *New York University Journal of International Law and Policy* 335.

[2] The Gulf War was the first sign of what has since been hailed by some as the 'revitalisation' of the Security Council. See Boutros Boutros-Ghali, *An Agenda for Peace* (New York, 1992), pp. 7, 28.

by the five permanent members – China, France, the United Kingdom (UK), the USA and, since December 1991, the Russian Federation (formerly the Soviet Union).[3] From the time of the creation of the UN in 1945 until 31 May 1990, the veto was exercised 279 times in the Security Council, rendering it powerless to deal with many conflicts. The permanent members used that veto power to ensure that no actions that threatened their spheres of interest would be taken. The ending of the Cold War meant an end to the automatic use of the veto power. The changed conditions of the post-Soviet era meant that the Security Council was suddenly capable of exercising great power, in a manner that appeared largely unrestrained.[4]

Although the jurisdiction of the Security Council under Chapter VII is only triggered by the existence of a threat to the peace, a breach of the peace or an act of aggression, the Security Council has, since 1989, proved itself increasingly willing to interpret the phrase 'threats to the peace' broadly.[5] The range and nature of resolutions passed by the Security Council since the Gulf War, relating *inter alia* to the former Yugoslavia, Somalia, Rwanda, Haiti and East Timor, have been interpreted as suggesting that the Council is willing to treat the failure to guarantee democracy or human rights, or to protect against humanitarian abuses, as either a symptom, or a cause, of threats to peace and security.[6] In this climate, some international lawyers began to argue in favour of Security Council action based on the doctrine of 'collective humanitarian intervention'.[7]

---

[3] Article 23 of the Charter of the United Nations (UN Charter), San Francisco, 26 June 1945, in force 24 October 1945, Cmd 7015, provides that the Security Council comprises ten non-permanent members elected for two year terms, and five permanent members.

[4] With the revitalisation of the Security Council came the realisation that there are very few formal or constitutional restrictions on the exercise of its power. This has led some international lawyers to claim that there is a constitutional crisis in the UN, due not only to the inability of the General Assembly, where all member states are represented, to control the Security Council, but also to the relatively powerless position of the International Court of Justice as revealed by the Lockerbie incident. See further José E. Alvarez, 'Judging the Security Council' (1996) 90 *American Journal of International Law* 1; W. Michael Reisman, 'The Constitutional Crisis in the United Nations' (1993) 87 *American Journal of International Law* 83.

[5] Under Article 39 of the UN Charter, where the Security Council determines that there is a threat to the peace, a breach of the peace, or an act of aggression, it may decide what measures shall be taken to maintain or restore international peace and security, including the use of force or of economic sanctions.

[6] See further Chapters 3 and 4 below.

[7] For the argument that a doctrine of 'collective humanitarian intervention' had emerged in the aftermath of operations authorised by the Security Council in Iraq,

For these commentators, military intervention has achieved a new respectability and has come to represent, amongst other things, a means for the liberal alliance of democratic states to bring human rights, democracy and humanitarian principles to those in undemocratic, authoritarian or failed states. Such liberal internationalists argue that collective humanitarian intervention has become necessary to address the problems of local dictators, tribalism, ethnic tension and religious fundamentalism thrown up in the post-Cold War era. While the Gulf War was generally justified in traditional collective security terms, as a measure that was necessary to restore security to the region and to punish aggression, later actions in Bosnia, Somalia, Rwanda, Haiti and East Timor have been supported by a very different interpretation of the legitimate role of the Security Council. There is now a significant and influential literature arguing that, in light of the post-Cold War practice of the Security Council, norms governing intervention should be, or have been, altered to allow collective humanitarian intervention, or intervention by the Security Council to uphold democracy and human rights.

The enthusiastic embrace of multilateral intervention has extended in some quarters to support for military action undertaken by regional organisations without Security Council authorisation, most notably in the case of NATO action over Kosovo during 1999.[8] Arguments in favour of NATO intervention in Kosovo represent a new phase in the progression of international legal arguments in favour of humanitarian intervention. In the case of Kosovo, international lawyers argue that there are situations in which the international community is justified in undertaking military intervention even where such action is not authorised by the Security Council and is thus (arguably) outside the law.[9] According to this argument, a commitment to justice required the

Somalia, Haiti, Rwanda and Bosnia, see Fernando R. Tesón, 'Collective Humanitarian Intervention' (1996) 17 *Michigan Journal of International Law* 323.

[8] See also the discussion of humanitarian intervention as a possible basis for the regional intervention undertaken by the Economic Community of West African States (ECOWAS) in Sierra Leone, in Karsten Nowrot and Emily W. Schabacker, 'The Use of Force to Restore Democracy: International Legal Implications of the ECOWAS Intervention in Sierra Leone' (1998) 14 *American University International Law Review* 321.

[9] It should be noted that not all NATO members have agreed that a doctrine of humanitarian intervention formed the legal basis for the military action undertaken in Kosovo. According to Michael J. Matheson, then Acting Legal Adviser to the US State Department, many NATO states, including the USA, had not accepted the doctrine of humanitarian intervention as an independent legal basis for military action at the time of the intervention in Kosovo. As a result, NATO decided that the legal justification for action in Kosovo was based on 'the unique combination of a number

international community to support the NATO intervention in Kosovo, despite its illegality.[10] While earlier literature about international intervention saw the Security Council as the guarantor of humanitarian values, literature about the Kosovo intervention has begun to locate those values in a more amorphous 'international community'. Legal literature discussing the legitimacy of the actions undertaken by NATO appears to indicate a loss of faith in international law as a repository of the values that should underpin the actions of international organisations. Yet while the bases upon which commentators justify international intervention have shifted since the days when a 'revitalised' Security Council was hailed as the guarantor of a new world order, the arguments made by international lawyers supporting intervention share a certainty about the moral, ethical, political and humanitarian imperatives justifying military action.

Those critical or anxious about expanding the legal bases for military action have also shifted ground in the years since the Gulf War. Many legal scholars working in the areas of human rights and international humanitarian law were highly critical of the actions undertaken in the Gulf. Criticisms ranged from analyses of the merely rhetorical nature of the Security Council's commitment to human rights, to criticism of the effects of the bombing and sanctions on the Iraqi people, to concern about the apparent domination of the revitalised Council by the United

---

of factors, without enunciating a new doctrine or theory. These particular factors included: the failure of the Former Republic of Yugoslavia to comply with Security Council demands under Chapter VII; the danger of a humanitarian disaster in Kosovo; the inability of the Council to make a clear decision adequate to deal with that disaster; and the serious threat to peace and security in the region posed by Serb actions.' Michael J. Matheson, 'Justification for the NATO Air Campaign in Kosovo' (2000) 94 *American Society of International Law Proceedings* 301. While the Security Council did not authorise the NATO action in Kosovo, the Security Council subsequently defeated a Russian resolution condemning the air campaign by a vote of twelve to three on 26 March 1999, and later authorised member states and international organisations to establish a security presence in Kosovo under UN auspices with Security Council Resolution 1244, S/RES/1244 (1999), adopted on 10 June 1999.

[10] For arguments that the use of armed force employed by NATO in the Kosovo crisis was illegal due to the lack of Security Council authorisation, but that the intervention is nonetheless legitimate, see Bruno Simma, 'NATO, the UN and the Use of Force: Legal Aspects' (1999) 10 *European Journal of International Law* 1; Michael J. Glennon, 'The New Interventionism: the Search for a Just International Law' (1999) 78 *Foreign Affairs* 2. For the argument that the NATO action is illegal although justified from an ethical viewpoint, see Antonio Cassese, 'Ex Iniuria Ius Oritur: Are We Moving towards International Legitimation of Forcible Humanitarian Countermeasures in the World Community?' (1999) 10 *European Journal of International Law* 23.

States.[11] The response to later interventions, however, has been more ambivalent. There are certainly some legal commentators who have continued to express concern about the apparent willingness of a largely unrestrained Security Council to expand its mandate to include authorising the use of force to remedy human rights abuses or 'to make every State a democratic one'.[12] Many legal scholars, however, seem haunted by the fear that opposing military intervention in Bosnia, Haiti, Kosovo or East Timor means opposing the only realistic possibility of international engagement to end the horrific human suffering witnessed in such conflicts. The need to halt the horrors of genocide or to address the effects of civil war and internal armed conflict on civilians has been accepted as sufficient justification for intervention, even if other motives may be involved.

Perhaps the most interesting place in the debate about the legality of humanitarian intervention is occupied by the new human rights warriors. In the popular scholarship of human rights lawyer Geoffrey Robertson, for example, humanitarian intervention demonstrates the possibility, too often deferred, of an international rule of law.[13] Robertson suggests that the world is entering a 'third age of human rights', that of human rights enforcement.[14] His vision of this age of enforcement is a potent blend of faith in the power of media images of suffering to mobilise public sentiment or the 'indignant pity of the civilised world', and belief in the emergence of an international criminal justice system. According to Robertson, in future the basis of human rights enforcement will be a combination of judicial remedies such as ad hoc tribunals, domestic prosecutions for crimes against humanity

---

[11] Philip Alston, 'The Security Council and Human Rights: Lessons to Be Learned from the Iraq–Kuwait Crisis and its Aftermath' (1992) 13 *Australian Year Book of International Law* 107; René Provost, 'Starvation as a Weapon: Legal Implications of the United Nations Food Blockade Against Iraq and Kuwait' (1992) 30 *Columbia Journal of Transnational Law* 577; Henry J. Richardson III, 'The Gulf Crisis and African-American Interests under International Law' (1993) 87 *American Journal of International Law* 42; Oscar Schachter, 'United Nations Law in the Gulf Conflict' (1991) 85 *American Journal of International Law* 452; David D. Caron, 'Iraq and the Force of Law: Why Give a Shield of Immunity?' (1991) 85 *American Journal of International Law* 89; Judith Gail Gardam, 'Proportionality and Force in International Law' (1993) 87 *American Journal of International Law* 391; Middle East Watch, *Needless Deaths in the Gulf War: Civilian Casualties during the Air Campaign and Violations of the Laws of War* (1991).

[12] Martti Koskenniemi, 'The Police in the Temple. Order, Justice and the United Nations: a Dialectical View' (1995) 6 *European Journal of International Law* 325 at 343.

[13] Geoffrey Robertson, *Crimes against Humanity: The Struggle for Global Justice* (Ringwood, 1999).

[14] *Ibid.*, p. 450.

and an international criminal court. An important part of that system will be the willingness of states to use armed force to create this new world of enforceable human rights. Such force should ideally be authorised by the Security Council, according to the dictates of the UN Charter, but where Security Council approval is not politically feasible, international intervention should nonetheless go ahead, carried out by regional organisations or even a democratic 'coalition of the willing'.[15] As he concludes, 'there is as yet no court to stop a state which murders and extirpates its own people: for them, if the Security Council fails to reach superpower agreement, the only salvation can come through other states exercising the right of humanitarian intervention'.[16]

The muscular nature of this new breed of humanitarianism is illustrated well by the terms in which Robertson welcomes the shift in human rights activism away from a reliance on strategies of persuasion or shaming, towards enforcement through more direct forms of international intervention:

The most significant change in the human rights movement as it goes into the twenty-first century is that it will go on the offensive. The past has been a matter of pleading with tyrants, writing letters and sending missions to *beg* them not to act cruelly. That will not be necessary if there is a possibility that they can be deterred, by threats of humanitarian or UN intervention or with nemesis in the form of the International Criminal Court. Human rights discourse will in the future be less pious and less 'politically correct'. We will call a savage a savage, whether or not he or she is black.[17]

Thus Robertson has no doubt that the new right of humanitarian intervention, represented by NATO's action in Kosovo and the multilateral intervention in East Timor, is to be welcomed because it allows for more effective enforcement of human rights. The human rights movement will no longer be reduced to humiliating acts of begging and pleading with tyrants. Lawyers can now take a more active and forceful role in promoting and protecting human rights globally, offering salvation to those threatened by state-sponsored murder and genocide.

For Robertson, the test of whether such intervention is justified should not be whether it is lawful, or authorised by the Security Council, but rather 'the dimension of the evil' to be addressed by the intervention.[18] The extent of this evil can partly be ascertained through global media, where 'television pictures of corpses in Racak, Kosovo, put such obscure

---

[15] *Ibid.*, pp. 446–7.   [16] *Ibid.*, p. 420.   [17] *Ibid.*, p. 453.   [18] *Ibid.*, p. 444.

places on the map of everyone's mind and galvanize the West to war'.[19] Today's human rights activists are motivated by 'revulsion against atrocities brought into their homes through a billion television sets and twice as many radios', leading them to exert pressure on democratic governments to impel international and UN responses – 'modern media coverage of human rights blackspots is rekindling the potent mix of anger and compassion which produced the Universal Declaration and now produces a democratic demand not merely for something to be done, but for the laws and courts and prosecutors to do it'.[20]

This new support for humanitarian intervention is also evident in the work of NGOs such as Human Rights Watch.[21] In its *World Report 2000*, Human Rights Watch treats the deployment of multinational troops in East Timor and the NATO bombing campaign in Kosovo as examples of a new willingness on behalf of the international community to deploy troops to stop crimes against humanity or to halt genocide or 'massive slaughter'.[22] Like Robertson, Human Rights Watch welcomes these developments as marking 'a new era for the human rights movement', one in which human rights organisations can 'count on governments to use their police powers to enforce human rights law'.[23] It sees the 'growing willingness to transcend sovereignty in the face of crimes against humanity' as a positive development, one which promises that 'victims of atrocities' will receive 'effective assistance wherever they cry out for help'.[24] Any problems of selectivity or dangers that humanitarian intervention 'might become a pretext for military adventures in pursuit of ulterior motives' can be met by ensuring that criteria are developed for when such intervention should occur, and by ensuring that no regions are 'neglected' when it comes to the willingness to use force.[25]

The conviction about the need for intervention expressed in post-Cold War legal and human rights literature mirrored the arguments made by European, US and Australian political leaders justifying international intervention during the 1990s. To give one example, British Prime Minister Tony Blair portrayed the NATO intervention in Kosovo as a 'just war,

---

[19] *Ibid.*, p. 438.   [20] *Ibid.*

[21] To some extent these human rights activists and lawyers are now more in favour of using force in such situations than are many military leaders. For a discussion of historical precedents to their arguments in the work of de Vitoria and other early international lawyers, see Chapter 6 below.

[22] Human Rights Watch, *World Report 2000*, p. 1.

[23] *Ibid.*   [24] *Ibid.*, p. 5.   [25] *Ibid.*, pp. 1, 4–5.

based not on territorial ambitions, but on values'.[26] According to Blair, British foreign policy decisions in the post-Cold War era 'are guided by a...subtle blend of mutual self-interest and moral purpose in defending the values we cherish...If we can establish and spread the values of liberty, the rule of law, human rights and an open society, then that is in our national interest.'[27] The war in Kosovo was fought precisely to defend such values:

This war was not fought for Albanians against Serbs. It was not fought for territory. Still less for NATO aggrandisement. It was fought for a fundamental principle necessary for humanity's progress: that every human being, regardless of race, religion or birth, has the inalienable right to live free from persecution.[28]

This was the broad climate within which the argument for humanitarian intervention in the case of East Timor was made. My immediate response to these calls for intervention was that here was a case where the willingness to kill people in the name of the international community might be ethical. I was moved by the sense that urgent action was the only way to prevent a genocide. This fear was evident in many calls for military intervention. A student asked to address one of my classes, and announced that 'as we speak, people are being slaughtered in the streets of Dili. Timorese people in Australia are hysterical. Come and rally at Parliament House and demand intervention now.' A newspaper headline on the same day read 'Plea for peacekeepers as terror grips Timor'.[29] The story the news article told was that violent pro-Jakarta militia were rampaging through Dili in response to the UN's announcement on 5 September that the overwhelming majority of East Timorese had voted for independence in the UN-sponsored referendum. More than one hundred people had already been killed or wounded, and many including injured children were seeking sanctuary at the UN headquarters. An email message sent by the NGO network Focus on the Global South on 8 September was headed 'Act now for East Timor.' The message asked

---

[26] Tony Blair, 'Doctrine of the International Community', Speech given to the Economic Club of Chicago, Chicago, 22 April 1999, http://www.fco.gov.uk/news/speechtext.asp?2316 (accessed 2 May 2001).

[27] Ibid.

[28] Tony Blair, 'Statement on the Suspension of NATO Air Strikes against Yugoslavia', London, 10 June 1999, http://www.fco.gov.uk/news/newstext.asp?2536 (accessed 2 May 2001). In future, however, given the lack of support for humanitarian intervention expressed by members of the new Bush administration, it may be that human rights lawyers and activists will prove to be more enthusiastic supporters of the use of armed force to remedy human rights violations than are political and military leaders.

[29] The Age, 6 September 1999, p. 1.

me to sign on to a statement to be sent to the UN, ASEAN, the Government of Indonesia and Asia-Pacific Economic Cooperation (APEC) heads of state. The statement began with the words:

The world failed East Timor once, in 1975, when it offered little protest to the bloody annexation of that country by Indonesia. Key international actors, including Australia, the United States, and ASEAN, either supported the takeover behind the scenes or tacitly approved of it...The world cannot afford to fail the people of East Timor again. As Indonesian troops and Indonesia-supported militiamen wreak mayhem on the people after the historic vote for independence last week, it is imperative that we act to prevent an act of ethnic cleansing on the scale of Bosnia and Kosovo.

As I walked down to feed my son at the university childcare centre that afternoon, I was handed a leaflet advertising a rally. The leaflet stated that 'the next few days will be critical in saving the lives of thousands of East Timorese' and urged that I 'demand an international peace-keeping force'. My desire for intervention was made more urgent by the repeated representation of the Timorese as defenceless, powerless, 'hysterical' and unprotected, and by the focus on threats to babies, women and children. As one eyewitness cried on the radio, 'The East Timorese are being slaughtered. There's no-one there to protect them.'[30] Hearing these reports left me feeling as unbearably and frustratingly powerless and helpless as the East Timorese. At the same time, if Australians and the international community were willing to use military force in response to this slaughter and devastation, we could be potential saviours of the East Timorese, agents of democracy and human rights able to overpower those bent on killing and destruction. It was up to us to offer protection to the people of East Timor.

Yet despite my growing sense that in this case intervention was necessary, I also had some doubts about my response. I had spent the last few years writing and thinking about how the desire for military intervention is produced. I had been interested in exploring the effects of the ways in which internationalists spoke and wrote about collective security and international intervention in the post-Cold War era. Two features of the knowledge practices of international lawyers had interested me. First, I had been concerned to think about the claim that a right or duty of humanitarian intervention was somehow revolutionary, fulfilling the promise of a world based on respect for human rights rather than merely respect for state interests. My sense was that the

[30] Radio National, 8 September 1999.

way in which international law was narrated in fact served to confine any revolutionary potential inherent in human rights discourse, such that the right of intervention in the name of human rights became profoundly conservative in its meaning and effects. Any potentially revolutionary interpretations of humanitarian intervention as heralding a commitment to human rights over state interests had been constrained by the meanings that were made of international intervention in legal texts. I felt that in quite complicated ways, these legal intervention narratives served to preserve an unjust and exploitative status quo.[31]

Second, the way in which humanitarian intervention was narrated had other less obviously 'international' effects.[32] For example, the way in which international law portrayed the need to intervene in order to protect and look after the people of 'failed states', and the forms of dependence set up in post-conflict 'peace-building' situations, seemed to rehearse colonial fantasies about the need for benevolent tutelage of uncivilised people who were as yet unable to govern themselves. The focus in international law's intervention narratives on the ways in which violence could be used by good and righteous men to achieve the best for those against whom that violence was directed seemed to me to reinforce many of the stories of masculinity against which feminists had been writing for decades. So, intervention narratives had a domestic or personal effect, despite their overtly international focus. These representations of international intervention help to shape the identities and world-view of all those who engage with them. Intervention stories work 'by calling an audience into the story'.[33] Their appeal is premised upon learned assumptions about value based on old stereotypes of gender, race and class – assumptions that inform the way those who live inside such stories experience the world.

In the work that I published over that period, I had argued that the enthusiasm for the new interventionism of the post-Cold War period was dangerous. The image of military action being conducted by the 'international community' in the name of peace, security, human rights and democracy had meant that many inhabitants of industrialised states were increasingly willing to support militaristic solutions to

---

[31] Anne Orford, 'Locating the International: Military and Monetary Interventions after the Cold War' (1997) 38 *Harvard International Law Journal* 443. See further the arguments developed in Chapters 3 to 6 below.

[32] See generally Anne Orford, 'Muscular Humanitarianism: Reading the Narratives of the New Interventionism' (1999) 10 *European Journal of International Law* 679.

[33] Donna J. Haraway, *Modest_Witness@Second_Millenium* (New York, 1997), p. 169.

international conflicts. The choice of high-violence options which continued to threaten the security of many people was now once again marketable to citizens of the USA and other democracies, in ways rendered unimaginable in the immediate aftermath of the Vietnam War. As Cynthia Enloe has noted, the construction of the US military as a global police force in the post-Cold War period has meant that it is now 'more thoroughly integrated into the social structure than it has been in the last two centuries'.[34] The increasing militarisation of the cultures and economies of industrialised states was also a matter of concern for those living within those states, particularly those who suffer when there are cutbacks to civilian spending in order to fund increased spending on the defence budget.[35] There was evidence that violence against women increases in militarised cultures generally, and in military families in particular.[36]

Experience had shown that armed intervention had not necessarily been humanitarian in effect. Those active in humanitarian organisations had argued that armed intervention, particularly aerial bombardment, often impeded humanitarian relief and was indiscriminate in its targets, generally proving counterproductive to the tasks of democratisation and peace-building.[37] The disproportionate targeting of essential infrastructure and deaths of civilians through such air campaigns had itself been questioned as a breach of international humanitarian law.[38] In addition, the introduction of large numbers of militarised men as

---

[34] Cynthia Enloe, *The Morning after: Sexual Politics at the End of the Cold War* (Berkeley, 1993), p. 184.

[35] J. Ann Tickner argues that 'when military spending is high and social welfare programs are cut back, women, who are disproportionately clustered at the bottom of the socioeconomic scale, are usually the first to suffer. Women also assume most of the unremunerated caregiving activities that states relinquish when budgets are tight.' J. Ann Tickner, 'Inadequate Providers? A Gendered Analysis of States and Security' in Joseph A. Camilleri, Anthony P. Jarvis and Albert J. Paolini (eds.), *The State in Transition: Reimagining Political Space* (Boulder, 1995), pp. 125–37 at p. 130.

[36] *Ibid.*

[37] For a report of criticisms of NATO actions by aid workers in Northern Albania, see Jonathon Steele, 'Aid Workers Protest at Nato's Role', *Guardian Weekly*, 6 June 1999, p. 23. See also the arguments canvassed in Thomas Weiss, 'On the Brink of a New Era? Humanitarian Interventions, 1991–94' in D. C. F. Daniel and B. C. Hayes (eds.), *Beyond Traditional Peacekeeping* (New York, 1995), pp. 3–19 at p. 8.

[38] Amnesty International, *'Collateral Damage' or Unlawful Killings? Violations of the Laws of War by NATO during Operation Allied Force* (2000); Human Rights Watch, *Civilian Deaths in the NATO Air Campaign* (2000); Judith Gail Gardam, 'Proportionality and Force in International Law' (1993) 87 *American Journal of International Law* 391; Middle East Watch, *Needless Deaths in the Gulf War: Civilian Casualties during the Air Campaign and Violations of the Laws of War* (New York, 1991).

peace-keepers had repeatedly led to increased exploitation, rape, prostitution and abuse of women and children.[39]

The new enthusiasm for military intervention as a weapon of human rights enforcement also had systemic effects. The resort to *ad hoc* interventionist responses to human rights crises by major powers allowed them to avoid funding, supporting and strengthening the existing multilateral mechanisms for promoting and protecting human rights.[40] The use of force as a response to security and humanitarian crises continued to mean that insufficient attention was paid to the extent to which the policies of international institutions themselves contribute to creating the conditions that lead to such crises.[41] For example, the representation of the interventions in Bosnia and Kosovo as the actions of an international community interested in protecting human rights and humanitarian values served to obscure the extent to which the international community had itself contributed to the humanitarian crises that had emerged in those places.[42] While ancient hatreds and ethnic tensions continue to be represented as the cause of the violence that erupted in the former Yugoslavia, critics have suggested that the crisis was equally a product of modern capitalist international relations.[43] In the former Yugoslavia as elsewhere, the project of economic restructuring and liberalisation which remains central to the new world order contributed to creating the conditions in which such hatreds were inflamed.[44] For these and other reasons, I had argued that the desire to use violence and to take 'action' by sending armed forces to create security had to be interrogated. As Edward Said has shown, the belief that 'certain territories and people *require* and beseech domination' was at the heart of making colonialism palatable.[45] Given that it was so difficult for people

---

[39] Anne Orford, 'The Politics of Collective Security' (1996) 17 *Michigan Journal of International Law* 373–411

[40] Alston, 'The Security Council'.

[41] See the arguments made in Orford, 'Locating the International', and see further Chapter 3 below.

[42] *Ibid.*; Susan L. Woodward, *Balkan Tragedy: Chaos and Dissolution after the Cold War* (Washington, 1995).

[43] Peter Gowan, 'The NATO Powers and the Balkan Tragedy' (1999) 234 *New Left Review* 83.

[44] Woodward, *Balkan Tragedy*; Orford, 'Locating the International' (arguing that the economic policies that were designed to refinance and repay Yugoslavia's foreign debt played a role in the rise of republican nationalism and the sense that the federal government lacked legitimacy. Nationalist leaders, including Slobodan Milosevic, came to power as the IMF's 'shock therapy' stablisation programme radically altered the nature of Yugoslav constitutional and political arrangements, causing significant and unstable new alliances in the region).

[45] Edward W. Said, *Culture and Imperialism* (London, 1993), p. 9 (emphasis in original).

to stand back from the culture that produced and legitimised imperialism, it seemed necessary to be cautious about any arguments that made the use of force appear benevolent to us today.

Action and inaction

In light of these concerns, I began to attempt to think through the conditions that were producing my desire for intervention and such a uniform plea for peace-keepers in the case of East Timor. To begin with, I was moved by the idea that there was a need to take action immediately, to *do something* to support victimised people, especially children. The East Timorese had done no more than express their wish to be free from oppression, brutality and exploitation at the hands of Indonesian invaders. The only way to take action to end that violence seemed to be to produce a stronger, disabling force – to persuade the men and women whose profession it is to kill in the name of my country to take action. I felt anger on behalf of the innocent people caught up in these power plays, particularly the babies and children targeted by rampant, ruthless militias, and the mothers of those children who seemed powerless to protect them. I had seen the posturing machismo of the militia leaders in newspaper photographs, and it seemed appalling that they could simply assert their dominance through aggression, violence and the ownership of weapons that they were willing to use. I was also moved by the image evoked by the student addressing my class, conjuring up a picture of 'hysterical' Timorese people in Australia. The language painted a picture of people who were crazed by despair, confusion and disbelief at what was happening in their homeland. Inaction seemed impossible to contemplate in such a situation.

Some weeks later at dinner with friends, the subject of East Timor again came up. One of our group had marched against Australian involvement in Vietnam in the 1960s, yet she had also marched in support of UN intervention in East Timor. Despite those things that worried me about what intervention can and has stood for, she argued that those people who had taken to the streets throughout Australia were not (necessarily) lining up in support of the US or Australian militaries, or any of the other conservative messages that might later be taken from the support for intervention. Rather, they were lining up in solidarity with the East Timorese people. She asked me – 'What alternative can you offer at that moment when the choice is either intervention or genocide?' Surely, she implied, law must be able to respond at that moment of crisis?

Her question is a compelling one. It raises a central theme underlying the debate about the legitimacy of humanitarian intervention – the idea that the choice facing the international community in security or humanitarian crises is one between action and inaction. In the case of East Timor, the story by which I was moved to advocate intervention was one in which slaughter, genocide and massive human rights abuses had to be met by action, specifically in the form of military intervention. Both those arguing for and those against the legitimacy of humanitarian intervention accept that the international community is faced with a choice as to whether or not to take action in states where conflicts arise. The argument made by those who support humanitarian intervention is based upon an assumption that post-Cold War crises are in part attributable to an absence of law, including international law, and a lack of sustained engagement by international organisations. Accordingly, a commitment to humanitarian ideals is seen to demand action from the international community, in the form of intervention. Thomas Weiss, for example, argues that, while humanitarian intervention may be counterproductive to the tasks of democratisation and peace-building, ruling out the option of such action will render the UN powerless to act, destroy its credibility and condemn it to the fate of the League of Nations.[46] Weiss presents a stark choice:

Too many pleas for consistency or against inevitable selectivity amount to arguing that the United Nations should not intervene anywhere unless it can intervene everywhere...But in light of genocide, misery, and massive human rights abuses in war zones around the world, should Pontius Pilate be the model for both the American and the international response? The fatalism and isolationism that flow from most objections to humanitarian intervention are as distressing as the situation in the countries suffering from ethnic conflict where such an action is required...A purely noninterventionist position amounts to abstention from the foreign policy debate.[47]

Similarly, Fernando Tesón argues that it is better for states to take collective action to intervene in favour of the rights and interests of human beings, even if such action may do some harm, rather than to remain inactive and, as a result, incapable of providing either relief from brutality or assistance in the achievement of democratic government.[48]

It is...surprising to be told that the very crimes that prompted the massive, cruel and costly struggle from which the United Nations was born, are now immune from action by the organ entrusted to preserving the fruits of the

[46] Weiss, 'On the Brink', p. 8.   [47] Ibid., pp. 8, 15.
[48] Tesón, 'Collective Humanitarian Intervention', 342.

hard-won peace. The formalism of anti-interventionists thus not only rewards tyrants, but it betrays the purposes of the very international order that they claim to protect.[49]

Even those who reject the legitimacy of collective humanitarian intervention appear haunted by the fear that failure to act under the auspices of the Security Council may represent a betrayal of our duty to be engaged in the world in the interests of humanity. Richard Falk's critical analysis of the precedent set by Security Council resolutions concerning Haiti provides a good illustration of that concern.[50] While Falk mounts a strong case against Security Council action in Haiti, he admits to a fear that advocating non-intervention may equal advocating inaction. 'Having mounted this case against intervention, a haunting question must be posed: with all of its deficiencies, isn't it better to have confronted and deposed Cedras, to have provided relief to the Haitian people from the widespread daily brutality and to have given them an opportunity to compose a more democratic government that addresses the poverty of the people?'[51]

For many commentators, Rwanda stands as the clearest example of the terrible consequences that result if the international community does not take action to prevent crimes against humanity, human rights abuses and acts of genocide.[52] As the UN Secretary-General Kofi Annan states in his 1999 annual report to the opening meeting of the General Assembly, 'the genocide in Rwanda will define for our generation the consequences of inaction in the face of mass murder'.[53] The message that he takes away from the failure to intervene militarily in Rwanda sums

---

[49] *Ibid.*

[50] Richard Falk, 'The Haiti Intervention: a Dangerous World Order Precedent for the United Nations' (1995) 36 *Harvard International Law Journal* 341. See also Security Council Resolution 940, S/RES/940 (1994), adopted on 31 July 1994 (authorising member states to impose economic sanctions and use force to 'facilitate the departure from Haiti of the military leadership' and to return it to democratic rule under President Jean-Bertrand Aristide).

[51] Falk, 'The Haiti Intervention', 357.

[52] For analyses that unsettle the assumption that it was the international community's inactivity in Rwanda that should be criticised for enabling the genocide, rather than the impact of its *activities* prior to the genocide, see Peter Uvin, *Aiding Violence: the Development Enterprise in Rwanda* (Connecticut, 1998); Michel Chossudovsky, *The Globalisation of Poverty: Impacts of IMF and World Bank Reforms* (Penang, 1997), pp. 112–22. Both focus on the role of the development enterprise overseen by international economic institutions and international non-governmental organisations in contributing to the dynamics that fuelled the Rwandan genocide.

[53] UN, *Secretary-General Presents His Annual Report to General Assembly*, UN Press Release SG/SM/7136 GA/9596, 20 September 1999.

up well the choice that many commentators see facing the international community:

To those for whom the greatest threat to the future of international order is the use of force in the absence of a Security Council mandate, one might ask – not in the context of Kosovo – but in the context of Rwanda: If, in those dark days and hours leading up to the genocide, a coalition of States had been prepared to act in defence of the Tutzi population, but did not receive prompt Council authorization, should such a coalition have stood aside and allowed the horror to unfold?[54]

Similarly, Geoffrey Robertson treats Rwanda as representing the failure of the international community to take decisive and forceful action to prevent human rights abuses. Although he is committed to the notion of an international rule of law, Robertson echoes the notion that the law must not be hijacked by the approach of legal formalists immersed in technicalities and rules, but must be open to interpretation in the light of the demands of morality and the principles of justice.

If only, say, Kenya, Uganda and South Africa had invaded Rwanda in April 1994 to stop the genocide after the Security Council action had been vetoed by Britain and the US (as it undoubtedly would have been), who would now complain about its illegality?[55]

Despite the power of this argument, the assumption that the international community faces a choice between military intervention and inaction limits the capacity of international law to develop adequate responses to post-Cold War security and humanitarian crises. In Chapter 3, I suggest a way forward for the debate that may enable international lawyers to move beyond the perceived opposition between action and inaction. To do so, I examine the ways in which international law and international institutions have been present and active in places such as the former Yugoslavia, Rwanda and East Timor prior to, and during, the humanitarian crises that arose there. The international community had already intervened on a large scale in each of the above cases before the security crisis erupted, particularly through the activities of international economic institutions. Inactivity, in other words, is not the alternative to intervention. The international community is already profoundly engaged in shaping the structure of political, social, economic and cultural life in many states through the activities of, *inter alia*, international economic institutions. Indeed, intervention in the name of

---

[54] *Ibid.*   [55] Robertson, *Crimes*, p. 408.

humanitarianism too readily provides an alibi for the continued involvement of those interested in exploiting and controlling the resources and people of target states. The 'myopia' of international lawyers about the effects of the new interventionism means that, in general, international legal debate fails to address the ways in which the destructive consequences of coercive economic restructuring contributes to instability, leading to further violence and denials of human rights.[56]

The question my friend asked about the choices available when international law is confronted with genocide or mass human rights violations, like the discourse of humanitarian intervention more generally, adopts a particular temporal focus. International law is structured around a concern with serial security and humanitarian crises. The focus is always on the moment when military intervention is the only remaining credible foreign policy option. The question that is produced by law's focus on the moment of crisis is always 'What would you suggest we do if we are in that situation again?' The assertion that this is the only moment which can be considered renders it impossible to analyse any other involvement of the international community or to think reflexively about law's role in producing the meaning of intervention. At the moment of crisis, the demands on law are so immediate and important that they replace everything else in the field of analysis – it is the duty of lawyers only ever to focus on specific crises and 'facts' rather than studying the narrating of legal texts or law as fiction. This book attempts to resist that conservative pull of law's temporal focus.

Law and empire

Some of the appeal of the idea of humanitarian intervention lies in the moral authority of the notion of democracy. One of the promises made by those who speak on behalf of the international community is that intervention can bring people the opportunity to be governed democratically. For example, while still US Ambassador to the UN, Madeleine Albright argued that 'UN peacekeeping contributes to a world that is less violent, more stable, and more democratic than it would otherwise be.'[57] She uses as an example the intervention in Haiti, suggesting that

[56] On the myopia of international lawyers in the face of globalisation and its effects, see Philip Alston, 'The Myopia of the Handmaidens: International Lawyers and Globalization' (1997) 8 *European Journal of International Law* 435.

[57] Ambassador Madeleine K. Albright, 'International Law Approaches the Twenty-First Century: a US Perspective on Enforcement' (1995) 18 *Fordham International Law Journal* 1595 at 1599.

it led to 'the effort to place the law on the side of the people of Haiti for perhaps the first time in that nation's history'.[58] Similarly, Geoffrey Robertson sees the UN intervention in East Timor as a case where the international community acted to protect the right of people to determine their own governance. Robertson argues that the UN 'got lucky' in its 'last humanitarian operation of the century'.[59] He believes that the future of East Timor 'is clear and optimistic: nation-building begins apace for a people the protection of whose post-plebiscite right to self-determination was the acknowledged reason for the intervention'.[60]

In the human rights terms adopted by Robertson, the international community attempts to ensure through humanitarian intervention the creation of conditions for the exercise of the right to self-determination.[61] According to the UN Charter, self-determination of peoples is a principle to be respected as a basis for the development of peaceful and friendly relations among nations.[62] Self-determination was raised to the status of a right of peoples in the common Articles 1 of the two major human rights covenants, which provided that all peoples have the right freely to determine their political status and freely pursue their economic, social and cultural development.[63] The idea that states were committed to respecting, protecting and promoting self-determination was a central component of the promise that the creation of the UN would usher in an age of decolonisation. In the post-Cold War era, some international lawyers came to argue international law guaranteed peoples not only the right to choose a form of political, economic and social organisation, but also the right to democratic governance as the ideal form of political organisation.[64] The concept that under international law all peoples have a right to self-determination reflects most perfectly law's self-image as a guarantor of peace, human rights and democracy.

Yet the tensions that beset the attempt to guarantee the right to self-determination or to democratic governance through the use of force

---

[58] *Ibid.*, 1603.   [59] Robertson, *Crimes*, p. 425.   [60] *Ibid.*, p. 434.

[61] For an analysis that treats military intervention as a means of achieving self-determination, see Morton H. Halperin and David J. Scheffer with Patricia L. Small, *Self-Determination in the New World Order* (Washington, 1992).

[62] Articles 1(2) and 55, UN Charter.

[63] Article 1, International Covenant on Civil and Political Rights, New York, 19 December 1966, in force 23 March 1974, 999 UNTS 171; Article 1, International Covenant on Economic, Social and Cultural Rights, New York, 19 December 1966, in force 3 January 1976, 993 UNTS 3.

[64] See particularly Thomas Franck, 'The Emerging Right to Democratic Governance' (1992) 86 *American Journal of International Law* 46.

reveal the limitations of those modernist legal claims. In his Grotius lecture on law and empire, Nathaniel Berman argues that there is a reformist tradition of international legal scholarship which treats law as a solution to the problem of imperialism.[65] International lawyers narrate the story of the rise of the state in Western Europe as a triumph of reason, order and sovereign equality over tribalism, religion and hierarchical relations.[66] The moment that figures the final break between law and empire, or between a society grounded on imperial legitimacy and one grounded on mutual recognition between European sovereigns, is the Peace of Westphalia of 1648. Much later, the modern law of decolonisation implemented under the UN Charter would be treated as extending this notion of sovereign equality in what is portrayed as a clean break between law and old-fashioned colonialism. Berman argues, however, that the 'claim of an historical break can only work if you treat imperialism as a single phenomenon that disappears with the death of specific players and legal forms. But decolonisation was only the end of a specific form of imperial domination.'[67] This book explores the possibility that the law of intervention can be read as a component of just such a new form of imperial domination.

Those international lawyers who support the new interventionism of the post-Cold War era have tended not to discuss the potential imperial character of multilateral intervention. Instead, they present an image of international institutions and international law as agents of democracy and human rights. That representation operates to reinforce the identity of international institutions and of major powers, particularly the USA, as in turn bearers of those progressive values. The UN and other post-World War II institutions have embodied the faith of many people in the ability of international institutions to protect ideals of universalism, humanitarianism, peace, security and human rights. Multilateralism has seemed to offer an escape from unrestrained self-interest and power politics. That faith, if anything, has grown stronger in the post-Soviet era, with commentators treating multilateral and regional institutions, particularly the UN and now NATO, as essentially benevolent and able to bring not only peace and security, but also human rights and democracy,

---

[65] Nathaniel Berman, 'In the Wake of Empire' (1999) 14 *American University International Law Review* 1521 at 1523.

[66] David Kennedy, 'Images of Religion in International Legal Theory' in Mark Janis (ed.), *The Influence of Religion on the Development of International Law* (Dordrecht, 1991), pp. 137–46 at pp. 138–9.

[67] Berman, 'In the Wake', 1531.

to the world. Those who express concern about the potential for powerful states to abuse the emerging norm of humanitarian intervention tend to treat this as a problem for the future. For example, in his 1999 annual address to the General Assembly, Kofi Annan commented that the Kosovo action could set 'dangerous precedents for *future* interventions without a clear criterion to decide who might invoke these precedents, and in what circumstances'.[68] The faith in law's freedom from imperialist desire is clear in the general acceptance amongst legal commentators of the humanitarian motives behind intervention in the post-Cold War era.

The issues at stake in this confrontation between law and empire arose for me in a discussion I had with a second close friend who supported the multilateral military intervention in East Timor. For her, the military intervention was the lesser of two evils, the greater of which was the continued Indonesian military occupation of East Timor, with the attendant rapes and murders. She described images on television of desperate parents throwing their children over a barbed wire fence into the UN compound in Dili, trying to make sure that their children reached sanctuary, and of the horror of seeing the bodies of some of those children getting caught on the barbed wire and hanging there. She talked about the televised images of people lining the streets of East Timorese villages, cheering the troops. She told me of activists returned from Timor talking to people in her home town in country Australia. Their stories were of people who were willing to die to cast their vote and say they had had enough of the Indonesians, of people walking miles carrying children and pleading with the UN staff to keep the polling booths open. They expected to die the next day and did not care. Their courage, she told me, is inspiring. We should be willing to go and stand with them.

I wondered – does this mean that we should not be critical about the way in which our response is shaped by televised images of war that are approved by our militaries?[69] Does our solidarity have to mean unquestioning acceptance of the use of force, an option our government and its allies consider an increasingly appropriate response in the post-Cold War era? Having originally felt that maybe this was a case for intervention, I argued strongly and seemingly without ambivalence with my

[68] UN, *Secretary-General Presents* (emphasis added).

[69] For a critical account of the extent to which war correspondents are controlled and managed by governments and their militaries, with a focus on the Kosovo conflict, see Phillip Knightley, 'Fighting Dirty', *Guardian Weekly*, 30 March–5 April 2000, p. 23.

friend. I said that military intervention had not led to greater freedom or self-determination for subject peoples in places such as Kuwait or Bosnia-Herzegovina. As I suggest in Chapter 4, those people have instead seen one form of domination replaced by another. For example, in the case of Kuwait, this has taken the form of a denial of civil and political rights to most of the country's citizens. In the post-Gulf War elections on 5 October 1992, only 14 per cent of the country's 600,000 citizens were eligible to vote.[70] Despite the strong Kuwaiti women's suffrage move-ment, women as a whole were excluded from eligibility. For women struggling for political rights in postwar Kuwait, the Gulf War means that they are now 'faced with patriarchal barriers ... blessed militarily'.[71] Yet the systematic exclusion of a large percentage of the population from the Kuwaiti political process was not the subject of comment in analyses of the success of UN action in the Gulf, despite the UN's rhetorical com-mitment to the restoration of democracy, self-government and human rights to the people of Kuwait.[72] In the case of Bosnia-Herzegovina, this took the form of administration of the new state by international organisations and their appointees. As Chapter 4 shows, the Dayton Peace Agreement institutionalised the exclusion of the people of Bosnia and Herzegovina from vital economic and political decision-making.[73]

Yet according to many legal accounts, the tension between law and empire was neatly, if belatedly, resolved in the case of East Timor. Por-tugal had held East Timor as one of its colonies from 1893. In 1960, the UN General Assembly placed East Timor on its list of non-self-governing territories, with Portugal as the administering power. Portugal initiated

---

[70] Those eligible were Kuwaiti men, over the age of twenty-one, who could trace their origins in the emirate to before 1920: Dale Gavlak, 'Still Suffering Nonsuffrage in "Liberated" Kuwait' (Jan–Feb 1993) 3 *Ms.* 14. Gavlak reports that women activists conducted protests outside polling stations, election rallies for women's political rights and lobbied parliamentary committees about the need for women's political participation. Kuwaiti women also demanded the right to run for political office, the right to be judges and prosecutors, equal rights in housing and education, and full citizenship for the children of Kuwaiti women married to naturalised Kuwaitis.

[71] Enloe, *The Morning After*, p. 176.

[72] Philip Alston argues that while human rights rhetoric played an important role in securing for the allies the support they needed both from their own citizens and from other UN member states during the Gulf War, the allies did not pay much more than lip service to human rights having established their military objectives. See Alston, 'The Security Council'.

[73] The General Framework Agreement for Peace in Bosnia and Herzegovina with Annexes, 1995, (1996) 35 ILM 75. For a discussion of the effect of the Dayton Agreement in these terms, see David Chandler, *Bosnia: Faking Democracy after Dayton* (2nd edn, London, 2000).

a decolonisation process in 1974, and sought to establish a provisional government and popular assembly to determine the future status of East Timor.[74] The Indonesian invasion of East Timor in 1975 ended this move towards decolonisation. Nevertheless, despite Indonesia's purported integration of East Timor as an Indonesian province, the UN condemned Indonesia's aggression and continued to recognise Portugal as the administering authority over the territory. The more celebratory account of this period suggests that international law was able to oversee the chaotic and bloody end to the imperial overreach of Indonesia and the failed decolonisation attempt for which Portugal was responsible. In 1998, Indonesia proposed that East Timor be granted limited special autonomy within the Republic of Indonesia. The resulting talks involving Indonesia, Portugal and the UN Secretary-General saw the Secretary-General entrusted with the organisation and conduct of a popular consultation to ascertain whether the East Timorese people accepted Indonesia's special autonomy proposal.[75] When the vote rejecting the autonomy proposal in favour of independence resulted in a campaign of violence and destruction waged against the East Timorese, the international community responded by sending a multinational force to restore peace and security.[76] International financial institutions were also able to help protect the people of East Timor against the violence sanctioned by Indonesia by exerting pressure on the Indonesian government during the post-ballot period.[77] In the following months, the Indonesian armed forces, police and administrative officials withdrew from the territory and militia attacks were controlled.

According to this story, law champions the East Timorese and paves the way for the removal of imperialists, both old (Portugal) and

[74] See generally Catholic Institute for International Relations/International Platform of Jurists for East Timor, *International Law and the Question of East Timor* (London, 1995); Julie M. Sforza, 'The Timor Gap Dispute: the Validity of the Timor Gap Treaty, Self-Determination, and Decolonization' (1999) 22 *Suffolk Transnational Law Review* 481.

[75] Agreement between Indonesia and Portugal on the question of East Timor, 5 May 1999 and the Agreements between the United Nations and the Governments of Indonesia and Portugal, 5 May 1999, S/1999/513, Annexes I to III.

[76] Security Council Resolution 1264, S/RES/1264 (1999), adopted on 15 September 1999. The Security Council acting under Chapter VII authorised the establishment of a multinational force with the tasks, *inter alia*, of restoring peace and security in East Timor and facilitating humanitarian assistance operations.

[77] For example, on 6 September 1999 the IMF froze all lending to Indonesia in protest against the violence in East Timor. On 13 September, the World Bank froze all disbursements to Indonesia, both in protest at the Bank Bali scandal and to increase the pressure to end the atrocities in East Timor. See World Bank Group, 'World Bank Freezes All New Loans to Indonesia', *Development News*, 23 September 1999.

new (Indonesia). Secretary-General Kofi Annan certainly saw these actions as signifying an important moment for the international community. For Annan, 'the tragedy of East Timor, coming so soon after that of Kosovo, has focused attention once again on the need for timely intervention by the international community when death and suffering are being inflicted on large numbers of people'.[78] He therefore welcomed the 'developing international norm in favour of intervention to protect civilians from wholesale slaughter'.[79] Similarly, Australia's Foreign Minister Alexander Downer lauded the role played by Australian troops as part of INTERFET in supporting self-determination and relieving suffering in the territory.

Australia has played a very constructive, and wholly creditable, role in the process that has led to self-determination for the people of East Timor...We saw an opportunity to allow East Timorese to decide their own future, and we helped them realise that chance. And when those who lost the ballot sought to overturn it through violence and intimidation, we put Australian lives on the line to end that suffering.[80]

Yet a consideration of the role of international organisations in East Timor in the period following intervention complicates this picture, particularly in the context of international law's imperial history. The UN and the World Bank have adopted a major 'trusteeship' role, taking over responsibility for administration in East Timor during the period of transition to independence. On 25 October 1999, the Security Council established the UN Transitional Administration in East Timor (UNTAET) as a peace-keeping operation 'endowed with overall responsibility for the administration of East Timor and...empowered to exercise all legislative and executive authority, including the administration of justice'.[81] The UN granted itself a broad and ambitious mandate, including the provision of security and maintenance of law and order, the establishment of an effective administration, assisting in the development of civil and social services, supporting capacity-building for self-government and assisting in the establishment of conditions for sustainable development.[82] The Secretary-General's Special Representative

[78] Kofi Annan, 'Two Concepts of Sovereignty', *The Economist*, 18 September 1999, p. 49.
[79] *Ibid.*, p. 50.
[80] Alexander Downer, Minister for Foreign Affairs, 'East Timor: the Way Ahead', speech given to the Rotary Club of Sydney, 30 November 1999.
[81] Clause 1, Security Council Resolution 1272, S/RES/1272 (1999), adopted on 25 October 1999.
[82] *Ibid.*, clause 2.

and Transitional Administrator, Sergio Vieira de Mello, was made 'responsible for all aspects of the United Nations work in East Timor', with
'the power to enact new laws and regulations and to amend, suspend or
repeal existing ones'.[83] The UN's view of its role in East Timor is well illustrated by Jean-Christian Cady, the Deputy Transitional Administrator of
East Timor, who was to comment, 'the United Nations found themselves
in a situation without precedent in their history: to rebuild a country
entirely'.[84] The World Bank also plays a major role in the administration
of East Timor. It administers the World Bank Administered Multilateral
Trust Fund for East Timor, and works in consultation with the East
Timorese and UNTAET representatives to facilitate economic development. The Bank has made clear that certain familiar Bank programmes
and priorities are to be implemented in the management of East Timor.
Its plans focus on ensuring that East Timor has a small state and is
quickly inserted into the global market economy, albeit as one of the
poorest countries in the region.[85]

The economic and political management being developed by these
international organisations on behalf of East Timor sets the stage for
the kind of limited sovereignty that Antony Anghie has analysed in
his study of the operation of the mandate system under the League of
Nations after World War I.[86] Under that system, territories belonging to
defeated powers were placed under the control of mandate powers who
were responsible for the administration of those territories and required
to report back to the League concerning the measures taken to ensure
the well-being and development of mandate peoples. The mandate system appeared to be premised on the international community's desire to
move away from colonialism, and to represent a radical departure from
international law's acceptance of colonialism towards an expression of
condemnation of colonial exploitation and violence.[87] In fact, Anghie
argues that far from representing a move away from imperialism, the
mandate system merely changed its legal form, instituting a new form

---

[83] *Ibid.*, clause 6.

[84] Jean-Christian Cady, 'Building the New State of East Timor', lecture given at the
Centre for International and Public Law, Australian National University, 18 May 2000.

[85] See, for example, World Bank, *Report of the Joint Assessment Mission to East Timor*, 8
December 1999, pp. 3–5, 8; World Bank East Asia and Pacific Region, *Background Paper
Prepared for the Information Meeting on East Timor*, 29 September 1999, p. 2.

[86] Antony Anghie, 'Time Present and Time Past: Globalization, International Financial
Institutions, and the Third World' (2000) 32 *New York University Journal of International
Law and Politics* 243.

[87] *Ibid.*, 278.

of colonial power based not on political but on economic control. The neocolonial process would be overseen by an international institution, one which, like the World Bank in East Timor, saw its role as technical rather than political. Administration of a territory was to be undertaken by a disinterested body of international experts intent on ensuring the proper development and welfare of those subject to their trust.[88] The policies of such institutions were seen as scientific and objective, rather than self-interested. The system as a whole, however, operated to integrate the mandate society into the international economy. Mandate territories were inserted into that economy in a subordinate role. As a result, while those territories appeared to be freed from political control, they remained subject to the control of the parties that exercised power within the international economy.[89]

Many of the same arguments can be seen to apply in the case of East Timor. The new enthusiasm for international trusteeship evidenced there is 'linked in some equivocal way to imperial history',[90] a history in which international institutions came to play an important role in limiting the meaning given to the concept of self-determination for newly sovereign states. Indeed, in the months following the intervention critics were to argue that the reconstruction of East Timor was providing an opportunity for massive foreign direct investment in the areas of telecommunication, banking, tourism, construction and legal services. For example, George Aditjondro sees East Timor under UN and World Bank management as becoming 'a paradise for market-driven foreign investors, without considering the real need for foreign investment... a new outpost of global capitalism in the Asia-Pacific region, due to the absence of a democratically elected government'.[91] He suggests that such a government would 'rely more on its own people's resources and traditions, and would therefore put the brakes on this massive influx of foreign capital'.[92]

Thus one of the arguments this book develops is that the nature of post-conflict reconstruction in places such as Bosnia-Herzegovina and East Timor mirrors the way in which the international community supported colonialism in earlier periods. From its support for acquisition of territory belonging to uncivilised peoples through to the operation of the mandate system, the international community has systematically

---

[88] *Ibid.*, 284.   [89] *Ibid.*, 283.   [90] Berman, 'In the Wake', 1526.
[91] George Aditjondro, 'From Colony to Global Prize' (2000) 47 *Arena Magazine* 22 at 32.
[92] *Ibid.*

facilitated the enterprise of colonialism. Central to this support has been the limited meaning given to the concept of self-determination. Post-conflict reconstruction carried out under the auspices of international financial institutions is often concerned to create a secure environment in which foreign investment can produce profits for the shareholders of multinational and foreign corporations, free of the kinds of investment constraints that were the product of the efforts of decolonised states to create a new international economic order during the 1970s.

As a result, there appear to be limits on the capacity of those in whose name the exercise of reconstruction is conducted to participate fully in determining the conditions that will shape their lives. I argue throughout the book that only one 'choice' is being made available to the new subjects of international law, such as the nation of East Timor. That choice is to be governed by economically rational governments under the tutelage of the international economic institutions who follow the military as representatives of the international community. This illustrates a broader political problem facing the subjects of the international legal system. International law has always operated to constitute as its subjects those who resemble the idealised self-image of European sovereign peoples. The anxieties about who should count as international legal subjects generated by the nineteenth-century colonial enterprise were central to the ways questions about legal personality were posed and answered.[93] The doctrinal attempt to define the 'proper subjects of international law' was fuelled by the political imperative of European lawyers seeking to find a way to distinguish 'sovereigns proper from other entities that also seemed to possess the attributes of sovereignty, such as pirates, non-European states, and nomads'.[94] The natural law of earlier jurists, such as the Spanish theologian Francisco de Vitoria, did not prove useful, as natural law thinking was premised on the notion that all societies, whether European or 'barbarian', were bound by a universal law expressed in Christian doctrine and the Roman law of nations.[95] The answer for nineteenth-century positivists such as Thomas Lawrence and John Westlake was to create a distinction based on perceived essential

---

[93] Antony Anghie, 'Finding the Peripheries: Sovereignty and Colonialism in Nineteenth-Century International Law' (1999) 40 *Harvard International Law Journal* 1 at 17.

[94] *Ibid.*, 26.

[95] See the discussion in Antony Anghie, 'Francisco de Vitoria and the Colonial Origins of International Law' (1996) 5 *Social and Legal Studies* 321.

cultural differences between sovereigns and others.[96] Historically, the resulting refusal to recognise non-European peoples as 'sovereign' greatly
constrained their capacity to shape the development of what came to be
known as 'international' law. The ongoing struggle of indigenous peoples to be recognised as peoples entitled to self-determination and as
subjects of international law is one of the contemporary manifestations
of this history. The struggle of people in Bosnia, Haiti, Kuwait, East Timor
and Kosovo to determine the nature of their conditions of existence and
to be recognised as fully sovereign is another.

The subjects of international law are themselves always constituted
by the law. As Costas Douzinas argues, 'the law is not just the creation
of popular sovereignty: it is also the carrier of the dictates of social reproduction, the begetter of subjects and the vehicle of violence'.[97] In
'recognising' new entities entitled to self-determination, the law is creating new legal subjects. These subjects must fulfil what the spirit of
international law requires, excluding what the international community perceives as alien or other at any given time. In the era of free
trade and liberal democracy, the law's new subjects can determine their
own destiny only within the constraints imposed by liberal capitalism.
In other words, if we accept that it is better to allow the USA and Australia under the UN banner to choose to intervene militarily to 'protect'
some of those at risk of genocide, the next question must be: having
grudgingly and after twenty-four years helped the East Timorese to re-
gain their independence from the Indonesians, how do 'we' help them
gain their independence from the International Monetary Fund (IMF),
the World Bank and the international community? What language do
we have for talking about that? Here the liberal promises of ballot boxes
and humanitarian intervention seem to be of little help.

So, as I debated the promises of intervention with my friend, I argued that living under the administration of the UN and the World
Bank promises little change – no real independence and new threats to
life, health and security. I argued that the presence of the military as
representatives of the 'international community' provides an alibi for
exploitation – we are able to portray our presence as offering salvation
and protection. I argued that this is a revolution, that this has changed

---

[96] Thomas Lawrence, *The Principles of International Law* (London, 1895), pp. 1–25; John
Westlake, *Chapters on the Principles of International Law* (Cambridge, 1894), pp. v–xvi,
1–16. See the discussion of this feature of their work in Anghie, 'Finding the
Peripheries', 10–22.

[97] Costas Douzinas, *The End of Human Rights* (Oxford, 2000), p. 227.

people's hearts and minds, that now people are ready to go on to the streets and protest for intervention, for the increased presence of US and Australian militaries in our region. Yet even as I argued, I thought about all the people protesting on the street, and I wanted to be part of that optimism. I wondered if I was missing something very fundamental here, if I was choosing not to believe in the good intentions of the international community in this case because I was lacking the necessary faith (in humanity? in law? in international organisations?). For my friend, the choice was clear. Living under UN and World Bank trusteeship is better than living under Indonesian governance. If she had the choice to live in Papua New Guinea under the World Bank, or West Papua under the Indonesian military, she argued, she would choose Papua New Guinea. People there eat better and are more secure. They are less likely to be subjected to rape and murder than those who are subject to the terror tactics of the Indonesian military or the pro-Indonesian militias.

I asked whether the choice between living under Indonesian soldiers or under international governance is after all a choice – 'we', the 'international community', were part of the conditions of the life of the East Timorese under Indonesian soldiers. Now we have changed the manner of our intervention, but does this mean we can treat 'then' as somehow being about the East Timorese suffering purely under the governance of the Indonesian military? 'Then' involved the US, British and Australian governments and militaries, arms manufacturers from Britain and the USA and the involvement of the World Bank and the IMF, whether through action or omission, in supporting the Indonesian government and military in its occupation of East Timor. So the choice between life in West Papua and Papua New Guinea seemed to me a false dichotomy, as they are both symptoms of global capitalism. Perhaps my friend was right though – it was extreme of me to argue that one symptom is no better than another. Yet how does it come down to these choices, to people arguing over whether it is better to be governed by the IMF and the World Bank or by the Indonesian military?

I worried about this conversation for days afterwards. Maybe on this one occasion it was better for there to be military intervention with the attendant international supervision, administration and governance that it legitimises. And yet didn't supporting this intervention support a dubious line of 'humanitarian interventions' including the Gulf War and NATO's actions in bombing Kosovo? To support such a shift in policy towards the acceptability of humanitarian intervention surely increased the legitimacy of militarism in states such as the USA, the UK, France,

Nigeria, Australia and Canada. It threatened to limit the role for non-violent and principled means of addressing human rights abuses. It helped build the acceptance of the actions of the international community as unquestionably benevolent and charitable, a story that once played out as the civilising mission. Perhaps I am just wedded to this rejection of humanitarian intervention as an option because I am not able to see the particularity of the situation in East Timor. After all, justice is only possible in the particular case. If in the future this precedent is misused, that is something to be dealt with in the future. This case may indeed mean that the law has changed, and that may be a good thing. Certainly, that is what an increasing number of international lawyers have been advocating since the time of the Gulf War.

As I thought about these things, I started to watch a television programme about Sierre Leone. It showed terrible images of little boys, who, the story told us, were in fact members of rebel groups, forced by the rebels to conduct raids and atrocities, and drugged to enable them to do so. The images we saw were of rebel soldiers dressed in fatigues. In one scene one armed soldier stood on the leg of a naked child of about ten in a truck, while the child screamed in terror. Other soldiers stood around. The child was clearly terrified. It was a horrific scene. In another image, a skinny little boy sat on the ground in front of a building, crying. He was being interrogated by soldiers. I turned off the TV and went to look at my sleeping baby boy. I thought back to my discussion with my friend and decided that I have no right and no power to make any argument at all about these matters. There is no alternative. The best we can hope for in the world as it is today is to be on the side of the more powerful of the ruthless militarised men who seem to dominate all societies, and hope that they don't turn against us.

But the next morning I returned in my mind to those scenes. I began to think about the conditions that made those images possible, and of their effect on me. I was reminded of the 1972 essay by John Berger, 'Photographs of Agony'.[98] Berger wrote that our response to war photographs, photographs of agony, is to feel a sense of powerlessness, which we then interpret as a commentary about our lack of moral agency. Perhaps we then send money to an aid organisation, or resolve to support whichever army is fighting those responsible for the agony. He says we should think instead about the conditions of our powerlessness and understand the relationship of those conditions to our lack of ability to participate democratically. Berger points out:

[98] John Berger, *About Looking* (London, 1980), p. 37.

Newspapers now carry violent war photographs because their effect, except in rare cases, is not what it was once presumed to be. A paper like the *Sunday Times* continues to publish shocking photographs about Vietnam or about Northern Ireland whilst politically supporting the policies responsible for the violence. This is why we have to ask: What effect do such photographs have?[99]

This is clearly the case in Australia with respect to East Timor. The policies of the Australian government and the international community supported the Indonesian government and the Indonesian military in their repression of the East Timorese for over twenty years. Yet even as Australians are appalled by the images of the results of those policies on our television screens, the ordering principles of the international political economy which supported that violence are free from interrogation. Berger writes that our sense of powerlessness is a product of the conditions of photography itself, so that 'any response to that photographed moment is bound to be felt as inadequate'.[100] The camera records and isolates an image of a moment of agony, a moment which is itself experienced by those being photographed as a moment violently isolated from the flow of time. The paralysis and frustration the viewer feels when looking at such images are a result of the relationship such images set up between viewer and viewed.

Those who are there in the situation being photographed, those who hold the hand of the dying or staunch a wound, are not seeing the moment as we have and their responses are of an altogether different order. It is not possible for anyone to look pensively at such a moment and to emerge stronger...

The possible contradictions of the war photograph now become apparent. It is generally assumed that its purpose is to awaken concern. The most extreme examples...show moments of agony in order to extort the maximum concern. Such moments, whether photographed or not, are discontinuous with all other moments. They exist by themselves. But the reader who has been arrested by the photograph may tend to feel this discontinuity as his own personal moral inadequacy. *And as soon as this happens even his own sense of shock is dispersed:* his own moral inadequacy may now shock him as much as the crimes being committed in the war. Either he shrugs off this sense of inadequacy as being only too familiar, or else he thinks of performing a kind of penance – of which the purest example would be to make a contribution to OXFAM or to UNICEF.[101]

In the context of the Sierra Leone story his point is clear. If I was 'there in the situation being photographed' with armed men brutalising a naked child, I imagine that I would be moved by my anger to step forward and say something to them, and I am sure that many people would

---

[99] *Ibid.*, p. 38.   [100] *Ibid.*, p. 39.   [101] *Ibid.*, pp. 39–40 (emphasis in original).

be in the same position. 'Those who are there in the situation being photographed...are not seeing the moment as we have.' The television images produce a sense of powerlessness because someone stood by and focused steadily on that picture, and did not make any move within that frame to help the child. If the image was instead of the photographer rushing forward and telling those people to stop, then I would feel less powerless. As I discuss in Chapter 5, this relates to the arguments made by feminist film critics that the function of cinematic narrative is to stop us recognising our own passivity as viewers, by creating our identification with the active hero in the film.[102] Thus the response produced in those of us watching televised images of death and suffering is to call for action. I think back to the images my friend described of children being thrown into the UN compound in Dili, and getting stuck on barbed wire. Anyone who was there in person would not have the horror of passively watching that scene, but would be able to try and help the children, covering the barbed wire with clothes, climbing up to make sure the children did not get stuck, lifting them over. Our sense of passivity is a product of the way in which televised images are produced, as is our desire that violence be used in response. Perhaps the greater our frustration with our passivity, the greater our need to see action taken in our name. As I argue through this book, the relationship between viewer and viewed and the narrative effect of such images are central to the conservative meanings made of humanitarian intervention.

I think also of Rey Chow's argument, that the 'Third World' is produced as spectacle, entertainment and monstrosity for those of us watching the media in the 'First World'.[103] In her discussion of the meaning of the massacre in Tiananmen Square, Chow says:

The 'Third World', as the site of the 'raw' material that is 'monstrosity', is produced for the surplus-value of spectacle, entertainment, and spiritual enrichment for the 'First World'. The intense productivity of the Western newsperson leads to the establishment of clear boundaries. Locked behind the bars of our television screens, we become repelled by what is happening 'over there'.[104]

Televised images of suffering people in the 'Third World' function to explain the need for intervention, and in so doing act also as the forms

---

[102] Kaja Silverman, *The Subject of Semiotics* (New York, 1983), pp. 215–36; Laura Mulvey, *Visual and Other Pleasures* (Bloomington, 1989), pp. 14–29; E. Ann Kaplan, *Looking for the Other: Feminism, Film and the Imperial Gaze* (New York, 1997).

[103] Rey Chow, 'Violence in the Other Country: China as Crisis, Spectacle and Woman' in Chandra Talpade Mohanty, Ann Russo and Lourdes Torres (eds.), *Third World Women and the Politics of Feminism* (Bloomington, 1991), pp. 81–100.

[104] *Ibid.*, p. 84.

of entertainment and spiritual enrichment to which Chow directs our attention. It is easy to forget that television news is part of a highly profitable entertainment industry, and that 'entertaining' the audiences of that industry is at least one of the functions that the suffering Third World fulfils. In addition, we are shown nameless starving, weeping, mourning strangers as part of a narrative in which we are spiritually enriched by the knowledge of our superiority and capacity to rescue and redeem these others. In the context of US reporting on the Tiananmen massacre, Chow points out that we should not take for granted the image of a US journalist 'standing on the street in Beijing, speaking a language which is not Chinese, condemning the Chinese government'.[105] She argues that we need to question the conditions that make such a fantastic spectacle appear normal. The 'freedom' that makes it possible for such journalists to produce knowledge about the 'non-West' is '*not a basic existential condition to which all are entitled (though that is the claim that is made) but a network of demands, negotiations, and coercions that are themselves bound by historical determinants constructed on slaughter and bloodshed*'.[106]

Both Berger and Chow are arguing that our response to the kinds of images of suffering in the 'Third World' that give meaning to military intervention must be to think about the conditions that make those images possible, the relationship of that to imperialism and the history of the presence of the 'West' in those places. We take for granted, as Chow says, that there will be a person in Kosovo or East Timor speaking English, an observer, providing images of monstrosities for us to consume at home over dinner. We do not think about the violent history that creates the conditions that produce the 'Third World' as spectacle. And we therefore do not start to think about the political effect of that production of the Third World as spectacle.

A focus on those images of the West and the non-West, or the international and the local, is important in part because of the links that such a focus suggests with cultures of imperialism. Postcolonial theorists have argued that imperialism was made possible in part through narrative.[107] Stories about civilising missions were used to announce, argue, and promote the cultural superiority of colonising states, to justify democratising and civilising invasions by colonial powers and to

---

[105] *Ibid.*, p. 85.   [106] *Ibid.* (Emphasis in original).
[107] Said, *Culture*, p. xiii (arguing that 'the power to narrate, or to block other narratives from forming and emerging, is very important to culture and imperialism, and constitutes one of the main connections between them'). See further the discussion in Chapter 5 below.

consolidate the power of European and later American states. In much the same way, legal narratives about intervention contribute to making the oppression and exploitation of peoples in Asia, Eastern Europe, Latin America or Africa appear natural, inevitable and desirable. Intervention stories are premised upon an assumption about the capacity of, and the need for, the international community to bring democracy and human rights to the rest of the world. The narratives of the new interventionism portray an image of international law and institutions as agents of freedom, order, democracy, liberalisation, transparency, humanitarianism and human rights, protectors of those living in failed states or in regions devastated by civil war and armed conflict. Military intervention is not only justifiable but morally required to rescue the victims of ethnic cleansing, attempted genocide, religious fundamentalism and massive human rights violations. Monetary intervention and supervision is necessary to restore the economic fundamentals of states that have proved unable to govern themselves prudently, and to bring greater freedom and prosperity to the people living in those states. Such stories ignore a history in which imperial powers announced and celebrated their superiority in similar language, with tragic consequences.

The promise of humanitarian intervention

Humanitarian intervention draws its powerful appeal from the revolutionary discourse of human rights, which promises liberation from tyranny and a future built on something other than militarised and technocratic state interests. At its best, as Costas Douzinas comments, human rights expresses 'concern for the unfinished person of the future for whom justice matters'.[108] Many human rights activists see humanitarian intervention as unquestioningly a good thing precisely because it appears to enact a commitment to the emancipatory ideals of freedom from oppression, respect for human dignity and valuing of human life. For my friends, this is the meaning that was made of intervention by the people marching in the streets calling for UN action in East Timor.

Yet there has been little analysis of what happens to the revolutionary potential of human rights when those rights are invoked by lawyers and diplomats from powerful states in the name of the people of a territory they intend to invade, bomb or administer. Legal texts justifying interventions in the name of human rights protection offer a narrative in

---

[108] Douzinas, *The End of Human Rights*, p. 15.

which the international community as heroic saviour rescues those passive victims who suffer at the hands of bullies and tyrants. According
to this account of the current state of internationalism, the international community is motivated by the desire to promote and protect
core values such as freedom, democracy and humanitarianism. It is international institutions, whether the Security Council or the IMF, the
World Bank or NATO, who will operate to bring freedom and indeed salvation to the people of Africa, Asia, Eastern Europe and Latin America.
Intervention by international institutions in the name of human rights
and democracy provides a reason, or, as some have argued, an 'alibi,'
for the presence of the international community in many parts of the
world.

As Douzinas argues, rights undergo a significant shift when they 'are
turned from a discourse of rebellion and dissent into that of state
legitimacy'.[109] While on the one hand the appeal to human rights is
used to undermine the legitimacy of 'rogue', 'failed' or target states in
the context of intervention, that appeal also serves at the same time
to authorise or legitimise the actions of those powerful states who collectively act as the 'international community'. Human rights discourse
thus seems to contain forces moving in opposite directions in the debate
about intervention. The language of rights still appears to promise the
energy and moral authority of resistance to power, yet it is increasingly
spoken by officials seeking to convince their audience that the resort to
violence in a particular instance is justified. In the words of Robert Cover,
the law's officials are able to constrain the meanings that can count as
law – they 'characteristically do not create law, but kill it'.[110] Their role
is to confront 'the luxuriant growth of a hundred legal traditions', and
to 'assert that *this one* is law and destroy or try to destroy the rest'.[111] In
other words, humanitarian intervention may seem to promise a world in
which substantive democracy, dissent, social justice, human flourishing
and the end of poverty are privileged over narrowly conceived national
interests. Yet, as I argue throughout this book, attention to legal texts
suggests that a far more circumscribed and conservative interpretation
of the ends of intervention is being named as 'the law'. As human rights
become at once part of the 'texts of resistance' and an apology for state

---

[109] *Ibid.*, p. 7.
[110] Robert M. Cover, 'Foreword: Nomos and Narrative' (1983) 97 *Harvard Law Review*
4 at 53.
[111] *Ibid.* (Emphasis in original).

violence, the meaning of human rights and democracy is being radically circumscribed.[112]

In his discussion of the relationship between law and narrative, Cover argues: 'No set of legal institutions or prescriptions exist apart from the narratives that locate it and give it meaning…Once understood in the context of the narratives that give it meaning, law becomes not merely a system of rules to be observed, but a world in which we live.'[113] Law and narrative are, for Cover, inextricably intertwined – narrative supplies law with its 'history and destiny, beginning and end, explanation and purpose', while law supplies narrative with its moral.[114] As I explore in detail in Chapter 5, humanitarian intervention is located firmly within a familiar heroic narrative, in which international institutions are the bearers of progressive human rights and democratic values to local peoples in need of those rights and values in the post-Cold War era. The stories that explain and justify the new interventionism have increasingly become part of everyday language through media reports and political soundbites. As a result, these strategic accounts of a world of sovereign states and of authorised uses of high-tech violence become more and more a part of 'the stories that we are all inside, that we live daily.'[115] Legal texts about intervention create a powerful sense of self for those who identify with the hero of that story, be that the international community, the Security Council, the UN, NATO or the USA.[116] Law's intervention narratives thus operate not only, or even principally, in the field of state systems, rationality and facts, but also in the field of identification, imagination, subjectivity and emotion.

My discussions with friends who felt that intervention was necessary in the case of East Timor convinced me that there may be occasions where armed force is the only available option to deal with a security or humanitarian crisis, however that crisis has been reached. Their focus on solidarity, on standing with and beside the East Timorese, not as saviours but finally as comrades, helped me to see that there is more than one

---

[112] Ibid., 54 (discussing the 'texts of resistance' that appeal to 'those of us who would live by the law of their community', and the 'texts of jurisprudence' that are resorted to by those who would kill that community law).

[113] Ibid., 4–5. For a discussion of Cover's linking of law and narrative in the context of the Kosovo intervention, see Jules Lobel, 'The Benefits of Legal Restraint' (2000) 94 American Society of International Law Proceedings 304.

[114] Cover, 'Foreword', 5.

[115] Terry Threadgold, 'Introduction' in Terry Threadgold and Anne Cranny-Francis (eds.), Feminine–Masculine and Representation (Sydney, 1990), pp. 1–35 at p. 27.

[116] See further Orford, 'Muscular Humanitarianism'.

way to understand and narrate the meaning of intervention within a particular context. Yet my response to these conversations with my friends, and in particular my continued uneasiness about the implications of the official meanings made of humanitarian intervention, also reminded me that when we join our voices to the call for military intervention in a particular situation, we may find ourselves part of a different narrative. In this case, I remain concerned that the official narrative about intervention that was buttressed by the Security Council-authorised intervention in East Timor is a disturbing one. The challenge this book addresses is to understand the effects of that dominant narrative, and to find ways to ensure that 'humanitarian intervention' has a more radical meaning than simply support for a particular kind of state-based, capitalist and militaristic world order. The discussions I have recounted helped me to realise that this is a far more complicated question than simply being for or against intervention. It involves thinking through the nature of the dominant intervention narrative, the imperial and patriarchal fantasies that haunt this narrative and the effects of particular interventions. It involves a focus on the way in which meanings are made about intervention, and the way those meanings shut out potentially revolutionary ways of understanding what is at stake. These are the obsessions around which this book turns.

2   Misreading the texts of international law

When feminists deliberately and self-consciously read black letter law or critical legal scholars deliberately read judgments...in ways that such texts were generically and institutionally never meant to be read, they do it knowing that they are breaking the rules of the code, knowing that they are endeavouring to challenge those rules and to effect change by making the genres 'mean' differently (that is, making the genres tell a different story).[1]

My aim in this chapter is to explain why I have chosen in this book to read legal texts about intervention 'in ways that such texts were generically and institutionally never meant to be read'. The kind of productive misreading that I hope to develop here involves breaching some of the protocols that govern international legal scholarship, in order, as Threadgold suggests, to make these texts ' "mean" differently'. Much legal writing in the field of intervention aims either at doctrinal exegesis, the description, development and refining of legal rules, or at studying the relationship between legal rules and the situations in which they take effect. My intention is to show that focusing only on the distinctions that legal texts make between a lawful and an unlawful intervention is to miss much of the most interesting work that those texts do. In this chapter, I set out to explain the traditions that inform my critical reading of intervention narratives, and to address some of the criticisms that might be made of this reading by those who want to uphold the 'rules of the code' that govern the legal genre. My hope is that in so doing, I am able to persuade opponents of critical theory to join in the project of making legal texts 'mean differently' offered by this book, while seeking to locate the traditions which inform my approach for the kindly

---

[1] Terry Threadgold, 'Book Review: *Law and Literature: Revised and Enlarged Edition* by Richard Posner' (1999) 23 *Melbourne University Law Review* 830 at 838.

disposed reader who is already convinced of the utility of critical theory for reading law.

This chapter outlines some of the key theoretical concerns and debates that inform my approach to reading humanitarian intervention. The first part explores what it means to read and write legal theory after colonialism, and the demands this makes of international lawyers. I suggest that much of the existing literature on humanitarian intervention involves forgetting law's imperial history. I argue instead for an approach that pays careful attention to 'the great shifting currents of global imperialism',[2] rather than adopting the teleological narrative of Western progress and civilising missions as an ordering principle of a reading of international law. The second part of the chapter develops this further to think through how feminism comes to international law in the aftermath of colonial occupation. It explores 'gender's limits, where does it work, and where does it not work' as a category in attempting to think ethically about developing a new politics of reading humanitarian intervention.[3] I attempt in that part to develop a feminist methodology for reading international law that avoids the deployment of 'the axiomatics of imperialism for crucial textual functions'.[4] The third part of the chapter locates my reading of humanitarian intervention within a critical legal tradition which questions the dominant representation of power in the texts of international law. I argue there that, despite its 'repeated gesture against sovereignty', much international legal scholarship continues to be 'obsessed with the struggle somehow to reinvent at an international level the sovereign authority it was determined to transcend'.[5] The suggestion that law works through the creation of subjectivity and identity, rather than purely through the constitution of sovereign states and international institutions, is treated as an exercise in 'illusory radicalism, rhetorically colourful but programmatically vacuous' by the defenders of traditional legal method.[6] I suggest in contrast that it is helpful to understand power as operating beyond a 'juridical' or

---

[2] Gayatri Chakravorty Spivak, A Critique of Postcolonial Reason: toward a History of the Vanishing Present (Cambridge, 1999), p. 89.

[3] Rey Chow, 'Violence in the Other Country: China as Crisis, Spectacle, and Woman' in Chandra Talpade Mohanty, Ann Russo and Lourdes Torres (eds.), Third World Women and the Politics of Feminism (Bloomington, 1991), pp. 81–100 at p. 82.

[4] Spivak, A Critique, p. 133.

[5] David Kennedy, 'The International Style in Postwar Law and Policy' (1994) 1 Utah Law Review 7 at 13, 14.

[6] Brad R. Roth, 'Governmental Illegitimacy and Neocolonialism: Response to Review by James Thuo Gathii' (2000) 98 Michigan Law Review 2056 at 2057.

prohibitive model in order to think about the power relations involved in, and enabled by, the performance of humanitarian intervention.[7] In each part, I attempt to develop ways of reading directed at thinking through the cultural and economic effects of militarised internationalism, and the relationship of these effects to the texts of law.

Legal theory and postcolonialism

What does it mean to read and write legal theory after colonialism? Much international legal scholarship, particularly that written about humanitarian intervention, treats that question quite literally: that is, international law is understood to be operating today as if it were no longer part of a colonial or imperial project. Let me sketch briefly how that plays out in two apparently opposing positions that structure the international legal debate regarding humanitarian intervention.

First, there is a group of international lawyers who argue that the best interpretation of international legal doctrine allows for the right, and indeed the duty, of humanitarian intervention. These advocates of humanitarian intervention tend not to see any necessary relation between such intervention and imperialism, treating international law as an agent of liberation from domination by corrupt Third World elites or the violence of religious or ethnic groups within such states.[8] The liberal legal explanation of the increasing acceptability of humanitarian intervention distances law from imperialism through a narrative in which human rights law has gradually evolved from a regime based upon soft, unenforceable norms to a regime which is enforceable by the international community.[9] According to this account, the advances offered by the new world of global communications and media technology make it possible for audiences in all parts of the world to witness unmediated visual images of horror and suffering in other places. As a result, people have started to demand from their liberal democratic governments in Europe, the USA, Australia, New Zealand and Canada some commitment to humanitarian action in the form of military intervention to save those innocents who are suffering elsewhere.[10]

---

[7] For the discussion of the departure from the 'juridical' model of power in the work of Michel Foucault, see further 'The Power of International Law' below.

[8] See, for example, Fernando R Téson, 'Collective Humanitarian Intervention' (1996) 17 *Michigan Journal of International Law* 323.

[9] Geoffrey Robertson, *Crimes against Humanity: The Struggle for Global Justice* (Ringwood, 1999), p. 450.

[10] *Ibid.*, p. 438.

The proponents of intervention accept that there is a threat that law used in this way could become a tool of imperialism in the future. So, for example, the UN Secretary-General Kofi Annan suggests in his 1999 Annual Report to the General Assembly that while the interventions in Kosovo and East Timor should be welcomed, there is a danger 'of such interventions undermining the imperfect, yet resilient, security system created after the Second World War, and of setting dangerous precedents for *future* interventions without a clear criterion to decide who might invoke these precedents, and in what circumstances'.[11] There is no question for Annan that the effects of intervention to date might be part of an ongoing imperial enterprise.

Conservative international lawyers have responded by questioning the existence of humanitarian intervention as an exception to the prohibition on the use of force, and have argued that respect for the norms that are central to the UN Charter-based legal order represent the best hope for decolonised states and their peoples. Those norms include the right to self-determination, respect for sovereign equality of states and non-intervention in the internal affairs of states.[12] For legal scholars who oppose resort to humanitarian intervention on the basis that it undermines an 'international rule of law', it is the progressive development of these legal norms that offers the best protection of the interests of the weak by constraining the powerful.[13] Humanitarian intervention should be rejected because it can provide 'a broad-ranging legal license for external intervention in the affairs of weak states'.[14] The future of these decolonised states is best served by their acceptance of international law, enabling their progress towards achieving the economic and political strength of 'Western' states. In this view, states are by definition autonomous, and intervention involves only overt acts involving the use of force or economic coercion.

There is an interesting footnote to most of the texts of those traditionalists who argue against the emergence of a legal norm in favour of intervention. Writing in 1991, Oscar Schachter commented:

---

[11] UN, *Secretary-General Presents his Annual Report to General Assembly*, UN Press Release SG/SM/7136 GA/9596, 20 September 1999 (emphasis added).

[12] Articles 1 and 2 of the Charter of the United Nations (UN Charter), San Francisco, 26 June 1945, in force 24 October 1945.

[13] Simon Chesterman, *Just War or Just Peace? Humanitarian Intervention and International Law* (Oxford, 2001), pp. 232–6.

[14] Roth, 'Governmental Illegitimacy', 2060.

Even in the absence of such prior approval [by the Security Council], a State or group of States using force to put an end to atrocities when the necessity is evident and the humanitarian intention is clear is likely to have its action pardoned. But, I believe it is highly undesirable to have a new rule allowing humanitarian intervention, for that could provide a pretext for abusive intervention. It would be better to acquiesce in a violation that is considered necessary and desirable in the particular circumstances than to adopt a principle that would open a wide gap in the barrier against unilateral use of force.[15]

Similarly, Jonathon Charney argues that the NATO action in Kosovo was clearly illegal. Any suggestion that it 'stands for the right of foreign states to intervene in the absence of proof that widespread grave violations of international human rights law are being committed... leaves the door open for hegemonic states to use force for purposes clearly incompatible with international law'.[16] It is international law, particularly UN Charter law, that remains the best guarantor we have of peace and security, order, and the protection of human rights.[17] For Charney, humanitarian intervention, no matter how 'well-intentioned', poses a threat to the stability and promise of the international legal order.[18] Yet in an apologetic moment mirrored in other examinations of humanitarian intervention, Charney notes that powerful states can and do intervene in contravention of international law, and may want to retain 'their power to take actions for political reasons notwithstanding the law'.[19] The best, albeit not perfect, solution for 'weak states' lies in maintaining a formal legal prohibition against such intervention, so that powerful states are required 'to break the law in extreme circumstances' if they want to take military action.[20] To take one further example, Simon Chesterman reaches the same conclusion in his analysis of the illegality of humanitarian intervention, arguing that:

In the event of an intervention alleged to be on humanitarian grounds, the better view is that such an intervention is illegal, but that the international community may, in extreme circumstances, tolerate the delict. In judicial terms this might translate to a finding of illegality but the imposition of only a nominal penalty...Moreover, by affirming the prohibition of the use of force, recourse to military intervention is maintained as an extreme, and last, resort.[21]

---

[15] Oscar Schachter, *International Law in Theory and Practice* (Dordrecht, 1991), p. 126.
[16] Jonathon I. Charney, 'Anticipatory Humanitarian Intervention in Kosovo' (1999) 93 *American Journal of International Law* 834 at 841.
[17] *Ibid.*, 835.   [18] *Ibid.*   [19] *Ibid.*, 838.   [20] *Ibid.*
[21] Chesterman, *Just War*, pp. 231–2.

In these three examples, the international legal order is represented as coexisting with abuses of power without condoning such abuses. By maintaining a separation between law and power, law retains its purity of purpose. International law ends at the point where 'politics' and coercion begins. Yet those 'outlaws' who are favoured by the international legal order need not fear its wrath.[22] As Christine Chinkin notes in her commentary on the role of the 'West' in scripting the Kosovo intervention, 'it is hard to envisage that other states would be able to undertake such a campaign, either unilaterally or together, against the wishes of permanent members of the Security Council and without being challenged by them'.[23]

Nonetheless, the conservative argument in favour of preserving the 'contemporary sovereign state system' assumes that this system is the best available. Brad Roth describes the bleak choice facing international lawyers as one between supporting a potentially imperialistic 'new norm that would open the door to "prodemocratic" intervention', or favouring 'the right to be ruled by one's own thugs'.[24] Implicit in this position is the view that, because international law and international institutions operate on the basis of formal respect for the sovereignty of all states, international law is free of the desire for empire. The problem of powerful states exploiting or dominating the peoples and resources of decolonised states is limited to the question of overt coercion, whether military or economic. Colonisation and imperialism occurred in the past and were properly resisted (with the assistance of international law). The project of the development of international law is one to which the 'Third World' has been able to contribute since 1945.[25] The resulting international legal order thus represents a formal commitment to decolonisation, to self-determination and to the protection of human rights. For example, Brad Roth sees the driving, revolutionary force of both human rights and anti-colonial nationalism as reasons to preserve and conserve the existing state-based system. The energies of these movements for change are reflected in the creation of postcolonial states, and of international legal rules which grant those states formal equality, so that to use human rights or anti-colonial arguments to critique

---

[22] Gerry Simpson, 'Out of Law' in *International Legal Challenges for the Twenty-First Century: Proceedings of a Joint Meeting of the Australian and New Zealand Society of International Law and the American Society of International Law* (Canberra, 2000), p. 307.

[23] Christine M. Chinkin, 'Kosovo: a "Good" or "Bad" War?' (1999) 93 *American Journal of International Law* 841 at 847.

[24] Roth, 'Governmental Illegitimacy', 2060, 2064.   [25] *Ibid.*

that order is to betray those movements.[26] This posits international law and postcolonial nation states as the end of anti-colonial struggles, and ignores a history in which the granting of formal political sovereignty to decolonised states coincided with new techniques of international institutional control premised on limiting the economic sovereignty of those new entities.[27]

A number of scholars adopt positions somewhere between the two poles I have described so far. Many are uneasy about the recognition of a new norm allowing for unilateral humanitarian intervention because of its potential for abuse, yet want to allow for situations in which collective action without Security Council authorisation is permissible, particularly in light of the Kosovo precedent. Thus they adopt a natural law argument, suggesting that there are situations in which the international community must act outside *positive* law, in ways that are nevertheless legitimate because of the demands of morality and justice. This is the approach adopted by Michael Glennon. While acknowledging that the NATO air strikes against Serbia were not 'technically legal under the old regime', Glennon suggests that the 'death of the restrictive old rules on peacekeeping and peacemaking...should not be mourned'.[28] According to Glennon, 'in Kosovo, justice (as it is now understood) and the UN Charter seemed to collide'.[29] Similarly, for Bruno Simma the NATO intervention was required in order to promote justice and morality, despite the illegality of such intervention. 'The lesson which can be drawn from [the use of force by NATO] is that unfortunately there do occur "hard cases" in which terrible dilemmas must be faced, and imperative political and moral considerations may appear to leave no choice but to act outside the law.'[30]

Louis Henkin has also argued that in the case of Kosovo, the law was caught between needing to uphold the international legal order based on respect for state sovereignty as a protection against the dangers of unilateral intervention by powerful states, while making space for the development of 'bona fide, responsible, collective intervention' to

---

[26] *Ibid.*, 2064–5.

[27] Antony Anghie, 'Time Present and Time Past: Globalization, International Financial Institutions, and the Third World' (2000) 32 *New York University Journal of International Law and Politics* 243.

[28] Michael J. Glennon, 'The New Interventionism: the Search for a Just International Law' (1999) 78(3) *Foreign Affairs* 2.

[29] *Ibid.*

[30] Bruno Simma, 'NATO, the UN and the Use of Force: Legal Aspects' (1999) 10 *European Journal of International Law* 1 at 22.

protect against human rights abuses.[31] Henkin resolves this dilemma by arguing that Kosovo represents the movement towards a new norm of international law, according to which states engaging in humanitarian intervention will act without Security Council authorisation, and then challenge the Security Council to pass a resolution terminating the action. Such a resolution would reverse the burden of the veto, because 'a permanent member favouring the intervention could frustrate the adoption of such a resolution'.[32] For Henkin, the Kosovo intervention can be interpreted as 'a step toward a change in the law, part of the quest for developing "a form of collective intervention" beyond a veto-bound Security Council'.[33] This could be done without formal amendment of the UN Charter, on the basis of 'a "gentleman's agreement" among the Permanent Members'.[34]

In this narrative, the international order, which represents values such as humanitarianism and justice, is threatened by states and leaders who have no commitment to human rights or peace.[35] The legitimacy of military actions taken in response is established on this argument through reference to norms of justice or morality. These 'outlaw' interventions are guided by the transparency of motive required of multilateralism, the good faith required of politics, and the wisdom or bona fides of the states engaging in intervention. In the case of Kosovo, the international community may have been acting outside of the law, but such action was not taken in the name of self-interest or old-fashioned imperialist aggression, but for the collective good.

Central to each of the positions on humanitarian intervention I have sketched is an approach to international law that involves forgetting its imperial history. Each is suspicious that the alternatives may betray the liberatory promises of international law. Those broadly opposed to intervention argue that the emergence of a right of humanitarian intervention may allow increased interference by the powerful into the affairs of the weak, while those broadly in favour of intervention suggest that to advocate the protection of state sovereignty over human rights protection is to betray the universal principles of human rights protection and humanitarianism that underpin the UN system.[36] Each sees our era as one in which decolonisation has successfully taken place, in which international law and the international community are essentially

---

[31] Louis Henkin, 'Kosovo and the Law of "Humanitarian Intervention"' (1999) 93 *American Journal of International Law* 824 at 825.
[32] *Ibid.*, 827. [33] *Ibid.*, 828. [34] *Ibid.* [35] Glennon, 'The New Interventionism', 4.
[36] Roth, 'Governmental Illegitimacy'.

anti-colonial, and in which the only real debate is over how international law can best end human suffering, while not falling prey to abuse by powerful states. In the words of Brad Roth, 'colonialism is a legal aberration',[37] rather than, as James Gatthi has argued, 'ingrained in international law as we know it today'.[38] Roth suggests that 'characterizing contemporary international law as essentially continuous with patterns of past Western domination' is not useful politically and belittles 'the hard-won achievements of anticolonialist struggles'.[39]

Roth's comments illustrate a tendency that Nathaniel Berman has criticised in international lawyers, the readiness to draw a line between imperialism and law. As Berman has argued, the orthodox faith in the capacity of international law to renew itself in the wake of its involvement in many of the horrors of the past three centuries, empire being the most obvious, involves the belief that 'eliminating a particular kind of political domination will cleanse law of imperial taint, [just as] controlling a particular kind of sexual desire will cleanse pragmatism of colonial fantasies'.[40] Leela Gandhi has argued that the 'colonial aftermath' more generally is marked by the belief that we can 'successfully imagine and execute a decisive departure from the colonial past'.[41] The 'triumphant subjects' of postcolonialism, whether former colonists or the former colonised, 'inevitably underestimate the psychologically tenacious hold of the colonial past on the postcolonial present'.[42] Gandhi quotes Albert Memmi's response to this delusion, 'and the day oppression ceases, the new man is supposed to emerge before our eyes immediately. Now, I do not like to say so, but I must, since decolonisation has demonstrated it: this is not the way it happens.'[43]

Both this delusion, and the failure to realise it, shape international law. International legal texts embody the faith that a renewed law emerged with the creation of the United Nations and the birth of the era of decolonisation. In contrast, this book follows legal theorists such as Anghie, Berman and Gatthi in reading texts about humanitarian intervention as intimately connected with, rather than as a decisive

---

[37] *Ibid.*, 2065.
[38] James Thuo Gathii, 'Neoliberalism, Colonialism and International Governance: Decentering the International Law of Governmental Legitimacy' (2000) 98 *Michigan Law Review* 1996 at 2020.
[39] Roth, 'Governmental Illegitimacy', 2065.
[40] Nathaniel Berman, 'In the Wake of Empire' (1999) 14 *American University International Law Review* 1521 at 1551.
[41] Leela Gandhi, *Postcolonial Theory: a Critical Introduction* (St Leonards, 1998), p. 6.
[42] *Ibid.*   [43] *Ibid.*

departure from, colonialism. To read international law after colonialism is to try to remember its imperial past, and to become familiar with
the spectres of colonialism that haunt the law today.[44] I want now to
sketch some of the key ideas from postcolonial theory that are relevant
to the international legal moment I explore in this book.

First, postcolonial theory encourages attention to the possibility
that imperialism, as a 'largely economic rather than largely territorial
enterprise',[45] survived the era of decolonisation. It is true that we do not
today see reprised that form of imperialism premised upon the claiming
of sovereignty over invaded or occupied territory by a foreign, colonial
power. Yet a 'largely economic' enterprise of imperialism continues, in
the form of the exploitation of the colonised, their land and resources.
Intervention has been preceded in places such as Bosnia-Herzegovina and
Rwanda, and accompanied in Haiti, Kosovo and East Timor, by the facilitation of this imperial enterprise. One of the overt aims of pre-conflict
'aid' programmes, and post-conflict reconstruction, has been the establishment of the necessary conditions to make foreign investment secure
and profitable. As I argue in Chapter 4, postwar reconstruction guarantees that the peoples and territories of Asia, Africa, Latin America and
Eastern Europe continue to produce the wealth of Europe and North
America, while images of the suffering peoples of the Third World, and
of our benevolence in responding to them, are used to provide spiritual enrichment to audiences in those wealthy countries. Thus rather
than narrate a history in which humanitarian intervention facilitates
progress from a world of irrational, tribal, premodern, failed states to
one of free, democratic, developing states, humanitarian intervention is
read in this book as part of a history of global imperialism.

Second, intervention narratives also mirror imperial culture by providing 'the possibility of the cultural self-representation of the "First
World"'.[46] The literature on humanitarian intervention treats those
who lead or inhabit target states as the 'other' of the 'international
community': as disordered, chaotic, tribal, primitive, pre-capitalist, violent, exclusionary and child-like.[47] These texts treat as a given that we,

---

[44] See the brief discussion in Lacanian terms of the repudiation of the trauma of
colonialism and the return of this repressed past as phantasmic memories in Gandhi,
Postcolonial Theory, p. 10.

[45] Spivak, *A Critique*, p. 3.

[46] Gayatri Chakravorty Spivak, *The Postcolonial Critic: Interviews, Strategies, Dialogues* (ed.
Sarah Harasym, New York, 1990), p. 96.

[47] See further Chapters 3–5 below.

international lawyers and our audiences, can 'know' these primitive societies – we adopt Sartre's 'imperial conviction' that 'there is always some way of understanding an idiot, a child, a primitive man or a foreigner *if one has sufficient information*'.[48] Legal texts pay meticulous attention to establishing the specificity of the international legal tradition – the words of founding fathers are treated with reverence, the distinctions made within doctrine are awarded grave consideration, the relationship of each text to that tradition is established with care. Yet within the same texts no name or voice is given to the people of the states who are the objects of intervention – their suffering is inscribed in these texts merely as 'material evidence once again establishing the Northwestern European subject as "the same"'.[49] The narrative that founds these texts locates the causes of the violence of intervention with those who inhabit target states. Through the meanings created in these texts, the self of the 'international community' is created by defining that community against its others. Of necessity, as I show in Chapters 3 and 4, this involves ignoring the complicity between those local or national communities to be targeted by intervention, and the international community that is constituted by that intervention.

In making such a claim, this book takes a position on the question of the place of narration and the centrality of texts in the practice of imperialism. For Edward Said, the construction of knowledge about the colonised was central to enabling the kind of European culture that could make imperialism possible.[50] In his study of 'Orientalism' as a discourse, Said explores the extent to which academic, imaginative and bureaucratic European texts came to constitute 'the corporate institution for dealing with the Orient – dealing with it by making statements about it, authorizing views of it, describing it, by teaching it, settling it, ruling over it'.[51] For Said, in order to understand European domination of the territory that Europe imagined as 'the Orient', it is vital to understand how 'European culture was able to manage – and even produce – the Orient politically, sociologically, militarily, ideologically, scientifically, and imaginatively during the post-Enlightenment period... European culture gained in strength and identity by setting itself off against the Orient as a sort of surrogate and even underground self.'[52]

---

[48] Jean-Paul Sartre, *Existentialism and Humanism*, (trans. Philip Mairet, New York, 1948), pp. 46–7, cited in Spivak, *A Critique*, p. 171 (emphasis in original).
[49] Spivak, *A Critique*, p. 113.
[50] Edward W. Said, *Culture and Imperialism* (London, 1993).
[51] Edward W. Said, *Orientalism* (London, 1978), p. 3.   [52] *Ibid.*

In his later work, Said developed this idea further in an exploration of the enormous cultural work necessary to make possible 'the *idea* of *having an empire*', an idea that is as central for Said to the enterprise of empire as are guns, boats, soldiers and administrators.[53] The puzzle he seeks to solve in *Culture and Imperialism* is one that seems pertinent to a consideration of international intervention. Given the 'immense hardships' faced by those who were engaged in the imperial project, the lack of domestic, European resistance to the project of empire, and the energy and resources involved in ruling or managing people on their home territory, what produced the 'will, self-confidence, even arrogance necessary to maintain such a state of affairs'?[54] One answer for Said lies in the power to create a narrative that gave a moral and heroic purpose to empire.

The main battle in imperialism is over land, of course: but when it came to who owned the land, who had the right to settle and work on it, who kept it going, who won it back, and who now plans its future – these issues were reflected, contested, and even for a time decided in narrative...The power to narrate, or to block other narratives from forming and emerging, is very important to culture and imperialism, and constitutes one of the main connections between them.[55]

As Leela Gandhi has shown, this insight has been central to shaping the work of many scholars working as postcolonial literary critics, who 'take their cue from Said's monumental reading of imperial textuality' to undertake 'textual mappings of the colonial encounter'.[56] Gandhi notes that scholars have read the colonial novel, as well as letters, histories, biographies, censuses, newspapers and travel writing, to explore the ways in which empire 'came to define the textual self-representation and narrative sensibility of metropolitan [European] culture'.[57] Legal documents have also been studied for their part in the 'frenzied verbosity' of metropolitan European culture.[58] Indeed, writing and reading law has been a key textual practice in the constitution of the idea of having an empire.[59] In particular, international law and the narrative of empire are inextricably intertwined – as I noted in Chapter 1, the heroic narrative of the march of civilisation supplies international law with its 'history and destiny, beginning and end, explanation and purpose',[60] while international law as a universal system of humanitarian values supplies the

---

[53] Said, *Culture*, p. 10.   [54] *Ibid.*   [55] *Ibid.*, p. xiii.
[56] Gandhi, *Postcolonial Theory*, p. 142.   [57] *Ibid.*, p. 143.   [58] *Ibid.*
[59] Ian Duncanson, 'Scripting Empire: the "Englishman" and Playing for Safety in Law and History' (2000) 24 *Melbourne University Law Review* 952.
[60] Robert M. Cover, 'Foreword: Nomos and Narrative' (1983) 97 *Harvard Law Review* 4 at 5.

narrative of empire with its moral. Spivak argues that 'as the North continues ostensibly to "aid" the South – as formerly imperialism "civilised" the New World – the South's crucial assistance to the North in keeping up its resource-hungry lifestyle is forever foreclosed'.[61] She uses *foreclosed* here in the sense developed in Lacanian psychoanalysis – the ego rejects an incompatible (and here crucially needed) idea together with an affect. She adds 'this rejection of affect served and serves as the energetic and successful defense of the civilizing mission'.[62]

The study of the culture and texts of imperialism has not been without its critics. In her discussion of debates within the discipline of English, Gandhi points to hostility expressed by critics such as Aijaz Ahmad and Arif Dirlik to the work undertaken by those exploring the 'textual politics' of postcolonialism.[63] Such critics argue that there has been a tendency to treat reading practices as if they were revolutionary, when this is just an alibi for the academic migrant or self-styled marginal critic aspiring to a particular class position in the West. For Ahmad, postcolonial literary theory is an indulgence of elites, irrelevant to the stuff of revolution. Thus one theme that concerns postcolonial theory is the relationship between postcolonialism as a textual practice and as a political practice. In part, what is at stake in this debate is the place of the text as an instrument of power.

Law occupies an interesting place in this debate, for while the law is a product and effect of power relations, it is also clearly a text-based practice. International legal texts in particular can be read for their part in producing objects of knowledge as colonisable. Yet legal texts also explain and enable violence in a more traditionally political manner – the legal text is marked out as 'law' in part through the founding violence (neither legal nor illegal) that gives law its authority,[64] while legal texts themselves authorise particular violent acts as legitimate.[65] These texts exhibit many of the features discussed by postcolonial critics

---

[61] Spivak, *A Critique*, p. 6.   [62] *Ibid.*, p. 5.

[63] Aijaz Ahmad, *In Theory: Classes, Nations, Literatures* (Oxford, 1992); Aijaz Ahmad, 'The Politics of Literary Postcoloniality' (1995) 36 *Race and Class* 1; Arif Dirlik, 'The Postcolonial Aura: Third World Criticism in the Age of Global Capitalism' (1994) 20 *Critical Inquiry* 328. See the discussion of anti-postcolonial criticism in Gandhi, *Postcolonial Theory*, pp. 56–8.

[64] Jacques Derrida, 'Force of Law: the "Mystical Foundation of Authority"' in Drucilla Cornell, Michel Rosenfeld and David Gray Carlson (eds.), *Deconstruction and the Possibility of Justice* (London, 1992), pp. 3–67.

[65] Robert M. Cover, 'Violence and the Word' in Martha Minow, Michael Ryan and Austin Sarat (eds.), *Narrative, Violence, and the Law: the Essays of Robert Cover* (Ann Arbor, 1992), pp. 203–38.

of imperial culture – they are premised upon a narrative according to which the invaders bring civilisation, here humanitarianism, to those in need of saving; they provide a schema for making sense of intervention in a manner that is palatable to domestic constituents; they create characters for those doing the invading, formed against the other as an underground self; they authorise violence. At the same time these texts offer possible resources for those who are subject to intervention.[66]

Yet as with postcolonial literary theory, readings of legal texts in the terms I propose give rise to the kinds of criticisms made by Ahmad, who treats 'all postcolonial theoretical practice as purely recreational'.[67] For those who criticise such readings, any reflexive, theoretical engagement with law is a luxury, the stuff of recreation. The pragmatic focus of international legal scholarship requires that all critique be directed towards programmatic change. If theory is necessary in the field of humanitarian intervention, its aim should be to 'work to make law respond consistently' to incidents of human rights abuses or crimes against humanity.[68] The self-representation of international law as a discipline concerned with peace, security, decolonisation and humanitarianism reassures lawyers that there is no time to waste on dealing with theoretical irrelevancies, when our profession is engaged in more important life and death matters. Lawyers have to deal with the facts on the ground and the problems facing real people in the real world. There is no time for abstract theoretical questioning when issues of life and death are at stake. A recent response by Brad Roth to critical scholarship on governmental illegitimacy provides a good example of the demands that orthodox scholarship makes of critique.

'Critical' scholars frequently seem to imagine that, in struggling against the methodological norms of their disciplines, they are struggling against the very structure of the power relations that exploit and repress the poor and weak – the metaphor being, in their minds, somehow transubstantiated into reality. The result is, all too often, an illusory radicalism, rhetorically colorful but programmatically vacuous. The danger is that a fantasized radicalism will lead scholars to abandon the defense of the very devices that give the poor and weak a modicum of leverage, when defense of those devices is perhaps the only thing of practical value that scholars are in a position to contribute.[69]

According to such critics, legal scholarship is at best vacuous and impractical, at worst narcissistic, if it engages in reflection upon the textual

---

[66] See further Chapter 6 below.   [67] Gandhi, *Postcolonial Theory*, p. 56.
[68] Berman, 'In the Wake', 1544.   [69] Roth, 'Governmental Illegitimacy', 2056.

practices of the law, providing no programme for action, institutional design or norm creation. The important question that legal scholarship must address is what doctrinal and institutional changes would help to achieve systemic goals. In other words, the principal thing that is going on in legal texts is the derivation of rules and institutions. To suggest that anything else can be said about the texts of law is frivolous. Programmatic solutions or 'alternatives' are the necessary conclusion to any attempt at critique. As Roth suggests, 'it would be different if [this] methodological radicalism...entailed a programmatic alternative. But it does not. Instead, it disdains to engage in the only consequential struggle in which its adherents are, by training and position, equipped to participate.'[70]

Such comments are familiar within the legal tradition, when its proponents are faced with challenges to the traditional priorities and ordering practices of international law. For example, the marginalisation of critical approaches to international law, and thus the avoidance of any ethical reflection on law's role in facilitating imperialism and exploitation, is evident in those legal texts which engage with feminist and progressive scholars.[71] Responses to postcolonial and feminist critiques both within and outside of the law are 'premised upon the assumption that structural shifts in forms of governance affect people more directly than imaginative shifts in critical methodologies'.[72] Any method of engaging with texts, whether literary, legal or political, that departs from orthodox forms of interpretation, is portrayed as illegitimate, and a dangerous waste of time and energy. Such critiques are part of a broader pattern of negative reactions to the use of cultural and critical theory to study issues of capitalism, globalisation, neoimperialism and militarism, both within international law and within the social sciences more generally. They represent a tradition that treats as opposites 'real' political action and irresponsible critical theory. Writing in 1990, Terry Threadgold criticised a similar tendency emerging in feminist theory to support forms of feminist writing that privileged ' "real" political action', imagined as non-theoretical, over theoretical work seen as 'a kind of intellectual game'.[73] The approach taken by Roth and other critics of legal theory suggests that focusing on representation makes it impossible to think about these issues of the effects of power in the

---

[70] Ibid., 2065.   [71] See further the section on 'Disciplining Feminism' below.

[72] Gandhi, Postcolonial Theory, p. 56.

[73] Terry Threadgold, 'Introduction' in Terry Threadgold and Anne Cranny-Francis (eds.), Feminine–Masculine and Representation (Sydney, 1990), pp. 1–35 at pp. 11, 13.

'real' world. Such critiques set up false dichotomies between politics and the private, and between reality and theory. As Trinh T. Minh-ha argues:

Although much has been said and done concerning the 'apolitical' character of the narrow 'political', is it still interesting to observe the endlessly varying ways the boundaries of 'the political' are being obsessively guarded and reassigned to the exclusive realm of politics-by-politicians. Thus, despite the effectiveness and persistence of the women's movement in deconstructing the opposition between nature (female) and culture (male) or between the private (personal) and the public (political); despite the growing visibility of numerous Third Worldist activities in de-commodifying ethnicity, displacing thereby all divisions of Self and Other or of margin and center based on geographical arbitrations and racial essences; despite all these attacks on pre-defined territories, a 'political' work continues unvaryingly for many to be one which opposes (hence remains particularly dependent upon) institutions and personalities from the body politic, and mechanically 'barks at all the after-effects of past inhumanity' – in other words, which safely counteracts within the limits of pre-formulated, codified forms of resistance.[74]

Similarly, I argue for a reading of humanitarian intervention that does *not* assume that a 'political' response to militarisation and neocolonialism is one which 'opposes...institutions and personalities from the body politic'. It is necessary to consider intervention stories as the result of ongoing cultural processes in order to understand how it is that these stories do the work of making brutality and exploitation appear legitimate and useful. I argue throughout the book that it does not make sense to talk about separating representation from reality, or intellectual games from real political action.[75] While there may be limits on when such critique should take place, my sense of those limits is not the same as that proposed by Roth and others. I agree with the argument that theoretical work should not be simply a frivolous game, played as some kind of elitist distraction from something called 'reality'. I would put this somewhat differently, perhaps following Threadgold as she argues, 'the models for legal writing should come from the law first and only borrow from other contexts if they need changing for political, gendered, racial or other reasons'.[76] In my view, the abandonment of the disciplinary or generic rules of law is called for in the context of humanitarian intervention, as I hope this book will demonstrate.

[74] Trinh T. Minh-ha, *When the Moon Waxes Red: Representation, Gender and Cultural Politics* (New York, 1991), p. 95.
[75] Threadgold, 'Introduction', pp. 13, 18.   [76] Threadgold, 'Book Review', 841.

Cultural criticism is necessary to understand the apparent naturalness and inevitability of both militarism and economic globalisation. Critics of cultural and critical theory reproduce a gendered division and privileging of labour, where the real work of dealing with power and its effects involves an exclusive focus on a 'public' sphere of states, corporations and international organisations, while the soft option of dealing with fantasy, desire and identity is done in a pink ghetto of devalued scholarship.[77]

This book makes use of the insights of postcolonial theory in one further way, to explore law as a form of pedagogy. As I have already noted, despite the exploitative nature of imperial regimes, imperialists did not see their actions in those terms. Rather, as Edward Said has shown so clearly, while 'profit and hope of further profit were obviously tremendously important' in the expansion of European imperialism, so too was a particular imperial culture which supported the notion that 'certain territories and people *require* and beseech domination'.[78] Imperial culture 'on the one hand, allowed decent men and women to accept the notion that distant territories and their native peoples *should* be subjugated, and, on the other, replenished metropolitan energies so that these decent people could think of the *imperium* as a protracted, almost metaphysical obligation to rule subordinate, inferior, or less advanced peoples'.[79] Central to this civilising-mission rhetoric was the idea of colonialism as pedagogy, and the coloniser as an educator. As Gandhi notes, the 'perception of the colonised culture as fundamentally childlike feeds into the logic of the colonial "civilising mission" which is fashioned, quite self-consciously, as a form of tutelage or a disinterested project concerned with bringing the colonised to maturity'.[80] For example, as Thomas Babington Macaulay famously explained, the British in India understood themselves as 'governors' who owed a duty 'as a people blessed with far more than ordinary measure of political liberty and of intellectual light' to educate the Indians, 'a race debased by three thousand years of despotism and priestcraft'.[81] Colonial peoples were to

[77] V. Spike Peterson, 'The Politics of Identity and Gendered Nationalism' in Laura Neack, Patrick J. Haney and Jeanne A. K. Hey (eds.), *Foreign Policy Analysis in its Second Generation: Continuity and Change* (New Jersey, 1995), pp. 167–86 at p. 183 (arguing that the 'gendered dichotomy of public–private structures the study and practice of international relations and foreign policy' and that one result is the 'discipline's neglect of activities associated with the private sphere').

[78] Said, *Culture*, p. 8 (emphasis in original).   [79] *Ibid.*, p. 10 (emphasis in original).

[80] Gandhi, *Postcolonial Theory*, p. 32.

[81] Thomas Babington Macaulay, 'Speeches in the House of Commons, dated 2 February, 1835' in G. W. Young (ed.), *Speeches* (Oxford, 1935), pp. 153–4.

be educated in the operation of the state machinery that had been created to enable the governance and exploitation of colonial territories,
so that a smooth transition from colony to decolonised state could be
made. Both in India, and later in England when the techniques learnt
in the colonies were repatriated, the training of a docile bureaucracy
guarded against the dangers posed by decolonisation and democracy.[82]
As Gandhi argues, 'the simple transference of State machinery' from
colonial regimes to their 'decolonized' successors enabled a 'generic continuity' between the two forms of administration.[83]

The pedagogical imperative, and its conservative effects, continues to
shape intervention discourse. As I discuss in detail in Chapter 4, the
relationship between the international community and the people of
states subject to intervention is portrayed as one of tutelage, particularly in discussions of 'postconflict peacebuilding' or reconstruction. As
that chapter shows, some of the most 'productive' work done by the
law in the realm of intervention is focused on establishing the archi-
tecture of the new post-conflict state in the 'peacebuilding' phase.[84]
For example, in the case of Kosovo and of East Timor, the international
community has set itself the task of creating the machinery and institutions of a reconstructed state, such as a police force, a judiciary, local
administrators, and the institutions of the capitalist market.[85] Its role is
understood in the pedagogical terms that mark colonial discourse –
the international community brings its tutees in places like Kosovo
and East Timor to political and economic maturity through the creation and transfer of the bureaucratic machinery of the modern nation-
state, and the training of the functionaries required to operate that
machinery. Chapter 4 shows that the idea of the international community having a mission to educate and develop is reflected in Security
Council resolutions establishing post-conflict mandates, and in reports

---

[82] Duncanson, 'Scripting Empire', 962.   [83] Gandhi, *Postcolonial Theory*, p. 119.
[84] See generally Michael J. Matheson, 'United Nations Governance of Postconflict
    Societies' (2001) 95 *American Journal of International Law* 76; Ralph Wilde, 'From Bosnia
    to Kosovo and East Timor: the Changing Role of the United Nations in the
    Administration of Territory' (2000) 6 *ILSA Journal of International and Comparative Law*
    467.
[85] In the case of Kosovo, see clause 10, Security Council Resolution 1244, S/RES/1244
    (1999), adopted on 10 June 1999; UNMIK Regulation 1999/1 on the Authority of the
    Interim Administration in Kosovo, paras. 1 and 6, 25 July 1999, http://www.un.org/
    peace/kosovo/pages/regulations/reg1.html (accessed 28 November 2001); Report of the
    Secretary-General on the United Nations Interim Administration Mission in Kosovo,
    S/1999/779 (1999), 12 July 1999. In the case of East Timor, see clauses 1 and 2, Security
    Council Resolution 1272, S/RES/1272 (1999), adopted on 25 October 1999. These
    documents are discussed in detail in Chapter 6.

of those involved in the reconstruction of states under international administration.

The imperial feminist

My reading of international intervention is enabled by the energies and insights of feminism. Yet to develop a feminist reading of an international project is to be haunted by the shades of those nineteenth-century European feminists whose role in facilitating empire is undergoing much exploration.[86] In order to think through the ethical issues involved in the politics of producing such a reading of humanitarian intervention, this section will outline some of the ways in which feminist legal theory is invited to participate in the project of constituting both the women of target states, and the international community. I will consider some of the dangers involved in accepting this invitation, and propose alternative methodologies for undertaking the risky project of (mis)reading the law of international intervention.

Disciplining feminism

One gesture that feminist international lawyers may be tempted, or invited by our legal brethren, to perform when engaging with international law is to participate in the ongoing project of saving the Third World, or in the grammar of Spivak, 'white men ... saving brown women from brown men'.[87] 'White women' are seen as ideally placed, indeed duty-bound, to contribute to this project. For example, in his review of a book of essays entitled *Human Rights of Women: National and International Perspectives*, Anthony D'Amato admonishes Hilary Charlesworth for questioning the justice of the international legal order, arguing that feminists should line up behind the project of saving the vulnerable

---

[86] Gandhi, *Postcolonial Theory*, pp. 81–101; Anne McClintock, *Imperial Leather: Race, Gender and Sexuality in the Colonial Conquest* (New York, 1995); Chandra Talpade Mohanty, 'Under Western Eyes: Feminist Scholarship and Colonial Discourses' in Mohanty, Russo and Torres, *Third World Women*, pp. 51–80; Spivak, *A Critique*.

[87] Spivak, *A Critique*, pp. 284–311. Spivak there begins to plot the history that produces the sentence 'White men are saving brown women from brown men.' She borrows the general methodology developed in Freud's predication of the history that produces the sentence 'A child is being beaten' in Sigmund Freud, ' "A Child Is Being Beaten": a Contribution to the Study of the Origin of Sexual Perversions' in *The Standard Edition of the Complete Psychological Works of Sigmund Freud*, (trans. James Strachey, Anna Freud, Alix Strachey and Alan Tyson) (24 vols., London, 1955), vol. XVII, pp. 179–204.

women of the Third World.[88] D'Amato there reproduces a vision of a world structured according to stereotypes of race and gender. The role of international law is to 'compensate women' for their weakness and vulnerability, particularly during child-bearing years, thus contributing to the creation of an 'advanced civilisation'.[89] D'Amato argues that such a civilisation is marked by its distance from one in which we behave 'like animals'.[90] In the animal world, according to D'Amato, bullying behaviour is the norm: 'on the whole, animals decide questions of life and death on the basis of physical power and brute force', and 'if an animal is weak, lame or infirm, other animals of its own species may kill or abandon it'.[91] As women are 'on average' in this weaker position and thus likely to be murdered or abandoned, D'Amato argues that international law should aim to bring all cultures close to those of 'highly industrialized countries', where in recent times women have made great progress in resisting institutionalised bullying.[92] As women are weak and the likely targets for violence, the role of international law and international lawyers is to protect them.

According to D'Amato, feminists should commit themselves to this task, rather than seeking to dismantle the system set up to save women from the laws of the jungle. He is particularly scathing of those feminist scholars who go beyond a traditional critique of the content of international law by 'accusing international law itself for having an andocentric nature that privileges a male view of world society'.[93] He challenges that approach on the grounds that it is like 'criticizing a house for having oppressively straight walls that meet each other at 90-degree angles and unnaturally level floors that do not tilt, and then blaming the end

---

[88] Anthony D'Amato, 'Book Review: Rebecca Cook (ed.), *Human Rights of Women: National and International Perspectives*' (1995) 89 *American Journal of International Law* 840.

[89] *Ibid.*, 840–1. According to D'Amato, it is 'a fact of nature that women are on the average physically weaker than men. Moreover, they pay the physical price for perpetuating the human species; during their child-bearing and child-nurturing years they are especially weak and vulnerable.'

[90] *Ibid.*, 840. D'Amato assumes that 'we' are not animals.

[91] *Ibid.* For an analysis of the way in which such stories about animals and nature are produced in order to legitimate certain social hierarchies or methods of ordering, see Donna Haraway, *Primate Visions: Gender, Race and Nature in the World of Modern Science* (New York, 1989).

[92] Hilary Charlesworth, 'Cries and Whispers: Responses to Feminist Scholarship in International Law' (1996) 65 *Nordic Journal of International Law* 557 at 563. Charlesworth argues that D'Amato attempts 'to quarantine more generally the problem of women's oppression to a few hot countries' by drawing a distinction between 'highly industrialized' and 'patriarchal' states.

[93] D'Amato, 'Book Review', 843.

product on the fact that the T square was set at 90 degrees instead of 80, the saw was *not* warped, and the nails were excessively straight'.[94] If feminists want to 'use law to transform an oppressive society', they would be better off 'taking law as it is, with all its rationality, objectivity and abstraction'.

If you want an unusual house and are dissatisfied with existing models, you are better off using traditional tools rather than eccentric ones, because the latter are less likely to produce the house that you want – the resulting house may well be skewed, but in a quite different way from what you had in mind.[95]

The comparison of international law to an orderly, systematic and efficient 'end product' of a building project reassures D'Amato and his audience that feminist criticisms are no threat to international law's rationality, civilising mission and responsibility for world order. That mission and responsibility involves bringing 'oppressive societies' up to the standards we are used to in 'highly industrialised countries', a project to which feminists can contribute by seeking to protect the weak through the rule of law.

In a similar vein, Bruno Simma and Andreas L. Paulus have suggested that feminists should not 'dispense with neutrality and objectivity' to engage in 'highly subjective' readings of legal doctrine, but should instead join in 'the dialogue with decision makers' aimed at 'setting general standards for human behavior'.[96] Such norms are 'urgently needed to hold the perpetrators of crimes against women accountable under the rule of law'.[97] Thus for Simma and Paulus, the role of feminist critique is to harness the 'transformative potential of the adaptation of positive law to meet women's concerns'.[98] The appropriate audience for critique is 'decision makers', the object of feminist work is 'women's concerns' and the appropriate end of critique is development of the rule of law. While there may be many instances where justice is served by such an approach, I want to question here the command that feminist work should unthinkingly be limited to joining the humanitarian mission of international law.

Such responses suggest that feminists are not welcome to develop an alternative practice of reading international law, one that tries 'to

---

[94] *Ibid.* (emphasis in original).   [95] *Ibid.*
[96] Bruno Simma and Andreas L. Paulus, 'The Responsibility of Individuals for Human Rights Abuses in Internal Conflicts: a Positivist View' (1999) 93 *American Journal of International Law* 302.
[97] *Ibid.*   [98] *Ibid.*

effect change by making the genres "mean" differently'.[99] Instead, feminists appear authorised to contribute to international law in two ways. First, women from 'highly industrialised countries' can gain access to female 'native informants' and produce knowledge about the victimised women of the Third World. In my own and others' experience, feminist international legal theory that departs from this role is criticised as 'unrelated to the real world', insufficiently linked to 'particular cases' or unable to deal with the 'facts on the ground'. Such criticisms suggest that there is an identifiable 'real world', namely the Third World, about which international lawyers can discover facts and gather information. The production or reproduction of knowledge about the real world of women is one of the ways in which some feminist international legal texts continue to be part of a tradition of imperialism. In this version of the appropriate disciplinary role of feminist theory, the suffering of the Third World Woman becomes the object of knowledge of First World International Lawyers. Feminists, in other words, can take their place as part of a 'set of human sciences busy establishing the "native" as a self-consolidating other'.[100] This is a direction that may at first glance appear a helpful response to the discovery that the silence of women is one of the foundations of international law. Yet as Hilary Charlesworth has commented more generally, if we find that the silence of women is 'an integral part of the structure of the international legal order, a critical element of its stability', we cannot respond by simply undertaking some remedial 'reconstruction work'.[101] Spivak warns that we cannot usefully respond to the silencing of the 'subaltern' woman by 'representing' that figure, or by constructing her as a speaking subject. Even when undertaken with 'good intentions', the attempt to rewrite the Third World as the subject of a reconfigured, decolonised Law cannot succeed. 'No perspective *critical* of imperialism can turn the other into a self, because the project of imperialism has always already historically refracted what might have been an incommensurable, discontinuous other into a domesticated other that consolidates the imperialist self.'[102]

Throughout her work, Spivak points to the ethical problems that arise if imperial feminists try to 'speak for' or 'know' Third World Women. This is particularly so in the context of an internationalism that positively welcomes those forms of 'sisterhood' aimed at producing new female

[99] Threadgold, 'Book Review'.   [100] Spivak, *A Critique*, p. 131.
[101] Hilary Charlesworth, 'Feminist Methods in International Law' (1999) 93 *American Journal of International Law* 379 at 381.
[102] Spivak, *A Critique*, p. 130 (emphasis in original).

subjects of development without unsettling the priorities of globalisation. For example, Krysti Guest has criticised the absurdity of some of the 'grotesque' attempts to give voice to 'the poor' on the part of the UN,[103] using as one example the 'Seminar on Extreme Poverty'.[104] This was a seminar that 'broke new ground' by inviting thirty 'very poor persons' to New York to engage in 'direct dialogue' with UN bodies.[105] According to the report of the UN Special Rapporteur on Human Rights and Extreme Poverty, Mr Leandro Despouy, 'the seminar expressed a desire for knowledge while realising a partnership right for the very poor'.[106] Guest points to the dangerous effects of this belief that UN experts could 'gain a better understanding of the living conditions and thoughts' of a homogenous category of 'very poor people' through a process authored in the name of human rights and global partnerships.[107]

Ethical questions aside as to the implications of this exchange on the lives of those people, the audacity of the assumption that one can know 'the poor' through the reductio ad absurdum of flying thirty 'extremely poor people' to New York reveals the seminar as a paradigmatic site of imperialist homogenising of 'the poor'. This creation of an homogeneous 'poor' continues in the substance of the 'direct dialogue', which proceeds by way of the thirty extremely poor people telling their story to the attentive UN representatives, the governing assumption being that one can 'know the poor' through their concrete experience. However, by staging the speaking subaltern through the positivism of 'concrete experience', the seminar erases all trace of the ways in which any re-presentation of such experience is overdetermined by the historical circuits of imperialist law and education or by the epistemic violence wrought on 'the poor' by the international division of labour. Unsurprisingly, these overdetermined representations by 'the extremely poor' do not offer a subversive analysis of international political economy, but are merely depoliticised accounts of poverty as a vicious cycle of misery.[108]

As Guest argues, the idea of a 'partnership with the poor' operates to mask the ways in which the 'systemic logic' of economic globalisation as implemented by international institutions generates poverty.[109] Feminism in states like the USA can in turn operate to reinforce that dynamic,

---

[103] Krysti Justine Guest, 'Exploitation under Erasure: Economic, Social and Cultural Rights Engage Economic Globalisation' (1997) 19 Adelaide Law Review 73.

[104] Commission on Human Rights, Report of the Seminar on Extreme Poverty and the Denial of Human Rights, E/CN.4/1995/101, 15 December 1994.

[105] Leandro Despouy, The Realisation of Economic, Social and Cultural Rights: Second Interim Report on Human Rights and Extreme Poverty, E/CN.4/Sub.2/1995/15, 5 July 1995, paras. 14, 15.

[106] Ibid., para. 15.   [107] Ibid., para. 13.   [108] Guest, 'Exploitation', 88–9.   [109] Ibid., 90.

so that we are left with the image produced in a World Bank pamphlet discussed by Spivak, where 'a hard-hatted white woman points the way to a smiling Arab woman in ethnic dress' under the heading of 'Gender and Development'.[110]

As well as producing knowledge about Third World Women, the discipline of international law authorises feminists to design rules that contribute to the protecting or saving of other women within the realms of international human rights law or international criminal law. However, as the experience of some of the women who attended the Beijing Fourth World Conference on Women in 1995 revealed, feminists are neither welcome to question the broader international legal commitment to trade and financial liberalisation, nor to challenge the international community's practice of supporting certain kinds of militarism, while outlawing that conducted on the part of 'terrorists' or 'rogue states'.[111] Some of the risks of contributing to the 'readily identifiable and paradoxically impossible solutions' proposed for women by international institutions can be seen from two of the growing body of UN-sponsored resolutions and documents concerning women and security.[112] In October 2000, the Security Council held a meeting on women and peace and security. In his address to that meeting, the UN Secretary-General Kofi Annan provided an example of the ways in which a 'gender perspective' can be mapped onto existing ways of doing business without questioning any of the bases upon which peace, security or even the category 'woman' is understood.[113] The place of this address is a world divided into two groups – men and women. The time of this address is an 'age of ethnic conflict', in which militias and the proliferation of small arms are marked out as threats to the peace. Women need protection in these kinds of conflict situations. To think about the links between women and peace or security is therefore to think about women's 'special needs' in relation to the needs of 'men' as a general category. This staging of

---

[110] Spivak, *A Critique*, p. 148.

[111] Anne Orford, 'Contesting Globalization: a Feminist Perspective on the Future of Human Rights' (1998) 8 *Transnational Law and Contemporary Problems* 171 at 192–4.

[112] Security Council Resolution 1325, S/RES/1325 (2000), adopted on 31 October 2000; *Windhoek Declaration: the Namibia Plan of Action on 'Mainstreaming a Gender Perspective in Multidimensional Peace Support Operations'*, 31 May 2000, www.unifem.undp.org/ unseccouncil/windhoek.html (accessed 23 August 2001). On the 'readily identifiable and paradoxically impossible solutions' offered to women by liberalism, see Alison Young, *Femininity in Dissent* (London, 1990), p. 12.

[113] UN, *Secretary-General Calls for Council Action to Ensure Women Are Involved in Peace and Security Decisions*, UN Press Release SG/SM/7598, 24 October 2000.

a struggle between men and women as a central mechanism for under-standing conflict, peace and security threatens to obscure many of the issues that feminists and women's groups have attempted to raise, such as the relationship between insecurity and economic liberalisation, or the ways in which the international division of labour is itself a vio-lent process. Imagining a struggle in these terms strips the world of its imperial history – can we really talk about conflict in the context of globalisation without suggesting that some women may perhaps not see taking 'their rightful and equal place at the decision-making table in questions of peace and security' as the key issue facing them today?

The Secretary-General's text also reinforces stereotypical views about women. Women are understood principally as victims of conflict – 'from rape and displacement to the denial of the right to food and health care, women bear more than their fair share of suffering'. Women are innately peaceful – 'women, who know the price of conflict so well, are also often better equipped than men to prevent or resolve it'. Women support their men and those of the international community – 'we in the United Nations know, at first hand, the invaluable support women provide to our peacekeepers ... persuading their menfolk to accept peace'. As gentle handmaidens and victims of war, women have an important role to play in helping support peace-keeping and peace-making missions.

The limitations of this role for women are avoided to an extent in the statement to the Security Council meeting by the Australian Permanent Representative to the United Nations, Ambassador Penny Wensley.[114] Wensley seeks to move beyond seeing women as 'victims of armed con-flict, as sufferers, as vulnerable people whose rights need protecting', to seeing women as potentially 'contributors and active participants'. Yet women are not imagined as playing a part in changing the rules of the game or the way that game is understood. Instead, the Australian delegation seeks to ensure that women are able to contribute to the existing projects and priorities of the UN – women have been 'denied their full role in national and international peacekeeping and peace-making operations' and 'the mandates of UN preventive peace missions, peacekeeping operations and peacebuilding should include provisions for women's protection and address gender issues'.[115] An international

---

[114] Penny Wensley, Ambassador and Permanent Representative of Australia to the United Nations, *Statement at the Open Meeting on Women and Peace and Security of the United Nations Security Council*, 24 October 2000, www.un.int/australia/Statements/ PS Statements.htm (accessed 23 August 2001).
[115] *Ibid.*

feminism conducted in these terms would simply have as its end the pairing of women with men as subjects of militarisation and globalisation. Any more subversive questioning of the way threats to the peace are understood, of the desirability of peace-keeping and peace-making operations as currently conceived, or of the nature and priorities of peace-building, are swept away by the promise to increase women's participation in a project the terms of which are already set. The Australian position implies that the project of advancing women's role as part of the mission to achieve peace and security is to be understood in the old terms of educating colonial tutees – the Australian delegation is able to provide examples of practical steps that can be taken to support the role of women in peace processes from the practical steps taken in its own 'development assistance programs' in Bougainville, the Solomon Islands and East Timor.

Does gender work as a category in such situations, and if so, whose work does it do?[116] How does this officially sanctioned desire to 'include' women as participants relate to the current enthusiasm for exporting the institutions of the free market in the name of democracy?[117] What to make of a refusal or resistance of the form that peace reconstruction takes, when that resistance is carried out in terms of social conservatism and religion over the bodies of women?[118] Such issues are far more complicated than the picture painted by these UN documents of a world in which, to paraphrase Spivak, white women save brown women from brown men. Failing to ask such questions of the role played by 'gender mainstreaming' in the new world order may mean that feminism ends up simply facilitating the existing projects and priorities of militarised economic globalisation in the name of protecting and promoting the interests of women.

Feminist criticism and the axiomatics of imperialism

As I have already implied, I see the invitation to participate in the humanitarian mission of international law as one that carries with it old

[116] For an introduction to this question, see Hilary Charlesworth and Mary Wood, ' "Mainstreaming Gender" in International Peace and Security: the Case of East Timor' (2001) 26 *Yale Journal of International Law* 313.

[117] Anne Orford, 'The Subject of Globalization: Economics, Identity and Human Rights' (2000) 94 *American Society of International Law Proceedings* 146.

[118] Charlesworth and Wood, 'Mainstreaming Gender', 316, discussing East Timorese resistance to the operations of the Gender Affairs Unit established by the UN Transitional Authority in East Timor in April 2000.

dangers. As Spivak has argued, it is 'particularly unfortunate [if] the emergent perspective of feminist criticism simply reproduces the axioms of imperialism'.[119] Which of the truths of imperialism risk reproduction in the texts of international legal feminism?

First, just as imperialism was a 'subject-constituting project' which served to consolidate both Europe and Europeans as sovereign subjects by defining Europe's colonies as 'Others', so too was nineteenth-century European feminism.[120] Through her reading of the novel *Jane Eyre*, Spivak shows what this meant for feminism and its colonised others.[121] She focuses on the character of Bertha Mason, the 'madwoman in the attic' who is finally given a history in Jean Rhys' *Wide Sargasso Sea*.[122] Spivak reads the treatment of Bertha Mason in *Jane Eyre*, in particular her setting fire to Thornfield Hall and killing herself 'so that Jane Eyre can become the feminist individualist heroine of British fiction', as 'an allegory of the general epistemic violence of imperialism'.[123] The sacrifice of Bertha Mason was the condition of the freedom and individuation of Jane Eyre. More broadly for nineteenth-century English feminists, the imperial project of soul-making allowed those women of Empire to move out of domestic childrearing so as to take part in the broader mission of civilising the other.

What is at stake, for feminist individualism in the age of imperialism, is precisely the making of human beings, the constitution and 'interpellation' of the subject not only as individual but also as 'individualist'. This stake is represented on two registers: childrearing and soul-making. The first is domestic-society-through-sexual-reproduction cathected as 'companionate' love; the second is the imperialist project cathected as civil-society-through-social-mission. As the female individualist, not-quite-not-male, articulates herself in shifting relationship to what is at stake, the 'native subaltern female' (*within* discourse, *as* a signifier) is excluded from any share in this emerging norm... In a reading such as mine... the effort is to wrench oneself away from the mesmerizing focus of the 'subject-constitution' of the female individualist.[124]

This world of subject-constitution through civilising mission, of Europe and its Others, is the world of humanitarian intervention. The constitution of native women in the texts of imperial feminism served to found the individuality of European women, and to make possible their participation in the larger project of soul-making through civilising mission.

---

[119] Spivak, *A Critique*, p. 114.   [120] *Ibid.*, pp. 125, 199.
[121] Charlotte Brontë, *Jane Eyre* (New York, 1960).
[122] Jean Rhys, *Wide Sargasso Sea* (London, 1968).   [123] Spivak, *A Critique*, p. 127.
[124] *Ibid.*, p. 117 (emphasis in original).

In the texts of international law, the feminist individualist is again able to constitute herself in shifting relationship to what is at stake over the bodies of her sisters who function as material evidence. As I argue in Chapter 5, the narratives of humanitarian intervention hail readers as white, powerful, active and masculine, and this has historically been a way of producing white, middle-class, imperial men and women. Audiences in intervening states are asked to identify with the role assigned to the active, muscular, professional agents of democracy or security constituted in these narratives of salvation. Women reading and writing such texts are able to identify with those heroic characters, but only if we are willing to sacrifice others to the feminine role of pitiable victim. In a similar way, nineteenth-century feminists were able to experience increased agency, just as imperial men could. What then are women who are international lawyers required to do to 'other' women and to feminised men in order to participate in 'the spoils of freedom'?[125] How to ensure, as Jean Rhys does in *Wide Sargasso Sea*, that 'the woman from the colonies is not sacrificed as an insane animal for her sister's consolidation'?[126]

In addition, feminist theory threatens merely to facilitate and enable neocolonialism if it stages the key struggle in this globalised world in terms of 'the mesmerizing model' of 'male and female sparring partners of generalizable or universizable sexuality'.[127] Paying attention only to the protagonists in this drama blinds us to the way in which the Third World is staged as a backdrop, with a cast of nameless extras imagined as playing a part they have not written. A feminist analysis of intervention that focuses on gender alone, without analysing the exploitation of women in the economic 'South', would operate to reinforce the depoliticised notion of 'difference' that founds the privileged position of the imperial feminist.[128] Versions of feminism have been able to enter disciplinary debates without destabilising metaphors of race and class that operate within disciplines like science and law to establish knowledge hierarchies.[129] Attempting to broaden the questions asked in her field of sociobiology, Donna Haraway comments:

I am ... interested in sociobiology as a postmodern discourse in late capitalism, where versions of feminism readily enter the contest for meanings, at least in retrospect and over the tired bodies of gutsy sociobiological feminists. How

[125] Renata Salecl, *The Spoils of Freedom: Psychoanalysis and Feminism after the Fall of Socialism* (London, 1994).
[126] Spivak, *A Critique*, p. 127.   [127] *Ibid.*, p. 148.   [128] Guest, 'Exploitation'.
[129] Haraway, *Primate Visions*, p. 353.

have sociobiological feminist arguments, like other western feminisms, enabled deconstruction of masculinist systems of representation, while simultaneously both deepening and problematizing unmarked enabling tropes of western ethnocentrism and neo-imperialism?[130]

To some extent, the field of international law differs from the sociobiology that Haraway describes, in that international legal feminists have not been able to ensure that their versions of feminism can enter the contest for meanings in the security and economic areas in which I am interested here. Not even imperial feminisms have been able successfully to contest the meanings of international economic law and collective security. There is clearly a need, then, to continue the attempt to criticise the masculinist foundations of these discourses. Yet the point that feminists are capable of reinscribing race and class difference is an important one in this area. How is it possible to engage with the internationalist discourses that form the object of my study without deepening the 'enabling tropes of western ethnocentrism and neo-imperialism'? In the fields of military intervention and economic development, for example, the bodies of 'womenandchildren' already appear playing the roles of objects: victims of rape, objects of religious control, victims of the sex trade, victims of droughts and famines. Can feminist analyses avoid reproducing these staples of legal texts, avoid dreaming of saving other women in ways that enable us to feel a power that we are unable to feel in our everyday lives?

Errant theory – feminist readings of intervention

A feminist politics of reading international law therefore has to attempt to avoid the deployment of 'the axiomatics of imperialism for crucial textual functions'.[131] In particular, it has to avoid seeing the world in terms of a 'battleground of male and female individualism', in which the goal of feminism would be merely to move women from the female domain of sexual reproduction to the male domain of 'social subject-production' via the sacrifice of the Other Woman. In the texts of humanitarian intervention, for example, the heroic subject is produced according to the logic of a narrative which legalises (or at least legitimises) aerial bombardment or sanctioned starvation. In the texts of international economic law, the belief that globalisation or development will result in liberated subjects ignores the ways in which economic

[130] Ibid.   [131] Spivak, A Critique, p. 133.

reconstruction produces a gendered international division of labour. What might a feminist reading that attempts to avoid reproducing the unarticulated assumptions of imperialism look like? How does this inform the ethics of feminist approaches to international law today?

In the essays collected together in *A Critique of Postcolonial Reason*, Spivak argues that critics (of literature, of law) must try to 'reopen the epistemic fracture of imperialism without succumbing to the nostalgia for lost origins';[132] that is, without trying to discover some kind of originary, exoticised, premodern, and always victimised, Third World Woman. Basing our 'global sisterhood' on the connections we imagine with such a figure supports the current processes of imperialism, militarism, financialisation and development – all can be more palatably conducted in the name of the suffering 'womenandchildren' of the Third World, with First World Feminists helping to constitute those marginalised figures.

A feminist reading practice thus might involve thinking through the conditions of the self-constitution of the international community, and the part that 'sisterhood' is called to play in that self-constitution. Chapter 5 attempts such a reading of the texts of intervention to explore the ways in which they constitute a heroic 'self' for the international community. The appeal of humanitarian intervention is produced through the process of identification with, or as, the heroes of intervention. Intervention narratives are premised on the notion of an international community facing new dangers, acting to save the oppressed and to protect values such as democracy and human rights. The reader of intervention literature is asked to identify with the active hero of the story, be that the international community, the UN or the USA, at the cost of the violence done to the imagined objects who form the matter of the hero's quest. The hero possesses the attributes of that version of aggressive white masculinity produced in late twentieth-century US culture, a white masculinity obsessed with competitive militarism and the protection of universal (read imperial) values.[133]

My reading also attempts to undo the opposition between coloniser and colonised, by seeking to show 'strategic complicities' between the terms in which the 'other' is constructed in intervention texts, and the

---

[132] *Ibid.*, p. 146.

[133] For a discussion of the relationship between colonialism and universality, in which 'European practices are posited as universally applicable norms with which the colonial peoples must conform', see further Antony Anghie, 'Francisco de Vitoria and the Colonial Origins of International Law' (1996) 5 *Social and Legal Studies* 321 at 332–3.

self that is there constructed.[134] I look at the similarities between the production of the heroic, masculine self of the international community, and the constitution of the other against whom force is deployed in the name of the values of that community.[135] Legal texts justify intervention on the basis of the need to reject forms of nationalism that depend upon fundamentalism and religion, and to punish those who seek to found communities on violence, exclusion and the wounding of bodies in the name of the law. Yet the texts of intervention are structured in equivalent ways. Chapter 6 argues that the international community shares something with those fantasised national or 'tribal' communities against which it constitutes itself. It shares a commitment to the wounding and excluding of marked others as its founding act. This fact helps to explain the vehemence with which those who identify with the international community come to disavow the leaders of 'rogue' or 'failed' national or tribal communities as less than human. This disavowal is necessary precisely because these communities in fact share that which the international community rejects as illegitimate: an originary violence deployed against those who are marked out on the grounds of race, ethnicity and gender. That with which we charge the other – that it founds a masculinist, racially exclusionary, violent and nationalist political order on the expulsion and wounding of women and children – is in fact the basis of the international community as constituted through intervention narratives. The attempts to disavow this lead to more violence.

A feminist reading of humanitarian intervention that seeks to avoid enabling exploitation must pay careful attention to the context of increasing economic integration in which such intervention takes place. The ending of the Cold War has enabled the process of economic globalisation to be facilitated by the increasingly effective and rapidly shifting operations of international economic institutions such as the IMF, the World Bank and the World Trade Organization (WTO).[136] The consequences of economic restructuring, and the fact that international

---

[134] For a reading of the strategic complicities in the treatment of the play of law and history in a text of the coloniser and the colonised, see Spivak, *A Critique*, p. 46.

[135] For a similar reading of the Bosnian conflict as 'an exacerbation rather than an aberration of the logic behind the constitution of political community', see David Campbell, 'Violence, Justice and Identity in the Bosnia Conflict' in Jenny Edkins, Nalim Persram and Véronique Pin-Fat (eds.), *Sovereignty and Subjectivity* (Boulder, 1999), pp. 21–37 at p. 23.

[136] There are many other actors involved in formulating and implementing the process of economic globalisation. The activities of international economic institutions are of particular interest because it is through those institutions that much of the agenda

institutions play such a central role in furthering that project, require international lawyers to begin to rethink what internationalism means in the twenty-first century. Intervention discourse on the whole almost completely ignores the current historical context of rapid and massive global economic change within which security and humanitarian crises emerge and military interventions take place. International law has been criticised more broadly for this curious, ahistorical representation of 'the international'.[137] For example, international lawyers have not taken into account the role played by the activities of international economic institutions in contributing to security crises. While ancient hatreds, ethnic tensions, postmodern tribalism or emerging nationalisms are regularly treated as the causes of humanitarian and security crises, most international legal analyses do not ask whether such crises could better be understood as a consequence of ever more ruthlessly efficient divisions of labour and resources in the post-Soviet era. Nor has the international legal literature on post-conflict reconstruction attended critically to the nature of the economic order that is put in place through that reconstruction process.[138] This book argues that it is necessary to take such activities into account in order to assess the meaning of humanitarian intervention.

Finally, the feminist method I develop assumes that 'international law is not a finished system',[139] that legal texts are never fully enclosed because that which founds the law is itself always both legal and illegal.[140] In her reading of the ethics of international law, Outi Korhonen argues, following Jacques Derrida, that international law, like any other genre, constrains those who seek to communicate in its terms, as it imposes on them the necessity to speak in the language of the law.[141] At the same time, this allows for the openness of the law, precisely because there

of economic restructuring is pursued in the aftermath of the Cold War. Economic and investment liberalisation is largely carried out multilaterally, with unilateral or bilateral initiatives threatened or resorted to in order to strengthen multilateral negotiations and regulations.

[137] David W. Kennedy, 'A New World Order: Yesterday, Today and Tomorrow' (1994) 4 *Transnational Law and Contemporary Problems* 329; Philip Alston, 'The Myopia of the Handmaidens: International Lawyers and Globalization' (1997) 8 *European Journal of International Law* 435.

[138] For an analysis that does pay attention to the economics of reconstruction, from the position of advocating the increased participation of the 'private sector' in 'economic peace building', see Allan Gerson, 'Peace Building: the Private Sector's Role' (2001) 95 *American Journal of International Law* 102.

[139] Outi Korhonen, *International Law Situated: an Analysis of the Lawyer's Stance towards Culture, History and Community* (The Hague, 2000), p. 223.

[140] Derrida, 'Force of Law'.   [141] Korhonen, *International Law*, pp. 207–84.

can never be a purely autonomous legal language. International law is a common enterprise, and thus the meanings that can be made of international law cannot be fully controlled – for any actor to participate in that enterprise is to surrender autonomy. The very fact that there is no controlling agent of the law opens up the possibility of justice. While we are constrained by the protocols of the texts of law, the meanings of those protocols, constraints and texts is something we make in community. Korhonen argues, pace Ronald Dworkin, that 'although the "rules of the game" are often very autonomous and constraining, they cannot be absolutely so, for they never have a singular agent to operate them in a purely idiomatic way. There is no singular Herculean lawyer whose advice could be asked on every issue'.[142] Law is not the autonomous possession of any one agent who can control it and guarantee its purity.[143] In addition, the law can never be a purely self-referential system because 'the legal structure cannot be known or used without its agent (the jurist) who cannot be its agent alone'.[144] International law can only appear closed through the efforts of the international lawyer, who must continually draw the boundary between law and non-law, inside and outside.

> The jurist manages a larger realm than just the circle of law, for that circle is not closed without her constant efforts of providing closure...Therefore the jurist stands in a situational bind, for which there is no one-time solution, having to constantly make the difference between law and non-law, legally communicable and non-communicable, inclusion and exclusion – by assertion, detection, and silence.[145]

Here lies the possibility for remaking the law in the image of justice. The law depends upon those who read and write it for the sense of closure upon which its legitimacy depends, and the international community in turn depends upon the law to perform the acts of exclusion and violence which both make possible, and limit, the building of that community. For those of us attempting to avoid 'being made subject-matter of law, subject to these genres, unable to become speaking subjects of law', learning to recognise and engage with the narratives by which the authority of law is produced is an essential skill.[146] When as an Australian feminist I attempt to read and write international law differently, I am also answerable to law's others, those who are rendered

---

[142] Ibid., p. 222.   [143] Ibid., p. 221.   [144] Ibid., p. 223.   [145] Ibid., p. 219.
[146] Nina Puren and Alison Young, 'Signifying Justice: Law, Culture and the Questions of Feminism' (1999) 13 Australian Feminist Law Journal 3 at 5.

as outlaws, illegals, material evidence, by the discipline within which I am conditionally authorised to speak. This is not to say that it is possible to avoid these acts of exclusion, or the drawing of boundaries. Rather, the knowledge that 'the commitment to international law implies community-building', and that this process is always incomplete or inconclusive, leads us to understand the ethics of reading and writing law differently. To return to Spivak:

If we want to start something, we must ignore that our starting point is, *all efforts taken*, shaky. If we want to get something done, we must ignore that, *all provisions made*, the end will be inconclusive. This ignoring is not an active forgetfulness; it is, rather, an active *marginalizing* of the marshiness, the swampiness, the lack of firm grounding in the margins, at beginning and end... These necessarily and actively marginalized margins haunt what we start and get done, as curious guardians... [We must not] forget the productive unease that what we do with the utmost care is judged in the margins.[147]

Any writer or reader of legal texts, critical or otherwise, is always faced with the challenge posed by these curious guardians at the margins – for me, to remember this is to be reminded of the demands of justice. Reading a legal text as a feminist involves trying to find a way to avoid sacrificing 'other women' while I take part in the constitution of international communities. Yet the authority I have to speak as a lawyer has been produced through a tradition dependent upon the starving, warring, abused, passive, victimised, chaotic, disordered, ungoverned bodies of international legal texts. Thus my reading is itself disciplined by international law. It also attempts to work with and through the limitations of the law, to see whether the protocols of the texts of law make possible 'a moment that can produce something that will generate a new and useful reading... a moment of transgression in the text – or a moment of bafflement that discloses not only limits but also possibilities to a new politics of reading'.[148]

The power of international law

It follows from what I have written in this chapter to date that my approach to reading humanitarian intervention departs from that of many international lawyers in its understanding of the basis of the power of international law. The question of the relationship between law and power is one that has been firmly on the theoretical agenda of our discipline

---

[147] Spivak, *A Critique*, p. 175 (emphasis in original).   [148] *Ibid.*, p. 98.

since at least the nineteenth century. International lawyers in general are practised in articulating a nuanced account of the power of law. This is in part due to our training in responding to the attacks of domestic positivists such as the nineteenth-century English legal philosopher John Austin, whose well-worn argument is that international society lacks an overarching sovereign, and thus lacks the power to create law.[149] Since the inter-war period, international lawyers have also been concerned to respond to realist international relations scholars, for whom it did not seem at all clear that international law had the capacity to constrain abuses of power by powerful states or to create order out of the anarchic state of international relations.[150] International legal texts thus often open with an account of the nature of international law and a concern with the question: 'how can legal order be created among sovereign states?'[151]

The answer to that question may derive from a positivist focus on the consent of states to the laws governing international society,[152] from a more 'sophisticated attitude about the death of sovereign forms' and the need to work for the renewal of sovereignty at the international level, or from a pragmatic belief that the development of a strengthened international order and flourishing global market cannot ignore how power is actually distributed.[153] Either way, international lawyers do not usually conceive of international law as embodying or enacting sovereign power. Indeed, the question 'is international law really law', a question that haunts international legal theory, is a manifestation of the sense that international law lacks this sovereign force.[154] Yet while international lawyers recognise that international law does not emanate from a single, sovereign authority, the discipline has generally not questioned that such power vests somewhere, usually in those sovereign states that

---

[149] John Austin, *The Province of Jurisprudence Determined and the Uses of the Study of Jurisprudence* (London, 1954), p. 302.

[150] For literature discussing the division, and subsequent post-Cold War rapprochement, between the disciplines of international law and international relations, see David Kennedy, 'The Disciplines of International Law and Policy' (1999) 12 *Leiden Journal of International Law* 9 at 106–9; Gerry Simpson, 'The Situation on the International Legal Theory Front: the Power of Rules and the Rule of Power' (2000) 11 *European Journal of International Law* 439.

[151] As discussed in Anghie, 'Francisco de Vitoria'.

[152] For an elaboration of that position, see Michael Byers, *Custom, Power and the Power of Rules: International Relations and Customary International Law* (Cambridge, 1999).

[153] Kennedy, 'The International Style', 13.

[154] See, for example, Anthony D'Amato, 'Is International Law Really "Law"?' (1985) 79 *Northwestern University Law Review* 1293.

are the source of international law. The question as to whether international law is really law is never meant as a question about the utility of the sovereign model as a means of understanding the relationship between power and international law, but rather as a question about whether international law conforms to an otherwise self-evidently realistic model of power. As Kennedy has argued, while 'metropolitan' public international law 'remains obsessed with the struggle somehow to reinvent at an international level the sovereign authority it was determined to transcend', its more pragmatic, private international law twin is 'united by its fealty to a rejected sovereignty' and 'haunted by the ghost of a sovereignty it explicitly rejects'.[155]

Traditional international legal scholarship assumes that politics goes on in the public sphere, and that power is a commodity that can be held by particular entities. Those entities may be superpowers exercising power over the new world order, sovereign states exercising power over their peoples and territories, international organisations at times managing to exercise such power over 'failed' or disordered states during successful interventions, or the market disciplining states that have failed to organise their 'economic fundamentals'. International law is primarily understood as either in service to, or as an attempt to constrain, such powerful entities.[156] The principal disciplinary question relating to power is how to orient international law to power, or how best to deal with the realities of the operation of power in the international sphere. As a result, international lawyers focus most of our attention on analysing the ways in which international law can assist in constraining, disabling or negotiating with those who are imagined as holding power.

In this book, I follow in the tradition of an alternative approach to international law, which argues that 'a continuing unsatisfactory juridical image of sovereignty in mainstream internationalist commentary has resulted in an underestimation of law's constitutive role in civil society, of the fluidity of power throughout a culture, and of the potential for politics outside traditional discourses of public authority'.[157] A critical reading of humanitarian intervention needs to depart from a conception

---

155 Kennedy, 'The International Style', 11, 13, 14.
156 The structure of international argument has swung between apologetic or pragmatic approaches to the fact that international lawyers have to be realistic about where power lies and idealistic approaches that make great claims for the possibility that international law can constrain such power: see Martti Koskenniemi, *From Apology to Utopia: the Structure of International Legal Argument* (Helsinki, 1989).
157 Kennedy, 'The International Style', 10.

of power as a commodity or thing held by particularly powerful entities like states. One way this can be done is by following the methodological shift developed in the work of feminist scholars, postcolonial scholars and queer theorists, who have been arguing for decades that apparently organisational and public issues, such as militarism, imperialism, law and monetarism, are deeply personal, while the personal issues of subjectivity and experience are deeply political.[158] The theorist who has contributed a great deal to the articulation of this shift in understanding of the operation of power is Michel Foucault. In his influential text, *The History of Sexuality: an Introduction,* Foucault argues that power operates in liberal states in ways that differ from what he terms the juridical model of power that is accepted in much political and legal theory.[159] For Foucault, coercive juridical or sovereign power is no longer the dominant form of power operating within liberal states. It has been replaced as the central mode of exercise of power by what he has termed 'disciplinary power', a new mechanism of power that emerged in the seventeenth and eighteenth centuries in Europe.[160] Unlike the model of power that we see at work in positivist legal theory, Foucault suggests that disciplinary power is productive in that it constitutes subjects through 'a multiplicity of organisms, forces, energies, materials, desires, thoughts etc'.[161] Disciplinary power 'is more dependent upon bodies and what they do than upon the Earth and its products'.[162]

This has implications for the way power is studied. One aspect of the methodological shift proposed by Foucault is his suggestion that we move from looking to sovereign entities or beings we imagine as holding power, to thinking about the role of disciplinary power in constituting

---

[158] For an account of the ways in which a feminist post-structuralist rethinking of the relationship between power and the subject might be used to develop strategies for writing a legal theory for women, see Judith Grbich, 'The Body in Legal Theory' in Martha Fineman and Nancy Thomadsen (eds.), *At the Boundaries of Law: Feminism and Legal Theory* (New York, 1991), pp. 61–76.

[159] Michel Foucault, *The History of Sexuality: An Introduction,* (trans. Robert Hurley, 3 vols., London, 1980), vol. I. For other scholarship that makes use of the work of Foucault in an international legal context, see Simon Chesterman, 'Law, Subject and Subjectivity in International Relations: International Law and the Postcolony' (1996) 20 *Melbourne University Law Review* 979; Dianne Otto, 'Everything is Dangerous: Some Post-Structural Tools for Rethinking the Universal Knowledge Claims of Human Rights Law' (1999) 5 *Australian Journal of Human Rights* 17; Anghie, 'Time Present'.

[160] Michel Foucault, 'Two Lectures' in Colin Gordon (ed.), *Power-Knowledge: Selected Interviews and Other Writings 1972–1977* (trans. Colin Gordon, Leo Marshall, John Mepham and Kate Soper, New York, 1980), pp. 78–108 at p. 105.

[161] *Ibid.,* p. 97.   [162] *Ibid.,* p. 104.

subjects. An analysis of power 'must not assume that the sovereignty of the state, the form of the law, or the overall unity of a domination are given at the outset; rather, these are only the terminal forms power takes'.[163] Power does not operate from the top-down, as something seized by an all powerful sovereign and then used to oppress those with less power. Rather, power is employed and exercised in relations between people, rather than existing as a commodity that can be monopolised by a single entity. Thus, Foucault's methodology involves a shift from studying the sovereign to studying the process of subjectification:

> Let us not, therefore, ask why certain people want to dominate, what they seek, what is their overall strategy. Let us ask, instead, how things work at the level of on-going subjugation, at the level of those continuous and uninterrupted processes which subject our bodies, govern our gestures, dictate our behaviours etc. In other words, rather than ask ourselves how the sovereign appears to us in his lofty isolation, we should try to discover how it is that subjects are gradually, progressively, really and materially constituted...We should try to grasp subjection in its material instance as a constitution of subjects.[164]

It is important to stress that this argument does not imply that international lawyers and international relations scholars should forget the state in their theoretical work. Instead, the argument understands the meaning of state power differently. While sovereignty and the state must continue to be a focus of analysis for those who work in these disciplines, 'the power effects of the state must be radically retheorized'.[165] A reconceptualisation of power along the lines proposed by Foucault suggests that while sovereign states, international organisations, superpowers, the global market and at times international law are certainly effects of power, they are not the sources of power. The sense that these entities are omnipotent is itself an effect of power relations.[166] It is not that more coercive top-down models of power are useless in understanding international legal phenomena such as wars, violent military interventions, economic restructuring and the violence imposed in these ways.

---

[163] Foucault, The History, p. 92.   [164] Foucault, 'Two Lectures', p. 97.

[165] Nalini Persram, 'Coda: Sovereignty, Subjectivity, Strategy' in Edkins, Persram and Pin-Fat, Sovereignty, pp. 163–75 at p. 171.

[166] Eve Sedgwick, Tendencies (Durham, 1993), pp. 5–6. Sedgwick describes that sense of power with reference to the 'Christmas effect'. At Christmas time all kinds of institutions and relations (the Church, the state, commerce) line up behind the notion of Christmas. While it seems as if all these institutions speak in the same voice, the effect is not due to the power of some central body, but rather because of the sense of unitary power produced by all these disparate bodies and entities lining up in that way.

On the contrary, classical models of power and coercion are useful in understanding these phenomena. The exclusive adoption of that model of power, however, limits the capacity to explore other effects of the operation of power. For example, Foucault's model of power is useful in attempting to understand the 'private life of war', colonialism or capitalism within industrialised liberal democratic states.[167] By abandoning sovereign power as the central premise of analysis, it becomes possible to analyse the ways in which local effects of power and local tactics combine to make what those who live in democratic industrialised states are used to calling politics possible. In order to analyse the operation of power in such states, we can look to its local effects, rather than looking for, and reproducing in our analyses, some powerful sovereign figure from whom such power is supposedly emanating. The legal system based upon sovereign power is 'superimposed upon the mechanisms of discipline in such a way as to conceal its actual procedures'.[168] The effect of focusing only on the juridical or sovereign form of power is to mask the operation of power in its disciplinary form and, thus, to make that form of power all the more effective. Sovereign power and disciplinary power may coexist in ways that are very productive.

Gayatri Spivak has argued that Foucault's 'monist and unified access' to this new conception of power is itself 'made possible by a certain stage in exploitation'.[169] For Spivak, the new disciplinary mechanism of power in operation in seventeenth and eighteenth-century Europe 'is secured *by means of* territorial imperialism – the Earth and its products – "elsewhere"'.[170] Her argument is important if one is to attempt to use Foucault's reconceptualisation of power to think about international law. The following two examples suggest the relationship between disciplinary power, sovereign power and international law. First, legal texts about actions of the UN Security Council or the North Atlantic Treaty Organisation ('NATO') have an effect as cultural products that both produce subjects and legitimise domination. The new respectability of military intervention, like nineteenth-century imperialism and colonialism, is enabled through faith in the idea that 'certain territories and peoples *require* and beseech domination'.[171] Whether through arguments about

---

[167] Susan Griffin, *A Chorus of Stones: the Private Life of War* (New York, 1992).

[168] Foucault, 'Two Lectures', p. 105.   [169] Spivak, *A Critique*, p. 278.

[170] *Ibid.*, p. 279 (emphasis in original).

[171] Said, *Culture*, p. 9 (emphasis in original), commenting on the role of this narrative in nineteenth-century colonialism. On the ways in which these ideas enable military and monetary intervention in the post-Cold War era, see Chapter 3 below.

the need to control state aggression and increasing disorder, or through appeals to the need to protect human rights, democracy and humanitarianism, international lawyers paint a picture of a world in which increased intervention by international organisations is desirable and in the interest of those in the states targeted for intervention. The stories that explain and justify the new interventionism have increasingly become part of everyday language through media reports and political soundbites. As a result, these strategic accounts of a world of sovereign states and of authorised uses of high-tech violence become more and more a part of 'the stories that we are all inside, that we live daily'.[172] Legal texts about intervention create a powerful sense of self for those who identify with the hero of that story.[173] Law's intervention narratives thus operate not only, or even principally, in the field of state systems, rationality and facts, but also in the field of identification, imagination, subjectivity and emotion.

A related example is the way in which international economic texts provide an alibi for the presence of the 'international community' in states that are subject to economic restructuring. These texts make sense of the relations between 'investors' and 'developing states' in terms of a narrative of progress and development, in which a character called Foreign Capital is the agent of wealth and prosperity.[174] This creates the sense that actions undertaken to enable the exploitation and control of people and resources in such states are in fact about charity and benevolence. A belief in prosperity and progress as measures of worth, the justification of desperation and suffering in the name of the gods of efficiency and order, and assumptions about value based on gender, race and class are all necessary to be able to see the world in the terms required to accept economic narratives.

Both sets of texts (military and economic) can be seen as sites of disciplinary power, in that they play a part in the 'constitution of subjects': those who read these texts are invited to become part of the stories they tell. International legal texts operate as a form of representational practice, and such practice is itself an exercise of power. This form of power operates in part through shaping the way in which individuals within states engaging in military and monetary intervention understand

---

[172] Threadgold, 'Introduction', p. 27.   [173] See further Chapter 5 below.

[174] Judith Grbich, 'Taxation Narratives of Economic Gain: Reading Bodies Transgressively' (1997) 5 *Feminist Legal Studies* 131; Arturo Escobar, *Encountering Development: the Making and Unmaking of the Third World* (Princeton, 1995).

themselves and the world, and then regulate their behaviour in conformity with that image. Post-Cold War internationalism requires and is conditioned upon such personal, domestic acts of identification and imagination. This operation of disciplinary power can itself be seen as dependent upon the exploitation of 'the Earth and its products – "elsewhere" '.[175] Access to the bodies, labour and resources of people in states subject to military and monetary intervention is the condition of the prosperous lifestyles of international lawyers and their audiences in industrialised liberal democracies. In turn, the exploitation of the suffering of people in civil wars or famines enriches global media corporations and their shareholders, and produces 'the surplus-value of spectacle, entertainment, and spiritual enrichment for the "First World" '.[176]

The adoption of the sovereign model of power discussed above also limits the capacity of scholars to reflect upon the forms of power exercised by international lawyers. It is necessary to move away from a sovereign model of power in order to begin to think about the ways in which the reading and writing practices of international lawyers are themselves political. The understanding that many international lawyers have of their professional role is shaped by the centrality of the sovereign model of power in international law. International lawyers, like many other professionals in industrialised countries, often see ourselves as essentially performing a neutral, technical function, and have not traditionally conceptualised power as something that we ourselves exercise. At least since the publication of Edward Said's *Orientalism*,[177] such an understanding of the role of knowledge producers in fields that engage with 'other' countries and cultures has been difficult to sustain. Yet international lawyers have continued to reproduce and refine an image of ourselves and our role as apolitical and outside of power relations. International lawyers may write about power, but we less commonly acknowledge that we are implicated in reproducing or making relations of power.

The understanding of knowledge production as a value-free exercise, involving the process of observing and describing a real world that exists externally to the observer, has been subjected to criticism from many quarters. In particular, it has been criticised by those scholars who analyse the ways in which many disciplines perpetuate race, gender and class as organising categories for understanding the world, and mask acts of exploitation and violence with narratives of progress and civilising missions. A different approach to power can enable critical theorists

---

[175] Spivak, *A Critique*, p. 278.   [176] Chow, 'Violence', pp. 81, 84.   [177] Said, *Orientalism*.

to explore the ways in which lawyers participate in the deeply political process of making particular narrow ways of being appear normal and natural, thus delegitimising other ways of imagining what it is to be in the world.[178] The assumption that all power rests with sovereign states or international organisations allows for little reflection upon the power relations that international lawyers reproduce and make possible through our intellectual and legal practice. For example, international lawyers are offered the roles of experts on 'development' in Africa, Asia or Eastern Europe; producers of knowledge about populations or post-conflict institution-building in states that have been involved in civil wars; or agents of human rights, democracy and the rule of law in far-away places. International legal texts produce knowledge about 'other' people and tell stories about the horrors and atrocities that occur in distant lands. All of these roles involve the reproduction of power relations. The imperial desire to know and to access 'other' peoples and territories is transformed through the practice of international law into a sense of expertise and authorisation to speak about those who can be constructed as in need of 'our' help.

Taking a broader approach to power also raises questions that are important for the kinds of feminist and anti-colonial political projects in which I am interested. When I first started writing about international law as a feminist woman in the academy, the temptation was to present my position as largely powerless, as a marginal or oppositional critic, voicing my protests about the actions of all-powerful institutions and processes, such as patriarchy, capitalism, globalisation and militarism. Gradually, I have come to realise that there are a number of problems that arise if such a position is assumed. The first is that, by understanding and presenting myself as powerless and those I am criticising as omnipotent, I run the risk of creating in myself and my audience a sense of hopelessness. If the patriarchy, the UN, the World Bank, the USA or the faceless process of globalisation are indeed all-powerful and extremely destructive, it is hard to see exactly what use seeking to resist, or writing about, their actions will be.[179] What can a reader who has learnt about the destructive consequences of military or monetary intervention conceptualise as a useful form of response or resistance if the image of those carrying out such interventions is one of totalising

---

[178] Andrea Rhodes-Little, 'Review Essay: Who Do We Think "We" Are' (1997) 8 *Australian Feminist Law Journal* 149.

[179] See the discussion in J. K. Gibson-Graham, *The End of Capitalism (As We Knew It): a Feminist Critique of Political Economy* (Cambridge, 1996), p. 263.

power? My fear is that, if I am complicit in producing this stereotype of an all-powerful enemy, my writing will close off possibilities for resistance.

The second problem that arises if I imagine myself as lacking in power is that I risk failing to take responsibility for the power that I do in fact exercise, and falling into the trap of a paranoid mode of understanding politics which assumes that there are all-powerful enemies who do exercise power over me and who must, if possible, be destroyed. The more I read and studied about the way in which people identify with leaders who act in brutal and evil ways, the more I realised that such people understand themselves first as victims and, thus, are able to feel a legitimate desire to destroy their enemies.[180] That raises difficult questions for me as a feminist: if to understand oneself as a victim is the prerequisite for being an oppressor, how could I be certain that such results were not the effects of my work?

Adopting a broader model of power allows me to think about how law disciplines its students and its officials, and to reflect upon the role that I play as an academic in that disciplining process.[181] It allows me to interrogate the desire that I share to be part of an international legal tradition that is built on imperialism, paternalism, elitism and the construction of others as exotic victims or enemies. It enables me to question what happens to people, including feminists, when they identify with a particular discipline or perform the narratives upon which it is founded. Is it possible to adopt the position, often adopted by feminist lawyers, of being somehow at once inside and outside of the discipline of law, critiquing it while making use of its assumptions, tools and power? Such questions are especially important for feminists engaging with an international legal tradition that has been resistant to self-reflection and analysis of the power relations involved in constructing and protecting legal authority.

---

[180] Jacqueline Rose, *The Haunting of Sylvia Plath* (London, 1992), p. 210: 'Perpetrators experience themselves as victims in order both to deny and to legitimate their role (to be a perpetrator you *have* first to "be" a victim)' (emphasis in original); Anita Eckstaedt, 'Two Complementary Cases of Identification Involving "Third Reich" Fathers' (1986) 67 *International Journal of Psycho-Analysis* 317 at 326: 'It is only a matter of time before the defence of experiencing oneself as a victim meets up with the repressed experience of harbouring the intentions of the perpetrator'; Anthony Elliott, 'Symptoms of Globalization: or, Mapping Reflexivity in the Postmodern Age' in Joseph Camilleri, Anthony Jarvis and Albert Paolini (eds.), *The State in Transition: Reimagining Political Space* (Boulder, 1995), pp. 157–72 at p. 167.

[181] See further Judith Grbich, 'The Body'.

This book explores international law as a discourse that involves the constitution of subjects whose authority and identity is made possible by their relation to those in turn constituted as 'other'. The positivist account of the relations between law and power does not allow us to think about how that process of exclusion of others might be resisted. Such issues can only be addressed by complicating the manner in which power is understood to be operating in and through international law. While doctrinal approaches to international law remain concerned primarily with attempts to develop constraints on the exercise of centralised power as it operates at the level of states or international organisations, they ignore forms of power that operate in more personal ways. Those who participate in shaping perceptions of the legality of the actions of states and international organisations need to develop further an intellectual practice which recognises that law's stories are both an exercise, and an effect of, power relations.

3   Localizing the other: the imaginative geography of humanitarian intervention

This chapter explores one of the ways in which international legal texts shape the meanings that are made of humanitarian intervention. My focus is on the ways in which such texts understand the causes of security and humanitarian crises in the post-Cold War period. In particular, I am interested in two key assumptions that underpin the arguments in favour of humanitarian intervention. First, state or local leaders or governments are presented as posing the major challenges to human rights and democracy, and humanitarian crises are seen as largely caused by actions and developments initiated and carried out by local or governmental actors or institutions. These actors are usually represented as being driven by forms of premodern tribalism, ethnic tensions and religious factionalism, which are channeled by ruthless political elites into genocidal violence.[1] This provides a motivating factor for intervention – in order to restore order or to guarantee human rights and democracy,

---

[1] See Fernando R. Tesón, 'Collective Humanitarian Intervention' (1996) 17 *Michigan Journal of International Law* 323 at 342 (treating state or local leaders or governments as the actors likely to threaten democracy or human rights); Leon Gordenker and Thomas G. Weiss, 'The Collective Security Idea and Changing World Politics' in Thomas G. Weiss (ed.), *Collective Security in a Changing World* (Boulder and London, 1993), pp. 3–18 at p. 14 (treating 'ethnic particularism' as a threat to peace and security); W. Michael Reisman, 'Some Lessons from Iraq: International Law and Democratic Politics' (1991) 16 *Yale Journal of International Law* 213 (arguing that 'tinhorn dictators' and 'contemporary tyrants' threaten post-Cold War peace and security); Michael Stopford, 'Locating the Balance: the United Nations and the New World Disorder' (1994) 34 *Virginia Journal of International Law* 685 at 686, 698 (suggesting that the breakdown of internal state structures and ancient ethnic and religious tensions are the major challenges to peace and security); Ambassador Madeleine K. Albright, 'International Law Approaches the Twenty-First Century: a US Perspective on Enforcement' (1995) 18 *Fordham Journal of International Law* 1595 at 1597 (suggesting that we 'live in an unsettled age, beset by squabbles, wars, unsatisfied ambitions').

military intervention is necessary.[2] International law and the international community are portrayed as the bearers of peace, democracy and human rights to local communities in need of saving. It is this vision, for instance, which underpins the portrayal of the role of the UN in then Secretary-General Boutros Boutros-Ghali's report, *An Agenda for Peace*:[3]

In these past few months a conviction has grown, among nations large and small, that an opportunity has been regained to achieve the great objectives of the Charter – a United Nations capable of maintaining international peace and security, of securing justice and human rights and of promoting, in the words of the Charter, 'social progress and better standards of life in larger freedom'. This opportunity must not be squandered.[4]

Collective humanitarian intervention in this view is necessary to address the problems of local dictators, tribalism, ethnic tension and religious fundamentalism thrown up in the post-Cold War era. For Boutros Boutros-Ghali, post-Cold War conflicts are 'often of a religious or ethnic character, and often involving unusual violence or cruelty'.[5] This 'new breed of intra-state conflicts' is marked by targeting of civilians and 'general banditry and chaos'.[6] Those who favour humanitarian intervention argue that, accordingly, international lawyers should abandon outmoded notions of sovereignty and non-intervention in order to enable states acting collectively to reach those who need their help.[7]

Second, the argument in support of the legality or legitimacy of collective humanitarian intervention treats the choice for the international community in the face of genocide or massive human rights violations

---

[2] For the argument that humanitarian crises require collective humanitarian intervention and a reconceptualisation of the principle of non-interference in the internal affairs of sovereign states, see Tesón, 'Collective Humanitarian Intervention' (arguing that the domain reserved to the exclusive jurisdiction of the state is quite small, and that matters such as democratic legitimacy are now subject to international scrutiny).

[3] An Agenda for Peace: Report of the Secretary-General, UN Doc A/47/277–S/24111(1992), reprinted in (1992) 31 *International Legal Materials* 956.

[4] *Ibid.*

[5] An Agenda for Peace, Supplement, UN Doc A50/60–S1995/1, 3 January 1995, paragraph 12.

[6] *Ibid.*, paragraph 13.

[7] See, for example, Tom J. Farer, 'Intervention in Unnatural Humanitarian Emergencies: Lessons of the First Phase' (1996) 18 *Human Rights Quarterly* 1, 15; Tesón, 'Collective Humanitarian Intervention', 371.

as one between action and inaction, or presence and absence. Post-Cold War security or humanitarian crises are represented as in part attributable to an absence of law, including international law, and a lack of sustained engagement by international organisations. Accordingly, a commitment to humanitarian ideals demands action from the international community, in the form of military intervention. Thomas Weiss, for example, argues that ruling out the option of using force will render the United Nations powerless to act, destroy its credibility and condemn it to irrelevancy.[8] Weiss characterises the choice as one between active interventionism or fatalistic noninterventionism:

Too many pleas for consistency or against inevitable selectivity amount to arguing that the United Nations should not intervene anywhere unless it can intervene everywhere ... But in light of genocide, misery, and massive human rights abuses in war zones around the world, should Pontius Pilate be the model for both the American and the international response? The fatalism and isolationism that flow from most objections to humanitarian intervention are as distressing as the situation in the countries suffering from ethnic conflict where such an action is required ... A purely noninterventionist position amounts to abstention from the foreign policy debate.[9]

Similarly, Fernando Tesón argues that it is better for states to take collective action to intervene in favour of the rights and interests of human beings, even if such action may do some harm, rather than to remain inactive and, as a result, incapable of providing either relief from brutality or assistance in the achievement of democratic government.[10]

It is ... surprising to be told that the very crimes that prompted the massive, cruel and costly struggle from which the United Nations was born, are now immune from action by the organ entrusted to preserving the fruits of the hard-won peace. The formalism of anti-interventionists thus not only rewards tyrants, but it betrays the purposes of the very international order that they claim to protect.[11]

In this debate, Rwanda stands as a spectacular example of what happens if the international community does *not* intervene to prevent crimes against humanity, human rights abuses and acts of genocide. This is well illustrated by the United Nations Secretary-General's 1999 Annual Report to the General Assembly, addressing the prospects for human security

---

[8] Thomas G. Weiss, 'On the Brink of a New Era? Humanitarian Interventions, 1991–94' in Donald C. F. Daniel and Bradd C. Hayes (eds.) *Beyond Traditional Peacekeeping* (New York, 1995), pp. 3–19 at p. 8.

[9] *Ibid.*, pp. 8, 15.   [10] Tesón, 'Collective Humanitarian Intervention', 342.

[11] *Ibid.*

and intervention in the next century.[12] Kofi Annan there reflected the view of many when he commented that 'the genocide in Rwanda will define for our generation the consequences of inaction in the face of mass murder'.[13]

The characterisation of intervention as active and productive, and non-intervention as inactive and negative, also appears to inform the popular response that we should do something to address the suffering and despair in Bosnia, Rwanda or East Timor, rather than do nothing. As Shashi Tharoor notes: 'In a world of satellite communications, with television images of suffering broadcast as they occur, few democratic governments are immune to the public clamour to "do something"'.[14]

This chapter is an attempt to unsettle the 'imaginative geography' of intervention, according to which the international community is absent from the scene of violence and suffering until it intervenes as a heroic saviour.[15] In order to reinscribe that which is erased by this cartography – the presence of the international community and its representatives at the scene of violence – this chapter foregrounds the post-Cold War economic project of the international community. In particular, I explore the practices of international economic organisations and development agencies that must be ignored in order to code as humanitarian the post-Cold War internationalism performed in the former Yugoslavia and Rwanda. Surprisingly little attention has been paid to the presence and activity of international institutions and agencies in countries prior to the outbreak of violence, ethnic cleansing or genocide. Yet the activity of these organisations unsettles both sets of assumptions – that humanitarian crises are caused by the absence of the international community, and that the international community prioritises human rights over other values. The aim of this chapter is to trace the effects, both doctrinal and cultural, of this failure to inscribe the presence of international actors in countries such as the former Yugoslavia or Rwanda prior to crises erupting.

The first part of the chapter questions the idea that the choice for the international community is between action (presence) or inaction (absence). I focus on two post-Cold War humanitarian crises, the genocidal

---

[12] UN, *Secretary-General Presents His Annual Report to General Assembly*, UN Press Release SG/SM/7136 GA/9596, 20 September 1999.

[13] *Ibid.*

[14] Shashi Tharoor, 'The Changing Face of Peace-Keeping and Peace-Enforcement' (1995) 19 *Fordham International Law Journal* 408 at 413.

[15] On the 'imaginative geography' of Orientalism and its representations, see Edward W. Said, *Orientalism* (London, 1978), pp. 49–73.

conflicts in the former Yugoslavia and in Rwanda. An examination of the role played by international economic institutions and actors in contributing to the conditions leading to the outbreak of violence complicates the dominant representation of an absence of international law and a lack of international engagement as contributing causes of those crises. I suggest that international, as well as local, passions and interests were a threat to peace and security in those instances.

The second part focuses more broadly on the project of economic liberalisation as carried out under the auspices of international economic organisations such as the IMF, the World Bank and the WTO. This project complicates both the idea that domestic politics are separable from internationalist actions, and that local institutions, actors or cultures pose the major threats to peace, democracy and human rights while international institutions and laws act primarily in the interests of human rights, democracy and stability. While these axioms justify greater scope for intervention by international institutions, actors and cultures at the state or local level, I suggest in contrast that it is necessary to rethink the understanding of international laws, international institutions and international culture as necessarily emancipatory.[16]

The third part explores the doctrinal effects of the failure to acknowledge the presence and activity of international actors and international law at the site of internal conflicts or genocide. I suggest that this failure limits the capacity of international law to develop adequate responses to post-Cold War security and humanitarian crises. The images of internationalism that appear in intervention texts are opposed to forms of nationalism variously represented as premodern, ethnic, tribal, chaotic, disordered and xenophobic. Such an opposition is made possible only by a selective focus on some areas of international activity as representative of the humane intentions and effects of international intervention, while other areas of activity are ignored. The failure to consider the involvement of international organisations or the role of international law in contributing to such crises has meant that, rather than examining the role played by the agenda of the international community in contributing to such conflicts, legal texts continue to understand the causes of such conflicts as ethnic or nationalist in origin.

---

[16] On rethinking the nature of 'the international', see David W. Kennedy, 'A New World Order: Yesterday, Today and Tomorrow' (1994) 4 *Transnational Law and Contemporary Problems* 329; and on rethinking the meaning of 'the global', see Vandana Shiva, 'The Greening of the Global Reach' in Wolfgang Sachs (ed.), *Global Ecology: a New Arena of Political Conflict* (London, 1993), pp. 149–56.

The final part concludes that this way of representing the causes of conflict serves to create a sense that the international community and those facing humanitarian or security crises are physically separate. This aspect of intervention narratives can be read as an attempt to create a distance between the space of the international community and the space of violence or terror.

Representations of the international

I want to start by questioning the assumption that the choice facing the international community is one between action and inaction. In order to do so, this part examines the presence of international law and international institutions in the former Yugoslavia and Rwanda prior to the humanitarian crises there.

The restructuring of Yugoslavia

The response by the Security Council and NATO to the conflict in the former Yugoslavia, and more specifically the 'ethnic cleansing' in Bosnia-Herzegovina, is treated by some commentators as an early example of the trend towards collective humanitarian intervention.[17] There, the Security Council appeared to treat violations of international human rights law as a threat to international peace and security. In a series of resolutions between 1991 and 1993, the Council showed itself increasingly willing to authorise arms embargoes and the use of force to facilitate the delivery of humanitarian assistance and protect safe havens in Bosnia and Herzegovina.[18] According to then Secretary-General Boutros Boutros-Ghali, this represented 'a new kind of UN operation', with the UN having

---

[17] See, for example, Sean D. Murphy, 'The Security Council, Legitimacy, and the Concept of Collective Security after the Cold War (1994) 32 *Columbia Journal of Transnational Law* 201 at 232; Tesón, 'Collective Humanitarian Intervention, 366.

[18] The Council 'deeply concerned by fighting in Yugoslavia which is causing a heavy loss of human life and material damage' and by regional consequences, and 'concerned that the continuation of this situation constitutes a threat to international peace and security', decides under Chapter VII that all States shall implement a general and complete arms embargo: UN Doc S/RES/713 (1991); the Council recognising that 'the situation in Bosnia and Herzegovina constitutes a threat to international peace and security and that the provision of humanitarian assistance in Bosnia and Herzegovina is an important element in efforts to restore international peace and security', and 'deeply concerned by reports of abuses against civilians', acting under Chapter VII 'calls upon states to take nationally or through regional agencies or arrangements all measures necessary to facilitate in coordination with the United Nations the delivery . . . of humanitarian assistance' in Bosnia and Herzegovina: UN Doc S/RES/770

'a humanitarian mandate under which the use of force is authorized'.[19] For Fernando Tesón, the NATO bombings undertaken pursuant to Security Council resolutions can be 'explained as a humanitarian effort, that is, an action undertaken by the military alliance authorized by the United Nations with the purpose of putting an end to the intolerable human rights violations taking place in the war'.[20] Similarly, Sean Murphy treats these resolutions as examples of 'a greater sensitivity to the importance of human rights abuses' on the part of the Security Council during the early 1990s.[21]

The literature on the former Yugoslavia shares the assumptions described in the introduction to this chapter. Whether the cause of the disintegration of Yugoslavia is understood to be ancient hatreds or Serbian aggression, those arguing that the Yugoslav conflict illustrates the necessity for collective humanitarian intervention treat international institutions essentially as agents of security, democracy and human rights.[22] The failure to use force, or the imposition of limits upon the use of force, on the part of the international community is seen as rendering it a largely passive observer to this conflict. Thomas Weiss, for example, describes the United Nations Protection Force for the former Yugoslavia (UNPROFOR) as 'eunuchs at the orgy', due to the constraints imposed on the capacity of UNPROFOR to use force in that conflict.[23]

An evaluation of the relationship between the actions of international institutions and the situation in the former Yugoslavia, however, suggests that this opposition between action and inaction misrepresents

(1992); the Council establishes a no-fly zone over Bosnia and Herzegovina to ensure the safety of humanitarian flights, implemented initially through a monitoring system associated with the UN peace-keeping operation, UNPROFOR: UN Doc S/RES/781 (1992); the Council acting under Chapter VII, authorises member states acting nationally or through regional organisations to take all necessary measures to ensure compliance with the no-fly zone over Bosnia and Herzegovina established to prevent Serbian assaults from obstructing the transfer of humanitarian aid supplies: UN Doc S/RES/816 (1993); the Council acting under Chapter VII authorises member states to take all measures necessary, through the use of air power, to protect safe areas in Bosnia and Herzegovina: UN Doc S/RES/836 (1993).

[19] An Agenda for Peace, Supplement, paragraph 19.

[20] Tesón, 'Collective Humanitarian Intervention', 368.

[21] Murphy, 'The Security Council', 230.

[22] See Noel Malcolm, Bosnia: a Short History (London, 1996), pp. xx–xxii, for an analysis of the way in which leaders such as John Major represented ancient hatreds as the cause of the Yugoslav conflict.

[23] Weiss, 'On the Brink', p. 8. For an analysis of violence as an expression of one form of masculine subjectivity as suggested by that metaphor, see Diana Taylor, 'Spectacular Bodies: Gender, Terror and Argentina's "Dirty War"' in Miriam Cooke and Angela Woollacott (eds.), Gendering War Talk (Princeton, 1993), pp. 20–40.

the engagement of the international community in the political and social life of Yugoslavia prior to the conflict. The programme of economic liberalisation and restructuring of the state implemented by the international financial institutions of the World Bank and the IMF during the 1970s, 1980s and indeed the 1990s contributed to the conditions in which such hatreds (whether ancient or otherwise) were inflamed.[24] Economic policies designed to refinance and repay Yugoslavia's foreign debt were a driving force behind major constitutional reforms and redefinitions of citizenship and workers' rights during the 1980s.[25] Such policies appear to have played a role in the rise of republican nationalism and the sense that the federal government lacked legitimacy. I want to outline briefly the nature of restructuring in the former Yugoslavia, and then to suggest how that project posed a threat to the peace.

The people of the former Yugoslavia were subjected to a stringent austerity programme during the 1970s and 1980s, partly as a result of decisions made by IMF officials and by economic liberals in the Yugoslav government.[26] The process of restructuring began in earnest in 1982, when the Yugoslav government sought a three-year standby loan from the IMF.[27] The loan was intended to be used to repay its foreign debt denominated in US dollars, the interest on which had ballooned during the oil crises of the late 1970s.[28] The conditions attached to that loan by the IMF were aimed at the introduction of domestic policy reforms which economists believed would better enable servicing of foreign debt.[29]

---

[24] See particularly Susan L. Woodward, *Balkan Tragedy: Chaos and Dissolution after the Cold War* (Washington, 1995); J. Petras and S. Vieux, 'Bosnia and the Revival of US Hegemony' (1996) 218 *New Left Review* 3, 9–11; Michel Chossudovsky, 'Dismantling Former Yugoslavia; Recolonising Bosnia', *Economic and Political Weekly*, 2 March 1996, 521.

[25] Woodward, *Balkan Tragedy*, p. 106; Petras and Vieux, 'Bosnia', 9–11.

[26] For the contrary argument that the austerity programme was *not* the result of IMF involvement but rather the 'result of domestic policy choices taken in response to external capital market constraints', see Laura Tyson, Sherman Robinson and Leyla Woods, 'Conditionality and Adjustment in Hungary and Yugoslavia' in Josef C. Brada, Ed A. Hewett and Thomas A. Wolf (eds.), *Economic Adjustment and Reform in Eastern Europe and the Soviet Union* (Durham, 1988), pp. 72–105 at p. 105.

[27] *Keesing's Contemporary Archives: Record of World Events*, Vol. 30, June 1984, 32932.

[28] *Ibid.* See also William R. Cline, *International Debt: Systemic Risk and Policy Response* (Washington, 1984), pp. 282, 287.

[29] *Keesing's Contemporary Archives: Record of World Events*, Vol. 30, June 1984, 32932. It is difficult to obtain precise information about the nature of the conditions attached to any IMF credits during that period, including those extended to Yugoslavia. IMF conditions were not published at that time, although they did tend to become public knowledge indirectly through governments, commercial banks and the media.

The original 'austerity' programme involved cuts in government expenditure, trade and price liberalisation, cutting of imports, and the promotion of exports.[30] Later programmes required capping wages, reorienting production towards exports which could compete in OECD markets, recentralising political and economic decision-making, privatisation and currency deregulation.[31] While the reasons for such reforms were always presented as purely economic and technical, the changes required by the IMF were 'fraught with political implications'.[32] Both directly and indirectly, the IMF reshaped Yugoslav politics throughout the 1980s and early 1990s.

The direct restructuring of Yugoslav politics occurred through the imposition of conditions requiring constitutional and institutional reforms. During the 1980s, the IMF began to make access to new credits for Yugoslavia conditional on such reform. The first change required by the IMF related to recentralisation, or the shifting of political and economic authority from republican governments and banks to the federal government and the National Bank.[33] Economists considered that the decentralisation of policy-making amongst Yugoslav republics that had occurred during the early 1980s was 'responsible for Yugoslavia's weak macroeconomic control'.[34] Accordingly, IMF conditions attached to the use of credits after 1982 included requirements for federal reassertion of economic authority over republican governments.[35] Further political changes resulted from the conditions attached to the 1987 and

Raymond Mikesell notes that while IMF agreements were secret and statements regarding their content limited to generalities, it is possible to judge IMF conditionality packages without seeing them, by evaluating the policies of countries that have been receiving IMF assistance. Raymond F. Mikesell, 'Appraising IMF Conditionality: Too Loose, Too Tight, Or Just Right?' in John Williamson (ed.), *IMF Conditionality* (Washington, 1983), pp. 47–62 at p. 53.

[30] Woodward, *Balkan Tragedy* p. 51; *Keesing's Contemporary Archives: Record of World Events*, Vol. 31, August 1985, 33808.

[31] See generally Cline, *International Debt*, pp. 281–90; Tyson, Robinson and Woods, 'Conditionality', pp. 91–6; Woodward, *Balkan Tragedy*; Marko Milivojevic, *The Debt Rescheduling Process* (London,1985), pp. 204–7.

[32] Woodward, *Balkan Tragedy*, p. 50; Petras and Vieux, 'Bosnia', 11.

[33] *Keesing's Contemporary Archive: Record of World Events*, Vol. 30, June 1984, 32932-3; Petras and Vieux, 'Bosnia', 11.

[34] Tyson, Robinson and Woods, 'Conditionality', p. 81. See also Milivojevic, *Debt Rescheduling*, p. 205.

[35] In 1982, the IMF required that control over foreign exchange allocation and operations be returned to the National Bank in Belgrade, after such functions had been decentralised and distributed amongst republican governments and banks five years earlier. In 1986/1987, when the IMF 'began to tie conditions for new credits to political reform', it focused on 'restrengthening the governing capacity of the federal

1988 IMF packages. In particular, the 'May Measures' of 1988 required the destruction of the socialist system of worker participation in firm decision-making, the removal of procedural protections against large-scale unemployment, and the cutting of public expenditure.[36]

Economic and political restructuring continued to be proposed by the IMF, economic advisers and the federal government during the period 1988–89, when the nationalist climate had become apparent and republican resistance to the proposed changes was clear. The federal government continued to be committed to drawing up and implementing new IMF-conditioned stabilisation restrictions as part of a process of debt rescheduling with private banks during that period, despite an escalation in nationalist rhetoric, nationalist revisions of republican constitutions, mass demonstrations against austerity measures, protests by newly defined minorities, strikes, police harassment of minorities, challenges to the Yugoslav army and racist attacks.[37]

At the end of 1989, after a decade of economic crisis, constitutional conflict and political disintegration,[38] the existing political system was failing,[39] and legitimacy of the federal government was being challenged by radical Slovene, Serb and Croatian nationalism.[40] Nevertheless, economic advisers to the Yugoslav government determined that 'the effectiveness of the program for global integration depended on speed', and the government announced a 'shock therapy' stabilisation programme, to begin in mid-December.[41] The programme aimed at completely

administration'. Economic planners wanted a more competent and effective federal government that could 'make and implement tough decisions'. In particular, having been critical of the consensual decision-making process that operated at the federal level and within the central bank as a means of ensuring equality between the republics, the IMF required a change in the voting rules of the National Bank from consensus to majority decision-making. Those changes were proposed by the IMF and supported by the federal cabinet. The significance of those changes can be seen in the packages for constitutional reform presented to the Yugoslav parliament as a result. In February 1987, the League of Communists recommended 130 amendments to the 406 articles of the federal constitution. See Woodward, *Balkan Tragedy*, pp. 57–74, 82.

[36] *Ibid.*, p. 96.   [37] *Ibid.*, p. 93–6.   [38] *Ibid.*, p. 148.

[39] *Ibid.*, p. 116.   [40] *Ibid.*, p. 117.

[41] *Ibid.*, p. 114. The principal adviser to the government was economist Jeffrey Sachs, who developed the 'shock therapy' model for dealing with states in transition from communism to capitalism. Sachs publicly espoused that model in a famous 1990 article: Jeffrey Sachs, 'What Is to Be Done?' *The Economist*, 13 January 1990, 19. He advised other Eastern European governments, the G7 and the IMF on the shock therapy model. For a critique of that model and its consequences, see Peter Gowan, 'Neo-Liberal Theory and Practice for Eastern Europe' (1995) 213 *New Left Review* 3.

removing 'political barriers to a market economy'.[42] During 1990, the year in which clear signs of civil war were emerging, the federal government continued to attempt to enact political reforms required by the shock therapy conditions. It did so under intense pressure from the IMF, which was concerned that the commitment to reform was flagging.[43]

IMF programmes had further indirect effects on political institutions and norms within Yugoslavia. The implementation of supposedly apolitical IMF conditions in fact required significant changes in Yugoslav politics. The goals of economic policy, for example, required 'fundamental changes in the locus of economic decision-making' and thus required constitutional reform.[44] Changes necessary to enable these reforms included altering the practice of distributing cabinet appointments on a nationality basis,[45] changing the composition of the governing board of the fund for development credits,[46] and shifting the balance of economic policy in favour of particular firms, sectors and republics.[47] Successive reformist Prime Ministers and their cabinets took steps to subvert established political processes in order to enable the adoption of unpopular measures supported by the IMF. The social impact of IMF economic liberalisation and shock therapy stabilisation programmes also had unacknowledged political effects. Those programmes arguably fuelled the nationalist dynamic by rapidly restructuring republican and federal levels of government, by implementing policies with divisive social consequences, and by advocating the removal of mechanisms that provided some state support to individuals who would suffer under unrestrained economic liberalism.[48]

Commentators on the former Yugoslavia point to a number of conditions that fuelled the republican nationalist dynamic that led to genocide. Those conditions include the destruction of existing federal

---

[42] Woodward, *Balkan Tragedy*, pp. 115, 129–30.

[43] Chossudovsky, 'Dismantling Former Yugoslavia', 521–2. 1990 saw the federal party collapse in January, competitive multiparty elections characterised by extreme racism and nationalism held from April to December, declarations of sovereignty and the right to secede by the republics of Slovenia and Croatia in July, and signs of civil war emerging. By June 1991, Slovenia and Croatia had announced their independence from the former Yugoslavia, and war had broken out.

[44] Woodward, *Balkan Tragedy*, p. 58.   [45] *Ibid.*, p. 73.   [46] *Ibid.*, p. 74.

[47] *Ibid.*, p. 101. In particular, producers in the southern republics tended to have fewer ties to Western European markets.

[48] Robin Blackburn, 'The Break-up of Yugoslavia' (1993) 45 *Labour Focus on Eastern Europe* 3; Petras and Vieux, 'Bosnia', 11; Chossudovsky, 'Dismantling Former Yugoslavia', 521–2.

constitutional arrangements during the 1980s,[49] the destruction of minority rights guarantees,[50] serious unemployment,[51] falling Yugoslav per capita income,[52] the growing role of nationalism in Yugoslav politics,[53] the role of the military as a political force,[54] and the growing gulf between rich and poor republics.[55] There are at least four ways in which IMF structural adjustment, stabilisation and later shock therapy programmes can be argued to have contributed to those conditions and thus to the political destabilisation of Yugoslavia.[56]

First, the programmes contributed both to a sense of insecurity for the people of Yugoslavia and to resulting social instability.[57] The destabilising consequences of the early IMF austerity programme introduced in 1982, for example, included inflation, falling real incomes, consumer goods shortages, unemployment and the threat of unemployment, the abandonment of food subsidies, and rising prices for commodities affected by import restrictions and the push for exports, such as gasoline, heating fuel, food and transportation.[58]

---

[49] Woodward, *Balkan Tragedy*, pp. 57–74, 82; Petras and Vieux, 'Bosnia', 11; Chossudovsky, 'Dismantling Former Yugoslavia', 521.

[50] Woodward, *Balkan Tragedy*, p. 381.

[51] Blackburn, 'The Break-up', 3; Petras and Vieux, 'Bosnia', 10; Chossudovsky, 'Dismantling Former Yugoslavia', 522.

[52] Valerie Bunce, 'The Elusive Peace in the Former Yugoslavia' (1995) 28 *Cornell International Law Journal* 709 at 712.

[53] *Ibid.*, 715.   [54] *Ibid.*, 710.

[55] *Ibid.*, 712; Catherine Samary, 'Behind the Breakup of Yugoslavia' (1993) 45 *Labour Focus on Eastern Europe* 27; Petras and Vieux, 'Bosnia', 10.

[56] Susan Woodward suggests a fifth way in which IMF conditions contributed to the crisis. Woodward suggests that the demands for political change made by the IMF also eroded the state's 'political capacity for managing the transition', and that the absence of a legitimate centralised authority meant that such claims could not be successfully mediated: Woodward, *Balkan Tragedy*, p. 379. She defines democracy as a system that enables peaceful resolution of conflict and entails a willingness to lose. I have less faith in benign central authority, given the absence of a willingness to lose, particularly on economically rational policy issues, amongst elites in existing democracies. Indeed, I do not see how any authority, whether or not it is benign, can mediate a system capable of reproducing and generating such extraordinary inequality and extremes of wealth and poverty, without resorting to violence.

[57] Andrew Williams, 'Economic Intervention by International Economic Organizations in Central and Eastern Europe: Will It Lead to More or Less "Security" for the Region?' in Pal Dunay, Gabor Kardos and Andrew J. Williams (eds.), *New Forms of Security, Views from Central, Eastern and Western Europe* (Aldershot, 1995), pp. 103–16 at p. 109; Woodward, *Balkan Tragedy*, p. 52; Petras and Vieux, 'Bosnia', 10; Chossudovsky, 'Dismantling Former Yugoslavia', 521–2.

[58] Woodward, *Balkan Tragedy*, p. 51; Petras and Vieux, 'Bosnia', 10.

Second, economically motivated political and constitutional reforms destroyed the means of protecting minority rights within the socialist system. That system of protection had been based upon the provision of government jobs distributed according to national status and state expenditure on cultural rights. Commentators argue that the 'multiple political arenas' created by Yugoslavia's extensive political decentralisation also operated to guarantee the protection of rights and freedoms: 'journalists who could not publish in one republic could get an audience in another; people facing discrimination in one republic could emigrate temporarily to another; and social movements repressed in one republic might hope for publicity and outside pressure in another'.[59] These mechanisms for accommodating ethno-national and other differences in socialist Yugoslavia were progressively broken down from 1982 onwards. The IMF conditions contributed to the destruction of those mechanisms, by requiring fiscal cuts, greater political centralisation, and an end to nationality-based distribution of voting and positions.[60]

Third, the effects of IMF programmes such as social polarisation, attacks on the protection of minority rights and constitutional and institutional 'reform', contributed to the nationalist dynamic developing during the late 1980s.[61] Those programmes played a role in the rise of republican nationalism and the sense that the federal government lacked legitimacy.[62] Critics of IMF programmes argue that, while Tito's Yugoslavia functioned as an 'imagined community' in the sense described by Benedict Anderson,[63] that sense of community depended upon the federal government having the ability to provide some level of economic and administrative support. When the IMF imposed the policy of structural adjustment in the 1980s, it led to the state, as usual, being stripped of most of its functions, except maintaining law and order.[64]

---

[59] Woodward, *Balkan Tragedy*, p. 381; Petras and Vieux, 'Bosnia', 10.

[60] Woodward, *Balkan Tragedy*, p. 381; Petras and Vieux, 'Bosnia', 10.

[61] Williams, 'Economic Intervention'.

[62] Chossudovsky, 'Dismantling Former Yugoslavia', 521–2.

[63] Benedict Anderson, *Imagined Communities* (London, 1991), pp. 6–7. Anderson defines the nation as an imagined community: 'imagined because the members of even the smallest nation will never know most of their fellow-members, meet them, or even hear of them, yet in the minds of each lives the image of their communion', and a community because 'regardless of the actual inequality and exploitation that may prevail in each, the nation is always conceived as a deep, horizontal comradeship'.

[64] Jochen Hippler, 'Democratisation of the Third World after the End of the Cold War' in Jochen Hippler (ed.), *The Democratisation of Disempowerment: the Problem of Democracy in the Third World* (London, 1995), pp. 1–31 at p. 24 (arguing that often after structural adjustment, the state is only left with 'the police, the army and the secret service: the

In that vacuum, ethnic nationalism offered a form of community and identity.[65] One of the reasons that the sense of community offered by nationalism is attractive under these circumstances is 'because the bases of existing communities have collapsed and governments are radically narrowing what they will or can provide in terms of previously guaranteed rights to subsistence, land, public employment, and even citizenship'.[66]

The attack on established systems of welfare also contributed to the anti-federal, republican focus of the nationalist dynamic.[67] While the federal government enacted rapid economic and political restructuring designed to meet with the approval of economic advisers, international institutions and private banks, republican leaders were able to appeal to those people who had to face the serious economic and social consequences of that rapid restructuring.[68] Nationalist republican governments thus gained popular support for the separatist policies of resisting federal taxation and opposing federal authority.[69] The 'gulf between richer and poorer republics' caused by economic restructuring also fuelled the separatist dynamic.[70] One major cause of the separation of Slovenia from Yugoslavia, for example, was the desire to abandon those republics that were 'slowing down insertion into capitalist Europe'.[71] Local leaders also gained support from ethnic minorities or those in poorer regions who resented the 'politics of capital cities' and its neglect of their interests.[72]

Fourth, the speed with which restructuring and, by 1990, shock therapy were carried out contributed to the rapid process of political disintegration that occurred once the Yugoslav crisis entered a 'nationalist dynamic'.[73] As the phrase 'shock therapy' suggests, economic logic dictated that speed was essential. The federal government and international institutions remained committed to implementing radical and

instruments of repression. By their nature, these can't [yet] be privatised or transferred to the North').
[65] Petras and Vieux, 'Bosnia', 10. See also Hippler's discussion of the ways in which 'other forms of identity, ethnic or ethnic-religious, become more important' in states subject to structural adjustment, as the 'national state' is stripped of its functions and becomes discredited: *Ibid.*, p. 25.
[66] Woodward, *Balkan Tragedy*, p. 17.
[67] *Ibid.*, p. 384; Chossudovsky, 'Dismantling Former Yugoslavia', 521–2.
[68] Woodward, *Balkan Tragedy*, p. 127; Blackburn, 'The Break-up'; Petras and Vieux, 'Bosnia', 10; Chossudovsky, 'Dismantling Former Yugoslavia', 522.
[69] Woodward, *Balkan Tragedy*, p. 384.   [70] Samary, 'Behind the Breakup', 27.
[71] *Ibid.* See also Woodward, *Balkan Tragedy*, pp. 105, 150.
[72] Woodward, *Balkan Tragedy*, p. 384.   [73] *Ibid.*, p. 17.

far-reaching political and constitutional reforms to enable a rapid transition from a socialist economic structure to a purely market-based regime, even after the nationalist climate and violent resistance to those radical reforms became apparent.[74] As Woodward notes, there was a clear conflict between the conditions necessary to ensure peace and those deemed necessary for economic liberalisation. While time was the commodity that was needed to build 'cross-republican, society-wide political organisations' to avoid civil war and genocide, rapid economic and political change was considered to be essential by the IMF, banks and financial institutions.[75]

The genocide in the former Yugoslavia was, of course, the work of violent, local men. The conditions imposed by the IMF and the consequences of those conditions were not the sole cause of that outbreak of violence. Structural adjustment and shock therapy programmes have been implemented in many states without leading to genocide. Yet it is not possible to say that this violent ethnic cleansing was a purely local event. To suggest that ethnic cleansing was the product of Yugoslav politics, interests, passions and ambitions alone is to absolve international institutions of any responsibility for taking account of the reception of the norms and culture they impose.

The development of Rwanda

I want now to develop this argument further by turning to look at the case of Rwanda in 1994. There, the Security Council infamously did *not* authorise military intervention in the face of genocide. Perversely, it chose the days after the genocide commenced to withdraw most of the UN peace-keepers who were on the ground to oversee the implementation of the Arusha peace accords between the Rwandan government and the rebel Rwandan Patriotic Front.[76] For many international lawyers, any criticisms of humanitarian intervention as a policy option must be

---

[74] See Sachs, 'What Is to Be Done', 21 (justifying the 'need for speed' in restructuring Eastern European political and economic institutions in 1990).

[75] Woodward, *Balkan Tragedy*, p. 384.

[76] The Arusha Accords consisted of a Peace Agreement, the N'Sele Cease-Fire Agreement and two protocols plus earlier completed protocols governing the rule of law, power-sharing and the repatriation of refugees. See *Letter from the Permanent Representative of the United Republic of Tanzania to the United Nations addressed to the Secretary-General, transmitting the Peace Agreement signed at Arusha on 4 August 1993, the N'Sele Cease-Fire Agreement and related Protocols of Agreement*, UN Doc A/48/824-S/26915 (1993).

read against the effects of the failure of the international community to intervene to prevent the Rwandan genocide.

The genocide began after the plane carrying Rwandan President Habyarimana and President Ntaryamira of Burundi was shot down on its approach to Kigali airport on the evening of 6 April 1994. Everyone on board was killed.[77] Almost immediately, militia roadblocks were set up throughout Kigali. Militiamen and Presidential guards began searching houses in Kigali and killing 'enemies', including prominent liberal politicians and democrats, Hutu sympathisers of democratic opposition parties, and Tutsi – purely because they were Tutsi.[78] According to Gérard Prunier, 'they started killing during the night and they managed to dispose of most of the "priority targets" – the politicians, journalists and civil rights activists – within less than thirty-six hours'.[79] The killing had spread beyond the city by 7 April. Over the course of the next hundred days between April and July 1994, over 800,000 people would be massacred in Rwanda.[80] The slaughter, rape and mutilations were vicious and horrifying. Yet as Prunier has argued, this was not a chaotic or anarchic event, but rather a highly organised enterprise: 'In Rwanda, all the preconditions for a genocide were present: a well-organised civil service, a small tightly-controlled land area, a disciplined and orderly population, reasonably good communications and a coherent ideology containing the necessary lethal potential.'[81]

Causes of the genocide included 'civil war, competition for power, racism, ideological radicalization, militarization [and] human rights violations'.[82] In particular, the mobilisation of racism was a means for Rwanda's elite, particularly the *akuzu* or group of people around President Habyarimana and his wife, to protect their privileges and status in the face of threats to their power. These threats were posed by the economic crisis of the 1980s, the 1990 invasion from Uganda by the Rwandan Patriotic Front, and the pressure for democratisation from the international community as part of the Arusha peace process.[83]

---

[77] *Report of the Independent Inquiry into the Actions of the United Nations during the 1994 Genocide in Rwanda*, UN Doc S/1999/1257, 15 December 1999 (hereinafter Independent Inquiry Report), http://www.un.org/News/ossg/rwanda report.htm (accessed 2 May 2002), 9.

[78] Gérard Prunier, *The Rwanda Crisis: History of a Genocide* (New York, 1995), pp. 230–1.

[79] *Ibid.*, p. 243.   [80] *Ibid.*, p. 265; Independent Inquiry Report, 1.

[81] Prunier, *The Rwanda Crisis*, p. 238.

[82] Peter Uvin, *Aiding Violence: the Development Enterprise in Rwanda* (Connecticut, 1998), p. 225.

[83] *Ibid.*, pp. 53–81; Prunier, *The Rwanda Crisis*, pp. 82–212.

The *akuzu* sought to legitimise their continued political dominance through making use of the ideology of the evil of Tutsis. In a practical sense, they organised and funded militias and spread racist propaganda, all of which paved the way for the genocide.[84] Thus for Gérard Prunier, the genocide was in part the end result of 'a fight for good jobs, administrative control and economic advantage...It was from that convergence of threatened privileges with ideological frustration that the genocide plans got their emotional fuel'.[85]

It is not difficult to feel anger and frustration at the appalling failure to act in the face of clear signs that genocide was going to take place in Rwanda. As the *Report of the Independent Inquiry into the Actions of the United Nations during the 1994 Genocide in Rwanda* (the Independent Inquiry Report) found: 'The international community did not prevent the genocide, nor did it stop the killing once the genocide had begun. This failure has left deep wounds within Rwandan society, and in the relationship between Rwanda and the international community, in particular the United Nations.'[86]

Much of the legal literature dealing with the genocide in Rwanda agrees, charging the international community with an absence of involvement and a failure to act to prevent the Rwandan genocide. The lesson to be learned from Rwanda, according to such accounts, is the need to establish better mechanisms to enable military intervention in the face of massive human rights abuses or genocide. For example, Ved P. Nanda, Thomas F. Muther, Jr and Amy E. Eckert argue that while there was sufficient early warning that a genocide might occur in Rwanda, 'the United Nations and member states took no effective action to prevent the disaster'.[87] They criticise the 'failure of the international community to prevent the 1994 massacre' and suggest that the genocide in Rwanda could 'have been halted by forcible intervention'.[88] For these authors, 'if there is a clear-cut case to be made for intervention, Rwanda was it'.[89] Similarly, for Dorinda Lea Peacock, the international community failed to intervene early enough in Rwanda, and 'was slow to take action to

---

[84] Prunier, *The Rwanda Crisis*, pp. 169, 182, 203, 220–9.   [85] *Ibid.*, p. 227.
[86] Independent Inquiry Report.
[87] Ved P. Nanda, Thomas F. Muther, Jr, and Amy E. Eckert, 'Tragedies in Somalia, Yugoslavia, Haiti, Rwanda and Liberia – Revisiting the Validity of Humanitarian Intervention under International Law – Part II' (1998) 26 *Denver Journal of International Law and Policy* 827 at 846.
[88] *Ibid.*, 847, 851.   [89] *Ibid.*, 851.

end or even to mitigate the killing'.[90] For Peacock, the key question in light of the Rwandan genocide remains: 'What level of horror would compel intervention?'[91]

This framework also underpins Samantha Power's critique of US foreign policy towards Rwanda.[92] Power is concerned to understand how the American system of policy-making allowed the US administration to fail Rwanda so spectacularly. Her analysis of the actions of US bureaucrats and officials is devastating, and testifies to a system in which there was no space for conceptions of justice, solidarity or humanitarianism to inform the making of decisions about foreign policy. Power's focus is on the failure to respond to the genocide. She suggests it was based on the creation by US policymakers of 'a nurturing ethical framework for inaction'.[93] According to Power, 'whatever their convictions about "never again", many [US officials] did sit around, and they most certainly did allow genocide to happen'.[94] Power argues that the USA could easily have done things differently, both before the genocide began and during its progress. She is particularly critical of the US failure to agree to pleas for UN reinforcements before the violence escalated, to deploy US troops to Rwanda once the genocide had begun in earnest, or at least to support those UN members who were themselves willing to deploy troops.

Common to many analyses is the suggestion that the international community is responsible for the Rwandan genocide due to its failure to use force to prevent or halt the genocidal killing. At the time the genocide commenced, there were in fact 2,519 UN troops in Rwanda as part of the United Nations Assistance Mission for Rwanda (UNAMIR).[95] UNAMIR's mandate included contributing to the security of the city of Kigali within a weapons-secure area established by the parties in and around the city, monitoring observance of the Arusha Peace Agreement, and monitoring the security situation leading up to elections.[96]

---

[90] Dorinda Lea Peacock, ' "It Happened and It Can Happen Again": the International Response to Genocide in Rwanda' (1997) 22 *North Carolina Journal of International Law and Commercial Regulation* 899 at 925.

[91] *Ibid.*

[92] Samantha Power, 'Bystanders to Genocide: Why the United States Let the Rwandan Tragedy Happen', *The Atlantic Online*, September 2001, http://www.theatlantic.com/issues/2001/09/power.htm, accessed 4 April 2002.

[93] *Ibid.*, 20.   [94] *Ibid.*, 2.   [95] *Ibid.*, 234.

[96] UN Doc S/RES/872 (1993). Although Dallaire asked for the approval of the Secretariat to use force in response to crimes against humanity and other abuses, the Secretariat never responded to that request: Independent Inquiry Report, 4.

The failure of the international community to take action in the face of the public and thorough preparations for the genocide is indeed remarkable. After all, as José Alvarez notes, 'there was nothing concealed about either the continuous public incitements to mass killing or the 1994 killings themselves'.[97] Much was known internationally about these preparations. For example, General Romeo Dallaire, head of UNAMIR, made repeated requests for more troops and resources in the months leading up to the outbreak of genocide.[98] Two major human rights reports were also published in 1993, setting out the potential for civil violence in Rwanda. The first, written by an International Commission of Inquiry established by four human rights NGOs to investigate human rights violations in Rwanda, documented massacres throughout the country, detailed the deaths of over 2,000 Tutsi murdered because of their ethnicity, and reported that extremist rhetoric was widespread and that militia groups had been formed.[99] The second was the UN report on the April visit to Rwanda by the Special Rapporteur of the Commission on Human Rights on extrajudicial, summary or arbitrary executions, Mr B. W. Ndiaye, published on 11 August 1993. That report detailed massacres of the civilian population fulfilling the definition of genocide, and described other serious human rights violations taking place in Rwanda, including death threats, political assassinations, and the absence of any system for protecting ethnic minorities from mounting violence.[100] It commented on 'the destitute condition of a whole sector of the population', the 'climate of mistrust and terror [that] currently prevails in Rwanda', and the 'profusion of weapons in circulation'.[101]

The Security Council failed to authorise the use of force to protect civilians in the face of such public preparations for genocide, and similarly did nothing to halt the genocide once it began. On the contrary, as the crisis erupted, the UN effectively removed its military presence, leaving only a token force. After ten Belgian peace-keepers were killed,

---

[97] José E. Alvarez, 'Crimes of States/Crimes of Hate: Lessons from Rwanda' (1999) 24 *Yale Journal of International Law* 365 at 392.

[98] Independent Inquiry Report, 5.

[99] The four NGOs were Human Rights Watch, International Federations of Human Rights, Inter-African Union of Human Rights, and the International Center for Human Rights and Democratic Development.

[100] *Report by Mr B. W. Ndiaye, Special Rapporteur on Extrajudicial, Summary or Arbitrary Executions, on his Mission to Rwanda from 8 to 17 April 1993*, UN Doc E/CN.4/1994/7/Add.1, 11 August 1993.

[101] *Ibid.*, para 11.

Belgium withdrew from UNAMIR on 14 April 1994. 'Belgian soldiers, aggrieved by the cowardice and waste of their mission, shredded their UN berets on the tarmac at Kigali airport.'[102] Despite Dallaire's declaration that with 5,000 soldiers he could stop the genocide, the Security Council voted unanimously on 21 April to withdraw all but 270 UNAMIR troops and to limit the mission's mandate.[103] A month later, on 17 May, the Security Council passed a further resolution expanding the mandate of UNAMIR and authorising the expansion of that mission to 5,500 troops.[104] Yet even this deployment was delayed due to disputes over the provision of troops and funding for the operation, so that over two months later UNAMIR still had only 550 troops.[105] On 22 June, the Security Council authorised the deployment of a multinational force under French control – the controversial *Opération Turquoise*.[106] For some commentators, this represents a (delayed) instance of humanitarian intervention, as the formal aim of this force was to establish a 'safe area' in south-west Rwanda.[107] However, its principal effects seem to have been 'to permit the slaughter of Tutsis to continue for an extra month, and to secure safe passage for the genocidal command, with a lot of weaponry, into Zaire'.[108]

The international community also failed to take action short of military intervention to prevent the genocide. For example, the continuation of development aid could have been made conditional upon the Rwandan government ending human rights violations.[109] As Linda Melvern notes, 'in the years immediately before the 1994 genocide there was a bewildering array of aid agencies involved in Rwanda and most of them were fully aware of the overt system of apartheid operated against the Tutsi'.[110] However, few attempts were made to use development aid to pressure the Rwandan government to ensure the protection of human rights and to end the incitement to genocide. Instead, international aid, structural adjustment and the business of development continued as usual.[111] Jamie Metzl suggests that the international community could

---

[102] Philip Gourevitch, *We Wish to Inform You that Tomorrow We Will Be Killed with our Families* (London, 1999), p. 150.

[103] UN Doc S/RES/912 (1994).   [104] UN Doc S/RES/918 (1994).

[105] Independent Inquiry Report, 15–17.   [106] UN Doc S/RES/929 (1994).

[107] Tesón, 'Collective Humanitarian Intervention', 365.

[108] Gourevitch, *We Wish to Inform You*, pp. 160–1.   [109] Uvin, *Aiding Violence*, p. 226.

[110] L. R. Melvern, *A People Betrayed: the Role of the West in Rwanda's Genocide* (London, 2000), p. 55.

[111] Uvin, *Aiding Violence*, p. 86.

have acted to jam the local radio broadcasts inciting genocide.[112] For Metzl, this was particularly pressing once it had become clear to those in Rwanda that genocide was imminent.[113] Many international aid workers and human rights activists were well aware of the pattern developing during the early 1990s, by which 'broadcasts would identify and criticize an individual, and Interahamwe [militia] groups would set out at once to find and attack the person named'.[114] Yet no action was taken to prevent the broadcasts. In addition, there was no attempt made to remove Rwanda from its seat on the Security Council, where it had become a non-permanent member on 1 January 1994.[115] The Independent Inquiry Report suggests that this created a problem in the Security Council's handling of the Rwandan situation, as the genocidal regime had full access to discussions at the Council and was able to try to influence decision-making there.[116] It also sent a message to those responsible for the genocide that the international community was not overly concerned about the conditions prevailing in Rwanda during that period.

All of these criticisms are important and damning. Yet I want to argue that this is only half the picture. As in the case of the break-up of Yugoslavia, the notion that the international community was missing in action during the preparations for the genocide can only be maintained if the international aid and development enterprise is treated as 'external' to Rwanda, and thus to the conditions that caused the genocide.[117] If we focus on the actions, presence and involvement of the international community in Rwanda during the preparations for genocide, it becomes far more difficult to present the Rwandan genocide as a purely local

[112] Jamie Frederic Metzl, 'Rwandan Genocide and the International Law of Radio Jamming' (1997) 91 *American Journal of International Law* 628. Initially this propaganda was broadcast by the government-controlled Radio Rwanda, and later by the semi-privatised Radio-Télévision Libre des Milles Collines (RTLM).

[113] *Ibid.*, 648. It is interesting to note, however, the reluctance of the US administration to name what was happening in Rwanda as genocide, even once the killings were well under way, for fear of bringing into play legal obligations (see Power, 10–12). Metzl's suggestion that the recognition of imminent genocide could be a trigger to the lawfulness of radio jamming may thus have limited utility.

[114] *Ibid.*, 631. See, for example, *Report by Mr B. W. Ndiaye, Special Rapporteur on Extrajudicial, Summary or Arbitrary Executions, on his Mission to Rwanda from 8 to 17 April 1993*, 17.

[115] Independent Inquiry Report, 39.

[116] *Ibid.*, 32. For example, the Inquiry noted that Rwanda voted against Security Council Resolution 918 (1994) which decided to increase the number of troops in UNAMIR and impose an arms embargo on Rwanda, 'a clear example of the problematic issue of principle raised by Rwandan membership of the Council', paragraph 15.

[117] Uvin, *Aiding Violence*, p. 225.

phenomenon. The large-scale presence of development workers is ignored in most analyses of the genocide, as is any exploration of the relationship between the processes that led to genocide and the development enterprise.[118] The debate relating to development is framed around the ways in which foreign aid could have intervened to prevent genocide, just as the legal literature is concerned with issues relating to military intervention. Yet the Rwandan genocide did not take place in a country that was isolated from the international community. Rwanda was seen as a 'model developing country' by the World Bank and most other development aid agencies.[119] As Peter Uvin notes:

Up to the last minute, thousands of technical assistants and foreign experts were building roads, extending credit, training farmers, protecting the environment, reorganizing ministries, advising finance officials, and distributing food aid, at a cost of hundreds of millions of dollars a year – the lion's share of all government expenditures. For most of these people, up to the end, Rwanda was a well-developing country – facing serious development problems, but dealing with them much more effectively than were other countries.[120]

How then might we write the presence of the international development community into our representations of the relationship between 'internal' or 'local', and 'external' or 'foreign', factors in causing the genocide? Does such a distinction between inside and outside even make sense in light of the degree of involvement of the 'international' in Rwanda prior to the genocide?

To begin with, aid provided 'a large share of the financial and moral resources of the government and civil society' in Rwanda.[121] Indeed,

---

[118] *Ibid.*, pp. 3–4 (arguing that there has been too little attention paid to the relationship between the development process and the Rwandan genocide); Todd Howland, 'Mirage, Magic, or Mixed Bag? The United Nations High Commissioner for Human Rights' Field Operation in Rwanda' (1999) 21 *Human Rights Quarterly* 1 at 5 (arguing that no UN agencies operating in Rwanda before the genocide have made a serious review of their work or projects to determine whether they facilitated or minimised genocidal actions and human rights abuses).

[119] Uvin, *Aiding Violence*, pp. 40–5. Those interested in economic development were impressed by the statistics relating to matters such as industrial production, investment, exports and paved roads (pp. 47–8). Those concerned with participation lauded the high density of NGOs (p. 48). Those who were concerned with technical indicators of 'human development' looked to achievements such as the high rate of vaccinations as markers of Rwanda's success (p. 160). In an unusually cynical aside, Peter Uvin comments there that 'one can point out that 85 percent of the Tutsi who were slaughtered and 85 percent of those who did the killing in Rwanda were vaccinated'.

[120] *Ibid.*, p. 2.   [121] *Ibid.*, p. 3.

'until the genocide, Rwanda was one of the most aided countries in the world'.[122] Bilateral donors, as well as multilateral donors such as the IMF, the World Bank and the ADB, continued to make large amounts of programme aid available to Rwanda during the early 1990s.[123] Aid agencies and the community of aid workers and foreign diplomats present in Rwanda during that period did little in response to the well-documented rise in government-sponsored human rights violations, racism, massacres and militarisation of society, all of which 'were constitutive elements of the drive to genocide'.[124] In fact, Uvin documents that during that period, aid from almost all countries increased, and most countries continued to provide military support to the Rwandan government.

This development aid helped to maintain the strong state necessary to organise and administer the genocide. Philip Gourevitch argues that genocide in Rwanda was not an instance of anarchy, but 'the product of order, authoritarianism...and one of the most meticulously administered states in history'.[125] In other words, it was precisely because of the excellent administration of this model developing state that genocide was possible. Similarly, Prunier argues that the *génocidaires* had believed they could carry off the genocide because, *inter alia*, they relied on 'their capacity to keep a reasonable degree of administrative efficiency during the slaughter process'.[126] This level of state capacity was made possible by the development enterprise. Uvin estimates that aid funding was responsible for close to 80 per cent of the investment budget and much of the operating budget of the Rwandan government. As a result, 'there was no way that the government could implement any policy, coherent or not, without the assistance of the foreign aid community'.[127] While this did not mean that donor governments or international economic organisations had a free hand in controlling what happened in Rwanda, those actors did have influence over policy developments.

The close relationship between aid agencies and governments also gave those agencies great leverage over elites within Rwanda. As Uvin comments: 'As most aid ends up with the upper crust in the cities – in the form of training, salaries, per diems, transportation, and entrepreneurial income – the elite could not live its lifestyle, make its

---

[122] *Ibid.*, p. 40.

[123] Michel Chossudovsky, *The Globalisation of Poverty: Impacts of IMF and World Bank Reforms* (Penang, 1997), pp. 115–20; Gourevitch, *We Wish to Inform You*, p. 94.

[124] Uvin, *Aiding Violence*, p. 229.   [125] Gourevitch, *We Wish to Inform You*, p. 95.

[126] Prunier, *The Rwanda Crisis*, p. 228.   [127] Uvin, *Aiding Violence*, p. 226.

money, buy its consumption products, and so forth without the support of the aid system.'[128]

The corollary of this is that a threat to withhold aid in the face of human rights violations could have had a significant, persuasive effect on members of that Rwandan elite. Uvin notes that this was in fact the result on the two short-lived occasions when the international community sought to force changes from the Rwandan government. The first took place in 1991, when the international community sought the release of 8,000 to 10,000 arbitrarily detained Tutsi. This diplomatic activity is considered to have been successful, and certainly most of the people detained were released.[129] Again, when the joint NGO human rights report was published in 1993, a number of countries threatened to (but never did) cut aid, the World Bank refused to give Rwanda the latter tranches of a structural adjustment loan, and Belgium and Switzerland briefly recalled their ambassadors.[130] The Rwandan government agreed to investigate the allegations and fewer massacres took place over the following months.

Even if it was felt that cutting off aid would have not worked, agencies could have shifted priorities away from structural adjustment and towards strengthening the judicial system, education of human rights, more equitable distribution of resources and repatriation and protection of refugees and internally displaced people. However, international economic institutions such as the World Bank continued with their usual policy prescriptions, and even praised Rwanda for its liberal approach to economics. So Uvin argues:

As Rwanda's farmers were facing crises without precedent, as inequality and corruption reached endemic proportions, as hope for the future was extinguished, and as violence, hatred, and human rights abuses became government policy, the [World Bank] was congratulating Rwanda for its improved capacity to overcome its 'limited absorptive capacity', to 'improve its capacity to design and implement development projects'...[131]

Commentators also argue that the racist violence in Rwanda was in part fuelled by rising frustration and unfulfilled expectations in Rwanda during a period of extreme economic and political change.[132] For Michel Chossudovsky, the 'sweeping macro-economic reforms imposed by the Bretton Woods institutions' between 1989 and 1992 contributed to 'exacerbating the climate of generalised insecurity' and 'precipitated the

---

[128] *Ibid.*, p. 227.   [129] *Ibid.*, p. 96.   [130] *Ibid.*   [131] *Ibid.*, p. 89.
[132] Chossudovsky, *Globalisation of Poverty*, pp. 115–20; Uvin, *Aiding Violence*, p. 210.

population into abject poverty and destitution'.[133] The conditions imposed by the IMF and the World Bank included the devaluation of the Rwandan franc, the lifting of agricultural subsidies and the privatisation of state enterprises. The combination of these austerity measures with falling commodity prices and civil war led to the collapse of public services such as health and education, sharp inflation accompanied by steep rises in fuel and food prices, a rise in the price of electricity following the privatisation of the state-owned Electrogaz, the collapse of the agricultural sector and a large increase in urban unemployed people.[134] Yet as Chossudovsky notes: 'No sensitivity or concern was expressed as to the likely political and social repercussions of economic shock therapy applied to a country on the brink of civil war. The World Bank team consciously excluded the "non-economic variables" from their "simulations".'[135]

Uvin's work also broadens the focus away from 'massive physical harm...done with arms by one group against another', to argue that structural violence in a more general sense was part of life for most people in Rwanda most of the time.[136] Ongoing inequality, exclusion, dispossession, alienation, disempowerment and humiliation had characterised life in Rwanda for decades, and development aid had played a central role in perpetuating this 'structural violence'.[137] Many Rwandans faced 'the permanence of social and economic exclusion; lack of access to information, education, health and minimal basic needs; and an authoritarian and condescending state and aid system'.[138] These conditions led to 'frustration, anger, ignorance, despair, and cynicism, all of which greatly increases the potential for acute violence'.[139] Many of the mechanisms that produced those effects were financed, legitimised and supported by the aid community.[140]

For example, aid contributed to growing income inequality in Rwanda. A small group of foreigners, technical assistants and 'big men of the state' benefited materially from development projects and foreign investment, and were able to live lavish lifestyles.[141] The spending patterns of aid projects disproportionately favoured a small, wealthy, well-connected, urban elite – almost two-thirds of project costs went to paying the salaries of a small number of technical assistants and consultants,

---

[133] Chossudovsky, *Globalisation of Poverty*, pp. 111, 117. See also Prunier, *The Rwanda Crisis*, p. 160.
[134] Chossudovsky, *Globalisation of Poverty*, pp. 115–20.   [135] *Ibid.*, p. 119.
[136] Uvin, *Aiding Violence*, p. 107.   [137] *Ibid.*   [138] *Ibid.*   [139] *Ibid.*
[140] *Ibid.*, p. 231.   [141] *Ibid.*, p. 117.

purchasing cars, and funding construction of project infrastructure, including 'houses for its top employees'.[142] The development aid enterprise also contributed to land concentration in Rwanda. Uvin notes that 43 per cent of farm households lacked the minimum land for survival, and that people living on those farms were chronically undernourished.[143] Yet most aid projects were conducted 'as if land were not scarce, liberally sprinkling offices, homes, storage buildings, demonstration and multiplication fields, and access roads across the countryside.'[144] Almost all rural projects started with 'the construction of big and expensive houses – the biggest ones for the foreign technical assistants, so they can live in conditions at least equal to those in their home countries, and smaller ones for the Rwandan cadres working for the project'.[145] The costs of such constructions were enormous and the space they took up deeply resented by local farmers.[146] Commentators describe a growing population of jobless and landless Rwandans who were becoming extremely unhappy with the spectacle of people associated with the government accumulating land and building huge houses.[147] 'In one of the few documents that present a farmer's opinion about the causes of the genocide, asset and income inequality figure in first and second place.'[148]

Uvin also argues that aid worked as a systematic form of humiliation. Farmers were confronted by a huge influx of foreign aid workers and their well-dressed, educated, urban, wealthy Rwandan assistants, arriving in air-conditioned cars, there to tell them how to improve themselves and their work practices. The lifestyle of this group was by implication the desirable one.

It can be argued that the whole development enterprise, with its ideas of material progress, its well-paid employees (whatever the color of their skin) with their four-wheel-drive vehicles, villas, foreign travel, and hundreds of small, daily status symbols, created a permanent reminder of the life that could be but that never would be for the majority of the population.[149]

Patricia Williams makes a similar argument about the seductive humiliation of Western capitalism.[150] 'Western flashing of cash and its ability to generate massive realignments troubles me less as ideology than as a

---

[142] *Ibid.*, pp. 146, 123.   [143] *Ibid.*, p. 113.   [144] *Ibid.*, p. 147.   [145] *Ibid.*, p. 123.
[146] *Ibid.*   [147] Prunier, *The Rwanda Crisis*, pp. 87–8.   [148] Uvin, *Aiding Violence*, p. 114.
[149] *Ibid.*, pp. 210–11.
[150] Patricia J. Williams, 'Law and Everyday Life' in Austin Sarat and Thomas R. Kearns (eds.), *Law in Everyday Life* (Ann Arbor, 1993), pp. 171–90 at p. 190.

deep discourtesy, a seductive humiliation, which teaches that self-worth derives from appearances and material possessions.'[151]

The gulf between Rwandans and foreign aid workers, however, is often rendered invisible in statistics concerning income levels, or the gap between rich and poor. Interestingly, the incomes of expatriates are never taken into account in the official data relating to income inequality produced by agencies like the World Bank.[152] Many foreigners lived and worked in Rwanda, most employed within the development enterprise and paid by NGOs, donor governments or international organisations. Those foreigners made up a particular class within Rwandan society, yet their physical presence is regularly ignored in analyses of the social divisions, distribution of resources and causes of violence in that country. According to Uvin:

All data on income distribution in Africa, for example, fail to include the well-known salaries and lifestyles of most technical assistants, foreign consultants, and the few lucky locals working with them. In other words, income inequality is calculated by leaving out the wealthiest, most visible segment of society. This is the segment of a thousand or so foreigners and maybe as many nationals who own almost all the beautiful houses, primarily in the capital, but also scattered throughout the countryside; who buy up most of the land from destitute farmers; who travel abroad and share the French culture. Most of these people work for the development enterprise and derive their wealth from it. Their salaries are hundreds of times higher than the incomes of farmers.[153]

Finally, the state system that existed to 'develop' the Rwandan peasant majority was inherited from the colonial era, and largely operated in an authoritarian fashion. Even if 'well-meaning foreigners' wanted to modify that system, they usually ended up working within it.[154] Aid workers continued, often unsuccessfully, to impose 'pre-conceived packages' designed by specialists upon farmers, and at best the method to achieve this goal was changed in the name of participation.[155] For Uvin, development aid in Rwanda and much of Africa promoted oppression, 'by reinforcing the humiliation and dehumanization brought about by authoritarian, top-down, controlling development agencies'.[156]

This discussion about the relationship between the development of a market economy and the Rwandan genocide does not explain why the frustration and aggression felt as a result of these conditions led to the form of violence that it did. Why did people not revolt and attack

---

[151] *Ibid.*   [152] Uvin, *Aiding Violence*, p. 115.   [153] *Ibid.*, p. 146.   [154] *Ibid.*, p. 132.
[155] *Ibid.*, p. 134.   [156] *Ibid.*, p. 232.

corrupt state officials or even foreign development experts, rather than killing their 'often equally poor Tutsi neighbours'?[157] Elite manipulation of racism takes us part of the way, but still fails to explain why there is such a willing audience for racist propaganda. The work of Slavoj Žižek suggests that one answer to this question lies in an understanding of the broader links between capitalism and violence. Žižek argues that such outbreaks of racist violence are in part a product of capitalism's economy of desire. Capitalism operates by producing an excess, a vicious circle of desire – it satisfies more human needs than any other economy, but also creates more needs to be satisfied; creates more wealth but also more need to produce wealth. Thus Jacques Lacan called capitalism the 'discourse of the hysteric: this vicious circle of a desire, whose apparent satisfaction only widens the gap of its dissatisfaction, is what defines hysteria'.[158] What is produced 'to fill out the lack only widens the lack'.[159] Žižek argues that it is here that we should understand what Lacan calls the discourse of the Master – 'its role is precisely to introduce balance, to regulate the excess'.[160] Prior to capitalism, societies could 'dominate the structural imbalance proper to the superego insofar as their dominant discourse was that of the Master' – this ethical system 'aimed to prevent the excess proper to the human libidinal economy from exploding'.[161] With capitalism, this ethical system breaks down – 'this function of the Master becomes suspended, and the vicious circle of the superego spins freely'.[162] Thus for Žižek, what is at stake in the new outbreaks of fascist or nationalist violence is precisely one kind of response to the excesses of capitalism. According to this reading, it should be no surprise that at those moments when shock economic restructuring is being imposed, the enjoyment of the other becomes most intolerable and racist violence results. Crises such as those that occurred in the former Yugoslavia or Rwanda suggest the need to rethink the 'vicious circle of desire' and the culture of control that are the conditions of possibility of this global economic system.

In conclusion, focusing on international law and international institutions that facilitate economic restructuring suggests that the opposition between collective humanitarian intervention and inactivity is a false one. The international community had already intervened on a large scale in Yugoslavia and Rwanda before the security crises erupted,

---

[157] Ibid., p. 211.
[158] Slavoj Žižek, *Tarrying with the Negative: Kant, Hegel and the Critique of Ideology* (Durham, 1993), p. 209.
[159] Ibid., p. 210.   [160] Ibid.   [161] Ibid.   [162] Ibid.

through the activities of international economic institutions and development agencies. The international community can be located inside, not outside, this space of violence. Inactivity is not the alternative to intervention. The international community is already profoundly engaged in shaping the structure of political, social, economic and cultural life in many states through the activities of international economic institutions.

The place of the international in a globalized economy

I have argued so far that 'the international' played a role in contributing to the conditions that led to violence in the former Yugoslavia and Rwanda, thus unsettling the assumption that the absence of the international community is a contributing factor in the conditions that led to the outbreak of violence in each case. I want now to explore the extent to which this level of international involvement is symptomatic of the place of the international in the global economy. In other words, can we neatly separate out domestic politics from international technical design, or are the two interconnected? And can we accept the broader assumption underlying the pro-intervention approach, that international institutions are the bearers of progressive human rights and democratic values to a 'local' in need of those rights and values in the post-Cold War era? In order to consider these questions, I want to focus on one major project of international institutions – that of trade and financial liberalisation. While there is no paucity of literature now dealing with the human consequences of this process, there is real debate over the extent to which globalisation either threatens or promotes human rights.

Proponents of economic globalisation argue that trade and investment liberalisation lead to benefits in the fields of human rights and political freedom by creating the economic conditions that allow these freedoms to flourish. Walden Bello has dubbed this the 'compassionate globalization' message.[163] This is the approach espoused by sociologist Anthony Giddens in his 1999 BBC Reith lectures.[164] Giddens there presents the impact of globalisation as broadly positive. It fundamentally reshapes public and private institutions, spreading democracy and

---

[163] Walden Bello, 'Global Conspiracy or Capitalist Circus?', 'An All-American Show?', *Focus on Trade*, February 2000.

[164] The Reith lectures were revised and published as Anthony Giddens, *Runaway World: How Globalisation Is Reshaping our Lives* (London,1999).

tolerance, liberating women and creating wealth.[165] Indeed, for Giddens, the 'battleground for the twenty-first century' will pit nationalism and fundamentalism against the cosmopolitan tolerance that is encouraged by globalisation.[166] Similarly, Frederick Abbott has argued that 'the success of the WTO is the success of democracy and the marketized economy that swept away the Berlin Wall'.[167] For such advocates of economic liberalisation, the key values to be promoted by globalisation are protection of private property, freedom to trade, the rule of law and formal equality.

International economic organisations increasingly portray their own actions in these terms. Official documents and speeches by representatives of the WTO speak of its role in providing the conditions that will lead to political liberalism and deepen democracy, while the World Bank speaks in the language of participation, good governance, anti-corruption and poverty alleviation.[168] For example, according to the former WTO Director-General Mike Moore, free trade and economic freedom are the conditions of political freedom. For Moore, the WTO has the 'opportunity to nurture and promote the core liberal values of justice and human progress... acting in the interests of all that is right and good'.[169]

The 'compassionate globalization' view is of course far from uncontroversial. A second view of economic globalisation suggests that it threatens human rights. Let me summarise some of the key features of that argument, by looking briefly at the activities of the IMF, the World Bank and the WTO.[170] The IMF and the World Bank have a significant effect on the policies of governments in those states seeking to make use of their resources through the imposition of conditions on access to credits and loans. Most people are by now familiar with the 'structural adjustment' conditions that have been attached to the use of IMF and World

---

[165] *Ibid.*, p. 5.   [166] *Ibid.*

[167] Frederick Abbott, 'Remarks' (2000) 94 *American Society of International Law Proceedings* 219.

[168] I should note that these organisations and the governments they represent have to date been careful to ensure that there is no linkage of these rhetorical statements to any of the human rights covenants negotiated under the auspices of the UN.

[169] Statement by Mike Moore to the 11th International Military Chiefs of Chaplains Conference, 9 February 2000, reprinted at http://www.wto.org/wto/speeches/mm22.htm, accessed 1 April 2000.

[170] See further Anne Orford, 'Locating the International: Military and Monetary Interventions after the Cold War' (1997) 38 *Harvard International Law Journal* 443; Anne Orford, 'Globalisation and the Right to Development' in Philip Alston (ed.), *Peoples' Rights* (Oxford, 2001), pp. 127–84.

Bank resources since the 1980s. Those conditions generally require countries to adopt policies of foreign investment deregulation, privatisation, cuts to government spending, labour market deregulation, lowering of minimum wages, and a focus on production of goods for export rather than domestic consumption. Equally controversial have been the so-called 'shock therapy' programmes discussed above and implemented since the late 1980s throughout Eastern Europe.

It can be argued that the imposition of such conditions threatens human rights in three broad ways. The first argument is that rights to political participation and self-determination are threatened in countries subject to IMF and World Bank conditions. Decision-making over ever larger areas of what was once considered to be central to popular sovereignty and substantive democracy is now treated as legitimately within the province of IMF and World Bank economists. People in such states are not free in any meaningful sense to choose forms of economic or social arrangements that differ from the models chosen by those who work for the IMF or the World Bank.

The second argument is that the model of development imposed by these institutions itself threatens the promotion and protection of economic, social and cultural rights. For example, structural adjustment conditions have resulted in the cutting of public expenditure on health and education, increased income disparity, greater unemployment and the marginalisation of women, the poor and rural populations. As the Committee on Economic, Social and Cultural Rights noted in 1998, rights such as the right to health or the right to adequate food are made significantly less relevant in states required to engage in those forms of economic restructuring.[171]

It may be that there has been something of a shift in the nature of the requirements imposed as part of structural adjustment programmes, as evidenced by the conditions attached to the use of resources by South-East Asian states since 1997. In Indonesia, for example, the IMF and the World Bank encouraged deficit budget spending to fund education projects and public sector job-creation programmes. While this was partly due to the way in which the IMF perceived the cause of economic problems there, this may also represent a trend away from the imposition of hard-line conditions in those areas. The World Bank also now uses the language of participation in its documents, although I have

---

[171] 'Globalisation and Economic, Social and Cultural Rights', Statement by the Committee on Economic, Social and Cultural Rights, May 1998.

elsewhere been critical of the limited meaning of that term in the Bank context.[172]

What has not changed, however, is the commitment of these institutions to imposing a particular capitalist model of market-driven development at any cost. Participation is only allowed within the framework determined by the institutions and their donor-states. This is summed up nicely by the following passage from the Bank's 1999 case progress report on Indonesia, written prior to the democratic elections in that country.

Today, Indonesians are understandably impatient for change. Calls for a "people's economy" and a redistribution of assets from the rich ... have acquired considerable popular support and need to be channelled in constructive ways, or else they could do considerable damage.[173]

This passage makes clear that the notion of a 'people's economy' premised on a real commitment to participation or proposals for the redistribution of assets are seen as dangerous, representing potential threats to the economic order that the Bank seeks to preserve or establish in Indonesia.

Third, the imposition of 'structural adjustment' and 'shock therapy' programmes also creates a climate in which abuses of civil and political rights such as the right to freedom from torture or the right to life are more likely to occur. Such programmes have too often led to increased levels of insecurity and political destabilisation in target states. The effect of IMF and World Bank policies has been to relieve many states of most of their functions, except maintaining law and order and facilitating private investment.[174] At the same time, the interests of investors are protected and secured. In situations where the state appears to address only the interests of international economic institutions and corporate investors, the insecurity, vulnerability and frustration of people increases. Violent protests, political destabilisation, attempted succession and populist nationalism have emerged as responses to governments that appear to be accountable only to foreign investors. This situation tends to be exacerbated by the refusal of the IMF and the World Bank to require cuts to military budgets.[175] The dangerous practice of imposing

[172] Anne Orford and Jennifer Beard, 'Making the State Safe for the Market: The World Bank's *World Development Report 1997*' (1998) 22 *Melbourne University Law Review* 196.
[173] World Bank, *Indonesia: Country Assistance Strategy – Progress Report*, 16 February 1999, 2.
[174] Hippler, 'Democratisation', p. 25.
[175] D. L. Budhoo, *Enough Is Enough: Dear Mr Camdessus ... Open Letter of Resignation to the Managing Director of the International Monetary Fund* (New York, 1990), pp. 69–72.

conditions that increase poverty, food scarcity, unemployment and insecurity, while failing to require cuts to military budgets, is a recipe for
human rights abuses. When governments attempting to comply with
IMF or World Bank programmes are faced with riots and protests, such
protests have been too readily met with repressive state action.

Membership of the WTO poses another source of constraint on the
choices open to peoples and governments. For many years the GATT
(General Agreement on Tariffs and Trade) regime was the insulated and
self-referential world of a 'specialized policy elite' of technocrats, officials and 'GATT-friendly academics'.[176] With the creation of the WTO at
the completion of the Uruguay Round of GATT trade negotiations in
1995, the political nature of free trade decision-making has become increasingly visible. This is in part due to the significant expansion in the
range of activities brought within the scope of the GATT/WTO regime.
The regulatory harmonisation required of WTO Members extends to
areas such as intellectual property protection, provision of services, foreign investment regulation, labelling, regulation of genetically modified
foods and biotechnology, and public and animal health and safety laws.
In addition, once a rule is agreed to as part of a trade negotiation it
is very difficult to alter it, while the importance of the WTO for all its
Members means that the costs of withdrawal are enormous. The resulting 'irreversibility' of rules agreed to at the WTO means that proposed
agreements are increasingly subject to intense scrutiny by 'outsiders' to
the regime, including human rights experts and NGOs.[177]

Some commentators have sought to respond to this political challenge by arguing that the trade regime is inherently protective of human
rights. For example, Ernst-Ulrich Petersmann argues that trade liberalisation does operate to protect human rights through furthering the right
to property, economic freedom and human dignity.[178] For Petersmann,
'liberal markets are a necessary complement of individual freedom and
constitutional democracy'.[179] Petersmann seeks to legitimate the trading
system by linking it with the moral authority of human rights.[180] In so
doing, he draws on a tradition in which the holder of rights is imagined

---

[176] Robert Howse, 'From Politics to Technocracy – and Back Again: the Fate of the
   Multilateral Trading Regime' (2002) 96 *American Journal of International Law* 94, 98–9;
   J. H. H. Weiler, 'The Rule of Lawyers and the Ethos of Diplomats' (2001) 35 *Journal of
   World Trade* 191.
[177] Howse, 'From Politics to Technocracy', 107.
[178] Ernst-Ulrich Petersmann, 'The WTO Constitution and Human Rights' (2000) 3 *Journal
   of International Economic Law* 19.
[179] *Ibid.*, 23.   [180] *Ibid.*, 24.

as a property-owning subject.[181] The ownership of property has been central to liberal conceptions of what it is to be fully human.[182] For John Locke, 'every man has property in his own person'.[183] A man owns his own person and thus his own labour. He can also appropriate the external world through putting his own labour into it, mixing himself with it and earning the right to exclude the rest of humanity from its use and enjoyment. This link between property and personality in the liberal philosophical tradition forms one of the conceptual links between capitalism and modern liberal law.[184] In this sense, the WTO does promote a narrow range of 'human rights'.

Yet human rights have also been conceptualised outside the purely individualistic framework developed in relation to some civil and political rights. Rights to political participation are conceived of as rights that we exercise in community with others, while rights to health or education presuppose a public sphere in which claims for a share of collective goods can be made. Collective rights such as the right to development or the right of self-determination focus on control over territory and resources, and allow for the development of a social, political and economic order that does not simply maintain exploitation.[185] It is the less atomistic approach offered by these rights that provides a challenge to the corporatism of the trade regime. Trade and financial liberalisation threaten this broader range of human rights in a number of ways.

First, post-Uruguay Round trade agreements reflect a move away from non-discrimination as the foundational premise of GATT, towards the dream of a world of sameness, or to adopt the language of free trade, harmonisation. In theory, most forms of regulation can operate as 'non-tariff barriers to trade', in that the existence of differing regulatory standards means that corporations may be prevented from selling the same product everywhere in the world. According to free trade logic, states should not be able to make use of non-economic bases, such as protecting consumer safety or environmental protection, to justify restrictive policies that inhibit the capacity of foreign producers to maximise their access to global markets. Harmonisation can ensure that profits are

---

[181] *Ibid.*, 23.

[182] Margaret Davies, 'The Heterosexual Economy' (1995) 5 *Australian Feminist Law Journal* 27, 30.

[183] John Locke, *Second Treatise of Government* (Cambridge, 1970), ch. V, s. 27.

[184] For a critique of this inscription of the property-owning subject as the representative of man, see Karl Marx, 'On the Jewish Question' in Jeremy Waldron (ed.), *Nonsense upon Stilts: Bentham, Burke and Marx on the Rights of Man* (London, 1987), pp. 137–50.

[185] See further Chapter 4 below.

maximised, entrepreneurialism is encouraged, and barriers to the sale of products are only created where the necessity of such regulations can be proved according to rational and rigorous scientific standards. In this imagined future, any national or indigenous differences, whether or not they are discriminatory, will be swept away in the march towards standardised regimes for intellectual property protection, health and safety regulations, foreign investment and provision of services.

The capacity to make decisions about what these harmonised standards should be is increasingly being removed from the democratic process, as trade agreements enshrine economics and science as privileged forms of knowledge. The 1994 Agreement on Sanitary and Phytosanitary Measures (SPS Agreement) offers a good illustration of this process.[186] That Agreement sets out obligations and procedures relating to the use of sanitary and phytosanitary measures, or human or animal health and safety laws. Members of the WTO are obliged to ensure that no such measure is maintained without scientific evidence.[187] States parties to the SPS Agreement agree to pass laws or regulations that protect animal and human health and welfare only where there are recognised and agreed international scientific standards necessitating such protection. Where there are no such standards, Members agree to pass such laws or regulations affecting foreign producers only where they can provide scientific evidence proving that a new technology is dangerous when used in animal or plant development. Scientific experts are recognised by the Agreement as legitimate sources of authorised knowledge upon which government policies can be based without breaching trade agreements.

That basis for decision-making excludes, or at the least marginalises, other community concerns or other forms of knowledge from consideration. The requirement that states privilege the knowledge produced by scientists, who are often paid and employed by interested corporations, over the knowledge of local consumers, workers, industry groups or farmers, operates to limit the scope for contesting and debating particular policies and laws. By restricting the bases upon which states can introduce laws relating to consumer safety, animal health and welfare or sustainable farming practices, the right of people and communities to participate in and shape their economic and social development is constrained. To require states to frame their objections or concerns about

---

[186] For a more detailed analysis of the SPS Agreement and its effects, see Orford, 'Globalisation', pp. 158–67.
[187] SPS Agreement, Article 2.

particular processes or products in the language of science necessarily excludes some bases for making decisions. For example, it can be difficult to address concerns about sustainable farming practices, the effects of agribusiness on small farmers in developing countries, or animal welfare, in the language of science. Such an approach shuts out other questions or issues, for example the appropriateness of adopting a precautionary approach to the safety of new processes, products or technologies. The decision to use caution in the face of new technologies involves a judgment about the commitment of corporations to consumer protection rather than profit. This involves a political judgment that should be made by democratic processes. As Joseph Weiler argues, the regulatory state and the detail of international economic law should not be outside the normal processes of democracy.[188] Such judgments, however, are precluded by the operation of the SPS Agreement.

The WTO agreements also embody an ideological preference for the commodification of resources, and for private over public ownership of such commodities. For instance, the Agreement on Trade-Related Aspects of Intellectual Property Rights (TRIPS) requires WTO Members to have in place laws that recognise and protect a broad range of private intellectual and industrial property rights.[189] In addition, Members agree to provide the legal and administrative infrastructure necessary to ensure that intellectual property rights can effectively be enforced under domestic law, both by their own nationals and by foreign rights-holders.[190] For some cultures in which traditional, community-based knowledge about seeds and plants was not commodified, TRIPS has meant the 'enclosure' of a common resource and its transformation into private property.[191]

A similar privileging of private interests underpins the General Agreement on Trade in Services (GATS). While GATS does not require Members to privatise public services, once services in sectors covered by GATS are privatised, the market for such services must be opened to foreign investors. The effect of this agreement is to make it far more difficult to

---

[188] J. H. H. Weiler, 'Balancing National Regulatory Sovereignty with the Discipline of Free Trade', The Sir Kenneth Bailey Memorial Lecture, University of Melbourne, 15 August 2001.

[189] TRIPS Agreement, Part II.

[190] TRIPS Agreement, Part III. For an examination of the legal and administrative changes required by developing countries to provide protection for patents relating to pharmaceutical and agricultural chemical products under TRIPS, see Appellate Body Report, *India – Patent Protection for Pharmaceutical and Agricultural Chemical Products*, adopted 19 December 1997, WT/DS50/AB/R.

[191] John Frow, 'Information as Gift and Commodity' (1996) Sept/Oct *New Left Review* 89.

reverse failed privatisations and return services to public ownership.[192] As states around the world experiment with the privatisation of services such as banking, water supply, electricity, telecommunications and urban transport, this kind of built-in privileging of private ownership reduces the scope for democratic participation in assessing such experiments.[193]

As these examples indicate, free trade agreements shift the boundary between public good and private interest in favour of the private interests of corporations. This has profound implications for the utility of liberal concepts of democracy and human rights in the public sphere.[194] The idea underlying such notions – the guarantee to individuals of formally equal access to public goods and participation in public decision-making – is undermined by the twinned processes of privatisation and commodification. By facilitating, or requiring, the reconceptualisation of aspects of the public sphere as private and thus outside the realm of liberal democracy, agreements such as TRIPS limit the relevance of concepts which imply power-sharing, claims to resources and entitlements against the state. The redrawing of boundaries between public and private operates to confine egalitarianism to an ever declining public sphere.

States and peoples are increasingly limited by such agreements in their capacity to choose models of development that do not suit the interests of powerful states such as the USA. One of the assumptions of much discussion in the trade and development area is that states and peoples are free to choose the development model, and in particular the legal and administrative system, that they believe best suits their conditions. If the choice is a bad one, it will be punished by foreign markets or investors. Agreements like TRIPS fundamentally unsettle that assumption. There, a powerful state, the USA, was able to make use of its market power to ensure that other states signed on to a far-reaching agreement relating to a form of property that will be at the heart of economic development into the next century.[195] Indeed, when states like the USA began to push to have intellectual property added to the Uruguay Round agenda, many trade negotiators and the GATT Secretariat itself had little familiarity with intellectual property regimes, and saw a conceptual

---

[192] See the discussion of the operations of GATS Article XXI in Scott Sinclair and Jim Grieshaber-Otto, *Facing the Facts: a guide to the GATS Debate* (Canada, 2002), pp. 33–5.

[193] Howse, 'From Politics to Technocracy', 113.   [194] Frow, 'Information', 105.

[195] Peter Drahos, 'Global Property Rights in Information: the story of TRIPS at the GATT' (1995) *Prometheus* 6.

tension between free trade and the monopoly privileges that intellectual property rights represent.[196] The USA was nevertheless able to make use of a process of economic coercion involving the threat and use of trade sanctions to ensure that the TRIPS Agreement was finally agreed to as part of the Uruguay Round of reforms.[197] That agreement goes further than perhaps any other international agreement to date in terms of stating in detail the kinds of laws and administrative systems that states must have in place, detailing not only the nature of the rights to be protected, but also the kinds of procedures and penalties that states must have in place to enforce these rights.[198]

Whatever view we adopt on the relationship between the activities of international economic institutions and human rights, we can say that it is not possible under such conditions to draw a firm line between national and international, domestic and foreign. Such distinctions are radically complicated by a globalised economy in which international organisations and agencies are intimately involved in making decisions that are far from technical. It is impossible to talk meaningfully about 'local' causes of conflict or 'local' threats to democracy and human rights in a world where the international community, through institutions like the IMF, the World Bank and the WTO, restructures the nature of daily life for most human beings.[199] Yet at present, 'the international'

---

[196] *Ibid.*

[197] *Ibid.*, 14–15. Drahos reveals that the USA made use of a range of coercive trade mechanisms at the bilateral level to ensure that states complied with US negotiating objectives relating to intellectual property protection. In addition, the US government in concert with major US corporations made use of an 'information' campaign in various countries to instil the idea that inventions and ideas were 'property' and that their 'theft' was a serious issue. The outcome of the negotiations over TRIPS was particularly remarkable given that most countries other than the USA are net importers of technological and cultural information, and yet have agreed to pay more for that information under TRIPS.

[198] Part III deals with the enforcement of intellectual property rights in great detail. It provides that states must implement enforcement procedures that are fair and equitable, and which are not to be 'unnecessarily complicated or costly, or entail unreasonable time-limits or unwarranted delays' (Article 41:2). Decisions relating to intellectual property matters are preferably to be in writing with reasons, and rights of judicial review are to be provided in the case of judicial decisions (Articles 41:3 and 41:4.). States are obliged to provide for criminal procedures and penalties, at least in the case of wilful trademark counterfeiting or copyright piracy on a commercial scale, and the remedies to be available under criminal procedures are to include 'imprisonment and/or monetary fines sufficient to provide a deterrent' (Article 61).

[199] Jim George, 'Quo Vadis Australia? Framing the Defence and Security Debate beyond the Cold War' in Graeme Cheeseman and Robert Bruce (eds.), *Discourses of Danger & Dread Frontiers: Australian Defence and Security Thinking after the Cold War* (St Leonards, 1996), pp. 10–48 at p. 33.

in pro-interventionist literature becomes that which major powers wish to claim or own – peace, democracy, security, liberty – while 'the local' becomes that for which major powers do not wish to take responsibility.

Engaging with the international

Those arguing in favour of expanding the humanitarian role of the Security Council or NATO present an image of international institutions and international law as agents of democracy and human rights. That representation operates to reinforce the identity of international institutions and of major powers, particularly the USA, as in turn bearers of those progressive values. The UN and other post-World War II institutions have embodied the faith of many people in the ability of international institutions to protect ideals of universalism, humanitarianism, peace, security and human rights. Multilateralism has seemed to offer an escape from unrestrained self-interest and power politics. Yet by representing international intervention as essentially humanitarian, pro-interventionist literature forecloses a number of important debates.

First, the focus on the role of international institutions and international law in intervening for human rights and democracy obscures the role played by international institutions and laws in contributing to economic liberalisation. By focusing only on norms of international law that relate to public issues, international lawyers fail to make visible the norms and institutions that facilitate the making of a global market. That failure contributes to the sense that economic liberalisation is natural and inevitable. Global economic restructuring is a given, and our role as humane international lawyers is only to consider norms relating to intervention, or issues such as the limits of self-determination. Accordingly, the conduct of business as usual appears both natural and politically neutral. As David Kennedy argues:

In [the dominant legal] view, only international government must be made; the international market makes itself...Of course, as has been recognised since the last century, this approach dramatically obscures the process by which a market is constructed – the ongoing choices required to elaborate, enforce, and interpret the background norms of private law, and the financial and other service institutions which must be put in place. It not only makes the State seem too active, too able to *will* (as all international institutionalists insist), it also underestimates the politics of the private.[200]

---

[200] Kennedy, 'A New World Order', 372 (emphasis in original).

Second, by failing to evaluate the relationship of the activities of international institutions to security and humanitarian crises, international lawyers avoid assessing the threats posed to security, human rights, life, substantive democracy, health and justice by economic restructuring. While the activities of international economic institutions, US and European economic advisers and private banks have arguably contributed to security crises, and certainly have substantial effects upon sovereignty, self-determination, statehood, the right to democratic governance and the protection of human rights, little or no attention has been paid to assessing the relationship of the activities of those institutions to security and humanitarian crises. Those institutions and laws have emerged untouched from the reassessment of norms and re-evaluation of the adequacy of international institutions that have taken place in light of these crises.

In other words, the project of economic liberalisation, an enormous and influential area of international engagement and intervention, appears sacrosanct when it comes to considering how a new world order might better guarantee peace, security, human rights, respect for humanitarian norms, genocide prevention and democracy. In the case of the Yugoslav conflict, the failure to consider the possibility that the causes of the crisis might be related to the activities of international institutions or the influence of international law, has meant that, rather than examining the role played by the international community in contributing to this situation, outside actors continued to understand the causes of the conflict as 'ethnic' or 'nationalist' in a premodern sense. The principal lesson we should have learned from Yugoslavia or Rwanda was, in other words, not primarily that we need a UN rapid deployment force, but that intellectuals and activists concerned about democratic and human rights issues should lobby their government's representatives and directors to oppose support for this model of economic liberalisation and marketisation in Eastern Europe. By structuring the debate around the use of force, we never get around to talking about those other issues.

José Alvarez makes a similar point about the way in which international lawyers understand the Rwandan genocide.[201] Alvarez argues that for international lawyers, the problem of genocide is defined in 'state-centric' terms – the mass atrocities committed in Rwanda are seen to have resulted from the combination of actions of 'state actors who

[201] Alvarez, 'Crimes', 370.

violated fundamental norms of civilized behaviour' and 'the failure of other government actors to respond'.[202] The crimes committed in Rwanda, and by implication the causes of those crimes, are treated as 'aberrant or exceptional deviations from the norms of interstate behaviour'.[203] Alvarez argues that for international lawyers, the 'solution' to the Rwandan genocide flows from the definition of the problem. If the genocide resulted in part from the failure of states or international organisations to enforce 'the international rule of law against rogue state actors', the solution 'needs to be provided, in top-down fashion, by the international community's most reputable enforcer, namely the United Nations'.[204]

This way of understanding the problem of genocide in Rwanda and elsewhere is compelling. In contrast to those who blame extreme violence on ahistorical and apolitical factors such as ancient hatreds, evil forces, primitive irrationality or inherent human (or masculine) aggression, 'international lawyers are proactive and non-defeatist'.[205] Even in the face of the horror that was the one hundred days of slaughter in Rwanda, international lawyers assert that 'international intervention to encourage accountability is neither useless nor counterproductive' and that 'there is always *something to be done*'.[206] I do not want to be cavalier about the internationalist faith in the capacity of human beings to create a different future and to challenge the existing order in such circumstances. But I do want to question *what* it is that we are called to do by the texts of law. The use of force appears as a necessary response to security and humanitarian crises where such crises are understood to be caused purely by localised ethnic or nationalistic tensions. The international community depicted the Yugoslav and Rwandan conflicts principally in ethnic or nationalist terms, and ignored the role that international institutions and outside actors played in contributing to the causes of the conflict. The result of constructing the crises in those terms had significant results for policies of intervention. The lessons learned from the Yugoslav and Rwandan crises turned upon how early and to what extent force should be resorted to in such situations. The apparent focus on the use of force as a response to security and humanitarian crises is problematic, both because it ignores the role that international institutions and policies of, *inter alia*, the EC and the USA, played in creating the conditions that led to violence, and because it appears that US

---

[202] *Ibid.*, 370–1.   [203] *Ibid.*, 369.   [204] *Ibid.*, 371.   [205] *Ibid.*, 382.
[206] *Ibid.* (emphasis in original, citation omitted).

and other governments are in any case reluctant to commit troops for collective humanitarian purposes. For a variety of reasons, citizens of states like the USA may not be willing to support military intervention, and thus force may in any case no longer be reliably available to contain crises resulting from the destabilising and oppressive consequences of economic restructuring. Accordingly, it seems timely to consider other ways in which changes to the policies of international institutions might contribute to peace and security.

Despite the lessons that might have been learned about the nature of international engagement in Rwanda and the former Yugoslavia, international institutions continue to cling, albeit somewhat more grimly, to the agenda of economic liberalisation and facilitation of a global division of labour.[207] Little has been done to absorb these lessons about the possibility that rapid economic liberalisation contributes to the conditions that make acute violence possible. Instead, as I argue in Chapter 4, the capacity of the international community to entrench economic restructuring has been strengthened as part of the post-conflict peace process in Bosnia-Herzegovina and East Timor.

The cartography of intervention

The representation of the conflicts in the former Yugoslavia and Rwanda as exacerbated by an absence of international involvement also serves to create a sense that the international community and those facing humanitarian or security crises are physically separate. As we have seen, there is little, if any, discussion of the presence of representatives of the international community in countries such as the former Yugoslavia or Rwanda prior to crises erupting. Edward Said described Orientalism as Europe's 'collective day-dream',[208] and texts such as those I have considered in this chapter indeed resemble a dream, in which an imaginative geography of the world is produced.[209] For Steve Pile, imaginative geographies function in such a daydream to: 'localize and distance the

---

[207] See Ana Stanič, 'Financial Aspects of State Succession: the Case of Yugoslavia' (2001) 12 *European Journal of International Law* 751; Cline, *International Debt*, p. 366 (discussing the fact that after the war, Yugoslav successor states cannot expect anything other than a modest amount of debt forgiveness, as debt indicators do not show particularly heavy indebtedness). See further the discussion of the economic programme for the internationally administered Bosnia-Herzegovina in Chapter 4 below.

[208] Said, *Orientalism*, p. 52.

[209] Steve Pile, 'Freud, Dreams and Imaginative Geographies' in Anthony Elliott (ed.), *Freud 2000* (Victoria, 1998), pp. 204–34 at p. 222.

East from the West, partly by displacing meanings. The border between East and West separates them off, so that the West can be sure that the other is somewhere else, outside. Nevertheless, the border joins as it divides. East and West lie side by side, simultaneously (too) close and far (away).'[210]

Humanitarian intervention narratives work in this way – to reassure the 'international community' that there is a differentiated other, and to locate this other 'somewhere else, outside'. Here, I have explored the conditions of that sense of separateness. It requires internationalist literature to ignore the presence of the international community in countries prior to violence erupting. The notion that the suffering or chaotic other is located elsewhere is reinforced through the act of intervention – we use force to maintain 'safe havens' or to protect (local) civilians at home, while at the same time evacuating foreigners.[211] As I will argue in Chapter 6, the refugee is the figure that unsettles this separation – through the claims or demands of the refugee from violence we are confronted with the spectre of a suffering other who does not stay at home, who seeks to unsettle our sense of safety and separateness.

This distancing of the other appears particularly necessary in the age of globalisation, when the kinds of crises to which humanitarian intervention is a response threaten to bring the other (too) close. Many accounts of the need for intervention discuss the role of televised images of suffering in creating a sense of the global village. So, for example, the quote from Shashi Tharoor in the introduction to this chapter suggests that it is 'television images of suffering broadcast as they occur' which gives rise to 'the public clamour to "do something"'.[212] Geoffrey Robertson agrees that the call for international and UN responses to human rights violations is inspired by a 'revulsion against atrocities brought into…homes through a billion television sets and twice as many radios, creating a vast audience beginning to think like global citizens'.[213] For Robertson, 'modern media coverage of human rights hotspots' and 'television pictures of corpses in Racak, Kosovo, put such obscure places on the map of everyone's mind and galvanize the West to war'.[214]

---

[210] *Ibid.*, p. 233.   [211] See the discussion of this practice in Chapter 6.

[212] Tharoor, 'The Changing Face', 413.

[213] Geoffrey Robertson QC, *Crimes against Humanity: the Struggle for Global Justice* (Ringwood, 2000), p. 438.

[214] *Ibid.*

In these ways, suffering in distant lands is made immediate through technology. Commentators like Robertson treat this as increasing a sense of common humanity, and as leading to the desire to 'do something' to respond to human rights abuses. But at the same time, the call made in response to these images is not to admit those suffering abuses as refugees, but rather to intervene militarily and prevent exodus.[215] The effect of military intervention is to keep a distance between those we wish to save and our own community. In other words, perhaps the idea that we are now one with the rest of humanity, that we are close to these suffering masses, inspires our fear as much as our compassion. Technology brings the other too close, the other threatens to invade our civilised world. As I argue in Chapter 6, this poses a threat to the sense of self of the international community, inherited from the identity created during the European encounter with the 'New World' and based on a faith that violence and barbarism are outside the developed, capitalist, civilised order of Western Europe and its colonial outposts.[216] Intervention narratives serve, both materially and ideologically, to maintain that separation. Intervention texts can thus be read as a response to this threat, an attempt simultaneously to locate and thus distance the colonised from the coloniser. Perhaps more importantly, as I explore in Chapter 6, this distancing is never final or successful – as we shall see, the space of dreams can never completely be controlled by the dreamer.

[215] See the discussion in James C. Hathaway, 'The Single Superpower and the Future of International Law' (2000) 94 *American Society of International Law Proceedings* 67, and further in Chapter 6 below.

[216] See generally Antony Anghie, 'Finding the Peripheries: Sovereignty and Colonialism in Nineteenth-Century International Law' (1999) 40 *Harvard International Law Journal* 1; Jennifer Beard, 'The Art of Development: Law and Ordering in the First World' (2002, unpublished doctoral thesis, on file with author).

4 Self-determination after intervention: the international community and post-conflict reconstruction

This chapter is concerned with the representation of the role of the international community in the wake of humanitarian intervention. In the cases of Bosnia-Herzegovina and East Timor, the challenges to be addressed by the international community are seen to include the design of new constitutional, legal and administrative arrangements, nation-building, and economic management through the creation of a stable environment in which foreign aid and investment can take place. This chapter explores the way in which legal texts about the administration of territories by the international community attempt to manage and narrate the consequences of humanitarian intervention.

The first part of the chapter outlines the role of territorial administrator that international actors have adopted in Bosnia-Herzegovina and East Timor. It explores the ways in which international reconstruction constitutes the international community – both materially in terms of the economic liberalisation facilitated by reconstruction, and symbolically through the notions of charity, pedagogy and functionalism that underpin representations of the role of international administration. The second part explores the ways in which the project of post-conflict reconstruction mirrors the support by the international community for colonialism in earlier periods. From its authorisation of the acquisition of territory belonging to uncivilised peoples through to the operation of the mandate system, the international community has systematically facilitated the enterprise of colonialism. Central to this support has been the limited meaning given to the concept of self-determination. As the cases of Bosnia-Herzegovina and East Timor illustrate, international administration following humanitarian intervention has a similar effect. As a result, there appears to be little opportunity for those in whose name intervention is conducted to participate fully in determining the conditions that will shape their lives. The final part of the chapter considers the possibilities, and limits, of self-determination as a foundation for challenging the legitimacy of the processes of intervention and reconstruction.

Self-determination in an age of intervention – a tale of two territories

The right of self-determination is one of the most compelling and contested ideas in international law. In legal debates about the status and meaning of this right, we see expressed modernist fantasies about the desirability, and the dangerousness, of national identity, territory, political community and autonomy. In the two cases of Bosnia-Herzegovina and East Timor, military intervention by the international community was hailed by at least some international commentators as contributing to the realisation of this right. For example, in 1996 then US Secretary of State Warren Christopher applauded the democratic outcome that he saw as resulting from the intervention in Bosnia and the Dayton peace process. 'Now the Bosnian people will have their own democratic say. This is a worthy goal in and of itself, because the only peace that can last in Bosnia is the peace that the people of the country freely choose.'[1]

Similarly, Australia's Foreign Minister Alexander Downer has lauded the role played by Australian troops as part of the UN-authorised International Force in East Timor (INTERFET) in supporting self-determination and relieving suffering in the territory. 'Australia has played a very constructive, and wholly creditable, role in the process that has led to self-determination for the people of East Timor...We saw an opportunity to allow East Timorese to decide their own future, and we helped them realise that chance.'[2] Geoffrey Robertson also sees the UN intervention in East Timor as a case where the international community acted to protect the right of people to determine their own governance.[3] He argues

---

[1] *Statement by Secretary of State Warren Christopher on Bosnian Elections*, United States Department of State, Office of the Spokesman, 18 September 1996, http://dosfan.lib. uic.edu/ERC/briefing/dossec/1996/9609/960918dossec.html (accessed 22 February 2002).

[2] Alexander Downer, Minister for Foreign Affairs, 'East Timor: the Way Ahead', speech given to the Rotary Club of Sydney, 30 November 1999.

[3] Geoffrey Robertson, *Crimes against Humanity: The Struggle for Global Justice* (Ringwood, 1999), p. 434.

that the protection of the 'post-plebiscite right to self-determination was the acknowledged reason for the intervention' in East Timor.[4]

Other international lawyers reject the argument that intervention in support of self-determination or democratic governance became lawful during the 1990s, arguing that there is little in the way of post-Cold War state practice or international texts to support that notion. For legal scholars who oppose resort to humanitarian intervention on the basis that it undermines the UN Charter, it is the progressive development of legal norms such as sovereign equality or non-intervention that offer the best protection for the right of self-determination.[5] Yet whether or not we accept the emergence of a principle supporting the legality of intervention in support of self-determination, we can adopt the suggestion by James Crawford that 'self-determination remains relevant in judging situations where intervention has occurred, and especially in dealing with their aftermath'.[6]

In both Bosnia-Herzegovina and East Timor, the international community has adopted the role of territorial administrator in the aftermath of its military intervention. The idea that the international community has a legitimate role as administrator of post-conflict territories and manager of the reconstruction process has gained increasing acceptance at the international level. These developments in international relations flow from a new faith in the international community as a benign, even civilising, administrator. Indeed, in light of this trend, it seemed almost unremarkable to be told in November 2001, in the aftermath of a war on terror, that the government of Afghanistan was being 'freely determined' by its people in Bonn, while the World Bank, the United Nations Development Program and the Asian Development Bank co-hosted a meeting in Islamabad to decide how to transform Afghanistan into a market economy.[7] Yet the role played by the international community in states subject to international administration would appear to be at

---

[4] Ibid.

[5] See, for example, Simon Chesterman, *Just War or Just Peace? Humanitarian Intervention and International Law* (Oxford, 2001), pp. 232–6.

[6] James Crawford, 'The Right of Self-Determination in International Law: Its Development and Future' in Philip Alston (ed.), *Peoples' Rights* (Oxford, 2001), pp. 7–67 at p. 46.

[7] See *Preparing for Afghanistan's Reconstruction*, Conference co-hosted by the United Nations Development Program, the World Bank and the Asian Development Bank, 27–9 November 2001, http://lnweb18.worldbank.org/sar/sa.nsf/91e66bec154b73d5852567 e6007090ae/72342fd95bbf24f085256b0a007b3f86?OpenDocument (accessed 22 February 2002).

odds with the realisation of the right of self-determination as one of the stated aims of humanitarian intervention. It is this tension, and the way in which it is managed by international lawyers and administrators in the context of Bosnia-Herzegovina and East Timor, that this part examines.

Staging democracy in Bosnia-Herzegovina

I want to begin by sketching the role of the international community in the implementation of the Dayton Peace Agreement in Bosnia-Herzegovina.[8] The Parties to the Dayton Agreement provided that military implementation of the agreement was to be overseen by an Implementation Force (later the Stabilization Force),[9] while implementation of the civilian aspects of the agreement was to be in the hands of the newly created Office of the High Representative (OHR).[10] Oversight of many aspects of civilian administration was allocated to other international actors.[11] For example, the Organization for Security and Cooperation in Europe (OSCE) was to supervise the conduct of free, fair and democratic elections;[12] the President of the European Court of Human Rights was to select three members of the Constitutional Court;[13] and the International Monetary Fund was to appoint the Governor of the Central Bank.[14]

Perhaps the most significant international body involved in the reconstruction process in Bosnia-Herzegovina is the Peace Implementation Council (PIC), an ad hoc group of fifty-five countries and organisations that was formed in 1995 to sponsor and direct the peace implementation process. The Steering Board of the PIC nominates the High Representative, who is then endorsed by the Security Council. The Office of the High Representative is funded by the PIC, and the Steering Board

---

[8] The General Framework Agreement for Peace in Bosnia and Herzegovina with Annexes, 1995 (1996) 35 ILM 75 (Dayton Agreement).

[9] *Ibid.*, Annex 1A, inviting the Security Council to adopt a resolution which will authorise a military implementation force. The Security Council established such a force by Resolution 1031 of 1995: S/1995/1031.

[10] *Ibid.*, Annex 10.

[11] Ralph Wilde, 'From Bosnia to Kosovo and East Timor: the Changing Role of the United Nations in the Administration of Territory' (2000) 6 *ILSA Journal of International and Comparative Law* 467.

[12] Dayton Agreement, Annex 3.   [13] *Ibid.*, Article VI of Annex 4.

[14] *Ibid.*, Article VII of Annex 4.

of the PIC provides the High Representative with 'political guidance'.[15] The PIC effectively decides policy for Bosnia-Herzegovina, and then directs the High Representative and other international institutions to facilitate the implementation of that policy.[16] The ongoing priorities for the PIC are 'deepening economic reform and creating the conditions for self-sustaining market-driven economic growth', accelerating the return of refugees and internally displaced persons, and 'fostering functional and democratically accountable common institutions supported by an effective, merit-based civil service and a sound financial basis'.[17]

The mandate of the High Representative has been interpreted extremely broadly. Under the Dayton Agreement, the 'High Representative is the final authority in theater regarding interpretation of this Agreement on the civilian implementation of the peace settlement'.[18] The High Representative has used this authority to impose legislation drafted by international actors but rejected by democratically elected state and entity bodies, to ban political parties, and to dismiss 'obstructive' elected and appointed officials. That interpretation has since been welcomed by the PIC.[19]

The former High Representative, Wolfgang Petritsch, made clear that this capacity to dismiss officials, ban parties and impose legislation extends to situations where parliamentarians refuse to pass legislation drafted by the international community implementing far-reaching economic reforms.[20] The language in which Petritsch discussed this stalemate is instructive in terms of the limits it suggests to a commitment to respect for the right of self-determination. In an interview with *Slobodna Bosna* in November 2001, Petritsch stated:

[15] Office of the High Representative, General Information, http://www.ohr.int/ohr-info/ gen-info/ (accessed 12 November 2001).

[16] David Chandler, 'Bosnia: Prototype of a NATO Protectorate' in Tariq Ali (ed.), *Masters of the Universe? NATO's Balkan Crusade* (London, 2000), pp. 271–84 at pp. 271, 272.

[17] Declaration of the PIC, 24 May 2000, http://www.ohr.int/pic/archive.asp?sa=on (accessed 13 November 2001).

[18] Dayton Agreement, Article V of Annex 10.

[19] In Paragraph XI.2 of the Conclusions of the Peace Implementation Conference held in Bonn, 9–10 December 1997, the Peace Implementation Council 'welcomes the High Representative's intention to use his final authority in theatre' by taking measures including 'actions against persons holding public office or officials ... who are found by the High Representative to be in violation of legal commitments made under the Peace Agreement or the terms for its implementation': http://www.ohr.int/pic/archive. asp?sa=on (accessed 13 November 2001).

[20] 'Interview: Wolfgang Petritsch, the High Representative in BiH: "What Message I Got across to the SDS"', 9 November 2001, http://www.ohr.int/ohr-dept/presso/pressi/ (accessed 13 November 2001).

It has been several months since the new authorities came to power in the Republika Srpska. Over this period we have been 'pressuring' the RS Government and the Parliament including the SDS [Serb Democratic Party] in particular, to be cooperative...I asked the representatives of the PIC to support me in taking more severe measures against the top RS officials because we have not seen the expected results. After this meeting, I went to Banja Luka and reiterated this to the politicians there. I think that such type of communication is really necessary – not some ambiguous political quibbling but very direct, open and intensive discussions with the relevant political actors in the RS.[21]

In a striking explanation of the ways in which the international community understands the meaning of democracy in a territory under administration, Petritsch explained that elected politicians do not have the right to reject legislation imposing radical economic reform:

I want to see the immediate adoption of the laws which are pending before the State Parliament. That is the first thing they have to do. If some representatives are concerned about the content of some laws, from the professional point of view, they can discuss it. However, it will not be acceptable whatsoever to reject the laws with the argument that they are unacceptable or that they do not want to deal with these laws at all. The laws concerning economic reform and development are essential, and they simply have to be passed. In case this does not happen, you can be sure that I will not hesitate to exercise my powers.[22]

Asked what kind of sanctions would be imposed because elected politicians had failed to produce 'the expected results' and had questioned international economic policy, Petritsch replied:

I will not hesitate whatsoever to exercise all the powers, as I did when I was compelled to do so in the past. I would like to remind you that to date I have removed about seventy local politicians. If the SDS compels me to do so, I will not hesitate to resort to such a measure in their case either. That is one of the options, but you know that I never mention any name in advance.[23]

Petritsch explains his motivation for treating elected representatives in these terms: 'investors, particularly those from abroad, look for security, the rule of law, and respect for human rights'.[24]

This mode of discourse has been taken up by the current High Representative, Paddy Ashdown. In an address to the BiH (Bosnia-Herzegovina) Parliament on 16 July 2002, Ashdown shifted between scolding and threatening the assembled parliamentarians as he explained that if they

[21] *Ibid.*   [22] *Ibid.*   [23] *Ibid.*   [24] *Ibid.*

did not conform to international policy prescriptions regarding fiscal priorities and services privatisation, the IMF, World Bank and EU 'would simply walk away from here'.[25] Ashdown made clear that the goal of international administration is to ensure that Bosnia-Herzegovina takes its proper place in the global market as a source of labour and a site for foreign investment:

Governments and Parliaments...can create the conditions in which private enterprise can flourish and generate employment. Inward investment is the key to this. But investment only flows to places where it is made welcome. Our aim must be nothing less than to make Bosnia and Herzegovina the most business friendly country in the region...That is why the various pieces of economic reform legislation that must pass through this Parliament are so important. Because together, they will help to create a business friendly environment, and a single economic space...[26]

The High Representative has explained that his vision for the future of the 'single economic space' of Bosnia-Herzegovina involves replacing the international community's military presence with its business representatives.

My goal here is to wind down the interventionist peace-building process of the postwar years, with its major North Atlantic Treaty Organization military component, and to help bring about a more normal presence based on extensive engagement by the European Union and private investors. In a few years' time there will be no more need for soldiers and international bureaucrats like me. Instead, I hope Sarajevo will be full of bankers and businessmen, the sort of people we increasingly see in all the other capitals of southeastern and central Europe.[27]

A formal commitment to democracy and the concept of local 'ownership' of the reconstruction process continue to be the stated aims of international administration in Bosnia-Herzegovina.[28] Yet there has been little concern expressed by the international community about the hollow nature of the democracy created under this administration. According

---

[25] 'Speech by the High Representative Paddy Ashdown to the BiH Parliament', 16 July 2002, http://www.ohr.int/ohr-dept/presso/presssp/default.asp?contentid=27319 (accessed 5 August, 2002).

[26] Ibid., 3.

[27] Paddy Ashdown, 'Collateral Costs in Fighting a New Court', The New York Times on the Web, 2 July 2002, http://www.nytimes.com/ 2002/07/02/opinion/02ASHD.html? todaysheadlines=&pagewant (accessed 3 July 2002).

[28] See Dayton Agreement, Articles I and II of Annex 4. On the commitment to 'ownership' as a governing principle, see OHR General Information; Report by the High Representative to the Secretary-General of the UN, 1 November 1999.

to David Chandler, this should not be a surprise, given that most international institutions involved in the 'transitional' administration of the state have expressed views about the 'incapacity of Balkan people to cope with democracy'.[29] The OSCE has stated that 'the "political level" of Bosnian voters is "not very high"'.[30] OHR representatives allege that 'Bosnia is a deeply sick society, ill at ease with even the most basic principles of democracy'.[31] Perhaps most strikingly, the Senior Coordinator of the Democratisation Branch of the OSCE Mission in Bosnia has argued that 'Bosnian people are incapable of handling electoral competition.'[32] As Chandler argues 'once the capacity of Bosnian people as rational political actors is negated, there is no reason, in principle, for international administration to be seen as merely temporary or transitional, nor for democracy to be seen as preferable'.[33]

The international community's mistrust of the Bosnian people as rational political actors does not only flow from the fact that they can not be relied upon to support legislation aimed at achieving non-negotiable economic and institutional goals set by the international community. In addition, it is due to a fear that minorities could again be persecuted if majoritarian rule is not in some way constrained by minority rights protections. This fear does appear to motivate some of those international actors who make a virtue of the political dispossession of the people of Bosnia-Herzegovina. This sense that the international community should be hostile towards nationalist politicians and organisations finds some support in the argument that nationalist identity is always dependent on belligerent othering, exclusion and violence. Let us then, one response might be, make a virtue of uncertain or fluid identities, of exile, of unbounded communities. The international community should reject any forms of political ordering based on exclusionary politics. However, as Jacqueline Rose has said:

> If certainty is belligerent and panicked, you cannot in this political context just make a virtue of its opposite, not in a world where the trauma of national indefinition – lack of a nation, yearning to be a nation – is what seems historically, and so dramatically, to engender the most ruthless of psychic and political states...

> You might say that the problem is the false securing of identity; or you might argue that it is only when you lose the minimal conditions for identity that the drive begins for an identity which is falsely and dangerously secure.[34]

---

[29] Chandler, 'Bosnia', p. 279.   [30] Ibid., p. 278.   [31] Ibid.   [32] Ibid.   [33] Ibid.
[34] Jacqueline Rose, States of Fantasy (Oxford, 1996), pp. 30–1.

David Chandler argues that this is precisely what is at stake in Bosnia-Herzegovina. In his view, 'the lack of cohering political structures has meant that Bosnian people are forced to rely on more narrow and parochial survival mechanisms, which has meant that ethnicity has maintained its wartime relevance as a political resource'.[35] The way in which international rule is being conducted is 'inevitably institutionalizing inter-communal divisions, setting back any long-term settlement for the region'.[36]

Charity and pedagogy – the reconstruction of East Timor

The complexity of issues raised by a commitment to the right of a people to control over their territory and resources can be seen in the case of East Timor. There, a deeply traumatised and divided society is confronting extraordinarily complex issues relating to ownership of land.[37] The East Timorese have experienced multiple waves of dispossession, beginning with Portugese colonisation in the eighteenth century, through Japanese occupation during World War II, to the Indonesian invasion of 1975.[38] The period of Indonesian occupation was characterised by famine, displacement, transmigration and loss of lands for purposes of public interest and private development (read development by military interests or government cronies).[39] Most of the population were again displaced in the militia violence of 1999 which followed the UN-sponsored autonomy consultation. As the work of Daniel Fitzpatrick has shown, the resulting competing claims to land and questions of justice are extremely complex, and have to be resolved in an institutional context in which all land title offices in East Timor were destroyed by the

---

[35] Chandler, 'Bosnia', p. 277.   [36] Ibid., p. 282.

[37] Daniel Fitzpatrick, 'Land Claims in East Timor: a Preliminary Assessment' (2001) 3 *Australian Journal of Asian Law* 135. Fitzpatrick analyses the extensive social and political conflict in East Timor caused by many competing claims to land and resources. He maps four sets of interests: those whose land claims are based on traditional or indigenous ownership; those with Portuguese-era titles; those with Indonesian-era titles, and those who have occupied land since the 1999 referendum. See also George Aditjondro, 'Mapping the Political Terrain' (2000) 46 *Arena Magazine* 27 (describing political division in post-referendum East Timor, including a generation gap between the 1975 resistance leaders plus the diaspora elite and those young Timorese who grew up under Indonesian occupation, and a gender gap); Hilary Charlesworth and Mary Wood, ' "Mainstreaming Gender" in International Peace and Security: the Case of East Timor' (2001) 26 *Yale Journal of International Law* 313 (discussing the exclusion of women from political and nation-building activities in East Timor).

[38] Fitzpatrick, 'Land Claims'.   [39] Ibid., 159.

militia violence in 1999. This resulted in the destruction, and possibly in some cases the removal, of all land title records.[40]

There will be no simple solution to resolving the enormous problems and dislocation caused by these waves of dispossession.[41] There is clearly a role in such a situation for sustained assistance from the international community. Self-determination here does not mean disengaging from the process of reconstruction. However, I want to compare the kind of subtle and careful analysis of its role that the international community needs to undertake in such a situation, with the language used by administrators at the UN and the World Bank to describe their function.

In order to understand the international community's activities in East Timor, it is useful to begin by considering the major role played by the World Bank. The World Bank, together with the Asian Development Bank, manages the Trust Fund for East Timor, established by the World Bank's Board of Governors following the December 1999 Tokyo Donor's Meeting. It has worked in consultation with the East Timorese and representatives of the former United Nations Transitional Administration in East Timor (UNTAET) to facilitate economic development. In the context of East Timor, the World Bank is departing from its structural adjustment model to provide funding for the building of health, education and public sector infrastructure. Yet it nonetheless still adheres to many of the features of its boilerplate blueprint for reform.[42] The Bank has made clear that certain familiar Bank programmes and priorities are to be implemented in the management of East Timor.[43] Its plans have focused on ensuring that East Timor has limited public sector employment, openness to foreign direct investment and is quickly inserted into the global market economy, albeit as one of the poorest countries in the region. The World Bank determined as early as 1999 that East Timor is to have a small state, with a concomitant contracting out of many areas of service provision to the private sector, and particularly to foreign investors. According to critics, East Timor under UN and World Bank management is becoming 'a paradise for market-driven foreign investors, without considering the real need for foreign investment'.[44] As Aditjondro has argued, in the short term East Timor

---

[40] *Ibid.*, 135.   [41] *Ibid.*, 164.   [42] See generally Chapter 3 above.

[43] See, for example, World Bank, *Report of the Joint Assessment Mission to East Timor*, 8 December 1999, pp. 3–5, 8; World Bank East Asia and Pacific Region, *Background Paper Prepared for the Information Meeting on East Timor*, 29 September 1999, p. 2.

[44] George Aditjondro, 'From Colony to Global Prize' (2000) 47 *Arena Magazine* 22 at 32.

has been overrun by foreign, mainly Australian, companies making large profits out of contracts negotiated with INTERFET or UNTAET.[45]

To give just one example, the hotel and tourism sector is one of the priority areas of the World Bank, and is the sector that is most ' "crowded" with investors and their Timorese or Timor-based partners'.[46] An early priority of development in this sector was to create accommodation for civilian UN and World Bank staff.[47] The expatriate business community operating in the tourism and services sector, including the UNTAET cafeteria, pay extremely low wages to East Timorese workers, while charging reasonably high rates for accommodation and meals.[48] Thus, says Aditjondro, 'Timorese workers are subsidising the Australian tourism business and the...United Nations and foreign NGO community in their country. So, who is helping whom, one could ask.'[49]

Of this situation, Xanana Gusmao said in December 1999:

It's an insult to the misery, the suffering of our people. Our people need soap, they need food. They have primary needs...Sometimes we felt that the Indonesian generals had no human feeling. Some businessmen also exploit the situation. It's very sad, because I cannot do anything about it. If I have a little power I can tell them to go, but I have no power.[50]

Aditjondro suggests that the East Timorese will be forced into honouring longer-term contracts which they had little say in negotiating, such as those made between INTERFET and Telstra, and the extremely lucrative construction contracts being awarded to Australian companies such as Multiplex Constructions Pty Ltd.[51]

Despite these concerns, international donors and international economic organisations portray their role in East Timor as essentially charitable. For example, the IMF's Head of Mission and Special Representative to East Timor, Luis Valdivieso, has been reported as saying, 'They [the people of East Timor] don't want to live on charity longer than they have to.'[52] Similarly, Peter Galbraith, Chief of UNTAET's Office of Political, Constitutional and Electoral Affairs, has commented that international donors are 'prepared to be generous over the short term', but do not

---

[45] Ibid.   [46] Ibid., 25.   [47] Personal communication with UN staff member.
[48] Aditjondro, 'From Colony', 24.   [49] Ibid.
[50] Xanana Gusmao, Socialist Worker, 19 December 1999, cited in Aditjondro, 'From Colony', 25.
[51] Aditjondro, 'From Colony', 24–6.
[52] 'The International Monetary Fund in East Timor', 2(3) The La'o Hamutuk Bulletin, June 2001, http://www.etan.org/lh/bulletinv2n3.html (accessed 20 February 2002).

want East Timor 'to be a permanent charity case'.[53] This portrayal of the role of international actors as charitable prefigures a careful analysis of the extent to which the political and economic relationship between East Timor and its donors is exploitative. As the authors of the *La'o Hamutuk Bulletin* comment:

'Charity' is a very problematic term by which to characterize international funding for East Timor. As many, if not most of the major donors to East Timor provided Indonesia with significant amounts of weaponry, funding, and diplomatic cover for its invasion and occupation of East Timor, such 'charity' is better seen as a very modest start to reparations.[54]

While the economic management of East Timor is in the hands of the World Bank, the UN has adopted a major 'trusteeship' role, taking over responsibility for administration in East Timor during the period of transition to independence. On 25 October 1999, the Security Council established UNTAET as a peace-keeping operation 'endowed with overall responsibility for the administration of East Timor and ... empowered to exercise all legislative and executive authority, including the administration of justice'.[55] The UN granted itself a broad mandate, including the provision of security and maintenance of law and order, the establishment of an effective administration, assistance in the development of civil and social services, support for capacity-building for self-government and assistance in the establishment of conditions for sustainable development.[56] The Secretary-General's Special-Representative and Transitional Administrator Sergio Vieira de Mello was made 'responsible for all aspects of the United Nations work in East Timor', with 'the power to enact new laws and regulations and to amend, suspend or repeal existing ones'.[57]

UNTAET achievements in East Timor include the registration of most of the resident population to vote, the holding of free and fair elections for the Constituent Assembly in August 2001, establishing an East Timorese civil service and judicial and legal system, reopening schools and technical colleges throughout the country, reconstructing over thirty major public buildings, and the re-establishment of basic infrastructure and services, including constructing roads and supplying electricity and water to urban areas. Yet as one journalist has noted:

[53] 'LH Editorial: Charity or Justice?', 1(2) *The La'o Hamutuk Bulletin*, July 2000, http://www.etan.org/lh/bulletin02.html (accessed 20 February 2002).
[54] 'The International Monetary Fund in East Timor'.
[55] Clause 1, SC Res. 1272 (1999), adopted on 25 October 1999.
[56] *Ibid.*, clause 2.   [57] *Ibid.*, clause 6.

Scratch the surface of East Timor's 'reconstruction' and the picture that emerges is a profoundly worrying one – there are serious questions about the bureaucracy, expense and paternalism of the UN presence and the appropriateness of the models of development being proposed and implemented by the UN in tandem with the World Bank and Asian Development Bank...The influx of foreign investors and comparatively wealthy UN and aid workers has led to the creation of a double economy and the perception of the UN as the new colonialists in East Timor.[58]

Many East Timorese and foreign activists reiterate this point. Groups such as East Timor's La'o Hamutuk and Australia's Aidwatch argue that the combination of UN paternalism, World Bank development models and unrestrained foreign investment is creating a new form of colonialism, and deepening divisions within the East Timorese community.[59]

While international donors and international economic organisations portray their role in East Timor as charitable, comments by UN administrators reveal that they see their relationship with the people of East Timor in terms of another colonial concept, that of pedagogy. The UN's role is understood in the pedagogical terms that marked colonial discourse – the international community brings its tutees in East Timor to political and economic maturity through the creation and transfer of the bureaucratic machinery of the modern nation-state, and the training of the functionaries required to operate that machinery. This view of the UN's role in East Timor is well illustrated by the comments of Jean-Christian Cady, then Deputy Transitional Administrator of East Timor.[60] For Cady, 'the United Nations found themselves in a situation without precedent in their history: to rebuild a country entirely'.[61] The UN had to 'create a State, with a constitution, administrative, judicial and

---

[58] Jenny Denton, 'Whose Agendas? East Timor Suffers under Weight of World Plans', *Canberra Times*, 14 April 2001.

[59] 'The World Bank in East Timor', 1(4) *The La'o Hamutuk Bulletin*, December 2000, http://www.etan.org/lh/bulletin04.html (accessed 20 February 2002); *Aidwatch Briefing Note: the World Bank in East Timor*, June 2001, http://www.aidwatch.org.au/timor/wb et.html (accessed 20 February 2002). See also Jorge Trindade Neves de Camoes, 'East Timor Today: Perspectives from the Grassroots', paper presented at a seminar on *UNAMET, INTERFET, UNTAET, International NGOs, World Bank, and 'Paraquedistas': Are They Helping or Obstructing the Nation-Building Process in East Timor?*, The Australian National University, 2 March 2000.

[60] Jean-Christian Cady was replaced by Dennis McNamara as Deputy Transitional Administrator in June 2001.

[61] Jean-Christian Cady, Deputy Transitional Administrator of East Timor, 'Building the New State of East Timor', lecture given at the Centre for International and Public Law, Australian National University, Canberra, 18 May 2000.

financial institutions, and a Public Service'.[62] UNTAET had to provide training for police, 'not only on police methods and techniques but also on the ethics of a democratic police and respect for human rights, which is of course a new idea in East Timor'.[63] Training of the Civil Service also posed difficulties for UNTAET: 'What UNTAET wants to achieve is a Civil Service independent from political affiliations and cronyism, competent and not corrupt. These are ambitious goals anywhere but perhaps more so in this part of the world.'[64]

Cady's vision is of East Timor as a blank slate in terms of existing knowledge and experience, marked by cronyism, incompetence and corruption. The people of East Timor are portrayed as lacking a state, ethics, skills and respect for human rights. This representation can be traced back to ideas about Europe's mission to educate and develop the peoples of its colonies – one aspect of the culture of imperialism explored by Edward Said. As Said has shown so clearly, while 'profit and hope of further profit were obviously tremendously important' in the expansion of European imperialism, so too was a particular imperial culture which supported the notion that 'certain territories and people *require* and beseech domination'.[65] As I argue in Chapter 2, central to this civilising-mission rhetoric was the idea of colonialism as pedagogy, and the coloniser as an educator. As Leela Gandhi notes, the 'perception of the colonised culture as fundamentally childlike feeds into the logic of the colonial "civilising mission" which is fashioned, quite self-consciously, as a form of tutelage or a disinterested project concerned with bringing the colonised to maturity'.[66] This pedagogical imperative, and its conservative effects, continue to shape the way in which international administration is understood.

East Timor formally gained its independence on 20 May 2002. Despite this, the international community is still heavily involved in administration of the new state. The Security Council, while 'recognizing the primary responsibility of the people of East Timor for nation building', notes international assistance will be required in the period after independence to assist in the 'development and strengthening of East Timor's infrastructure, public administration, law enforcement and defence capacities'.[67] It established the United Nations Mission of Support in East Timor (UNMISET) to succeed UNTAET on 20 May 2002, and to

[62] Ibid., 1.   [63] Ibid., 3.   [64] Ibid., 4.
[65] Edward W. Said, *Culture and Imperialism* (London, 1993), p. 8 (emphasis in original).
[66] Leela Gandhi, *Postcolonial Theory: a Critical Introduction* (St Leonards, 1998), p. 32.
[67] SC Res. 1410 (2002), adopted on 17 May 2002.

assist in maintaining political stability and security, providing law enforcement and demarcating borders with Indonesia.[68] Similarly, the IMF and the World Bank have both signalled their intention to maintain their role in the economic management of East Timor and its development post-independence.[69] The powers exercised by the UN and international financial institutions sit uneasily with the existence of bodies intended to represent the will of an independent people.

Self-determination after colonialism

The economic and political management being developed by these international organisations on behalf of East Timor sets the stage for the kind of limited sovereignty that Antony Anghie has analysed in his study of the operation of the mandate system of the League of Nations after World War I.[70] Under that system, territories belonging to defeated powers were placed under the control of mandate powers who were responsible for the administration of those territories and required to report back to the League concerning the well-being and development of mandate peoples. The mandate system appeared to be premised on the international community's desire to move away from colonialism.[71]

Anghie argues, however, that far from representing a radical departure from international law's acceptance of colonialism, the mandate system merely changed its legal form, instituting a new form of colonial power based not on political but on economic control. The neocolonial process would be overseen by an international institution, one which, like the World Bank in East Timor, saw its role as technical rather than political. Administration of a territory was to be undertaken by a disinterested body of international experts intent on ensuring the proper development and welfare of those subject to their trust.[72] The policies

---

[68] *Ibid.*, paras. 2, 4, 12.

[69] World Bank, East Timor: Donors Applaud East Timor's National Development Plan, Dili, 15 May 2002, http://web.worldbank.org/WBSITE/EXTERNAL/NEWS/0,contentMDK: 20045490~menuPK:34466~pagePK:34370~piPK:34424~theSitePK: 4607,00.html (accessed 28 June 2002); Donors' Meeting on East Timor, Staff Statement by Stephen Schwartz, Deputy Division Chief, IMF Asia and Pacific Department, Dili, 14–15 May 2002, http://www.imf.org/external/np/dm/2002/ 051402.htm (accessed 28 June 2002).

[70] Antony Anghie, 'Time Present and Time Past: Globalization, International Financial Institutions, and the Third World' (2000) 32 *New York University Journal of International Law and Politics* 243.

[71] *Ibid.*, 278.   [72] *Ibid.*, 284.

of such institutions were seen as scientific and objective, rather than self-interested. The system as a whole, however, operated to integrate the mandate society into the international economy in a subordinate role. As a result, while those territories appeared to be freed from political control, they remained subject to the control of the parties that exercised power within the international economy.[73] The resources and people of those territories were exploited just as efficiently under this new arrangement as they were under classical colonialism. Many of the same arguments can be seen to apply in the cases of Bosnia-Herzegovina and East Timor.

In some quarters, even this limited sovereignty is seen as posing too great a constraint on the freedom to act of the international community and private investors. For example, Allan Gerson has written that the direct degree of control exercised by the World Bank and the UN over the economic development of East Timor prior to independence provides a model which is greatly to be preferred to the situation in the Balkans. For Gerson, 'East Timor presents the most concerted effort at UN–World Bank coordination, *unhampered* by the type of self-imposed legal restrictions hindering the Bank's engagement in Bosnia and Kosovo.' This is particularly the case as 'in the latter, Serbia *nominally* retains sovereignty'.[74]

The questions these case studies raise for the legitimacy of international law are demonstrated in an article by Matthias Ruffert on the administration of Kosovo and East Timor by the international community. Ruffert struggles to find a legal category to capture the nature of the international personality of those territories under administration, given that all the existing categories that intuitively seem to fit – protectorate, trust territory – must be dismissed because of their links to colonialism.[75] He explains his reluctance to adopt these categories on the basis that 'the colonial context should not inadvertently be alluded to', despite his recognition that 'even if there are traces of self-determination, particularly in East Timor, the power of final decision remains with the UN-administration in all areas of government'.[76] For Ruffert, there is 'without any doubt' no colonising impulse at work

[73] *Ibid.*, 283.
[74] Allan Gerson, 'Peace Building: the Private Sector's Role' (2001) *American Journal of International Law* 102 at 110 (emphasis added).
[75] Matthias Ruffert, 'The Administration of Kosovo and East Timor by the International Community' (2001) 50 *International and Comparative Law Quarterly* 613 at 631.
[76] *Ibid.*, 627, 629.

here – both because 'the special status of both territories is temporary' and because of 'the benevolent character of international administration'.[77]

The colonial character of the categories to which Ruffert is drawn illustrates for me what is at stake for international law in the post-conflict reconstruction process. The narrative of humanitarian intervention operates to construct this sense of the 'benevolent character of international administration'. Participation in this narrative limits our understanding of what is taking place in those territories. As Homi Bhabha comments in the context of colonial governance:

The barracks stands by the church which stands by the schoolroom; the cantonment stands hard by the 'civil lines'. The visibility of the institutions and apparatuses of power is possible because the exercise of colonial power makes their relationship obscure, produces them as fetishes, spectacles of a 'natural'/racial pre-eminence.[78]

The texts of humanitarian intervention and of international economic law play a central part in making this relationship obscure. These texts make sense of the relations between barracks, 'investors' and 'developing states' in terms of a narrative of progress and development, in which a character called Foreign Capital is the agent of wealth and prosperity.[79] As a result, economic coercion as exploitation in the Third World is hidden from sight.[80] The international legal literature celebrating the achievement of post-intervention reconstruction plays its part in masking this relationship by failing to attend critically to the nature of the economic order that is put in place through the reconstruction process.

Attention to this colonial heritage suggests something else that is at stake in these texts, beyond economic questions of control over territory and resources. The international community constitutes itself in these texts of intervention and reconstruction as a designer of new worlds, a solver of problems, and a saviour of suffering peoples. As the work of Annelise Riles has shown, the aesthetics of international legal practice is premised upon an appreciation of the art of global design, and a faith in the ability of lawyers to create 'new and universally attractive

---

[77] *Ibid.*, 629.   [78] Homi K. Bhabha, *The Location of Culture* (London, 1994), p. 83.

[79] Judith Grbich, 'Taxation Narratives of Economic Gain: Reading Bodies Transgressively' (1997) 5 *Feminist Legal Studies* 131; Arturo Escobar, *Encountering Development: the Making and Unmaking of the Third World* (Princeton, 1995).

[80] Gayatri Chakravorty Spivak, *In Other Worlds* (New York, 1988), p. 167.

forms'.[81] International legal form brings problems into existence 'for it-self to solve'.[82] This is never clearer than in the literature on intervention, where problems of poverty, violence, ethnic tension and authoritarian-ism are a background against which to imagine the international com-munity as a designer of solutions and a manager of their implementa-tion. In their resolutions and statements on East Timor, the IMF applauds 'the UN's skilful management of the transition' and 'the effectiveness of the international community's financial and technical support',[83] while the Security Council pays tribute to 'the dedication and professionalism of UNTAET and to the leadership of the Special Representative of the Secretary-General in assisting the people of East Timor in the transition towards independence'.[84] The Secretary-General comments that UNTAET 'had a truly historic mandate in East Timor' and that 'few would have imagined that a de novo public administration could have been estab-lished within just 30 months'.[85] In this sense, the internationalisation of Bosnia-Herzegovina and East Timor contributes to the constitution of the 'international community', both materially and symbolically.

Imagining self-determination

I want now to ask whether the emancipatory promise of self-determination can offer a counter to the efficient management practices underpinning international administration. Are international lawyers doomed 'to manipulate a discourse gone dead in their hands',[86] or can the language of self-determination serve as a basis for responding to the issues I have raised about Bosnia-Herzegovina and East Timor?

The answers to these questions depend in large part upon the for-mulation of self-determination that is named as the law. A minimalist view of self-determination dominates the texts of law in the context of international intervention or peace-building. Catriona Drew has argued

---

[81] Annelise Riles, 'Global Designs: the Aesthetics of International Legal Practice' (1999) 93 *American Society of International Law Proceedings* 28 at 33.

[82] *Ibid.*, 34.

[83] Donors' Meeting on East Timor, Statement by Stephen Schwartz, Deputy Division Chief, IMF Asia and Pacific Department, Oslo, 11–12 December 2001, http://www.imf.org/external/np/dm/2001/121201.htm (accessed 28 June 2002).

[84] SC Res. 1410 (2002), adopted on 17 May 2002.

[85] Report of the Secretary-General on the United Nations Transitional Administration in East Timor, S/2002/432, p. 15.

[86] Gerry J. Simpson, 'The Diffusion of Sovereignty: Self-Determination in the Post-Colonial Age' (1996) 32 *Stanford Journal of International Law* 255 at 256.

persuasively that there has been much attention paid internationally to the procedural aspect of 'the right of a people to a free choice over its political and territorial destiny', at the expense of other substantive elements.[87] According to this narrow reading of the content of the right, self-determination merely guarantees the right to a process, by virtue of which all peoples 'freely determine their political status'.[88]

The implications of treating the right of self-determination as a right to a free choice in the absence of more substantive rights are well illustrated by the arguments of Rosalyn Higgins, then acting as agent for Portugal, in her oral argument before the International Court of Justice (ICJ) in the *Portugal* v. *Australia* case.[89] Portugal there claimed that Australia had violated its duties to respect the right of the people of East Timor to self-determination, by negotiating and concluding the Timor Gap treaty with Indonesia for the exploitation of the natural resources of East Timor.[90] Australia argued that the conclusion of this treaty did not prevent a future choice regarding their political status by the people of East Timor, and thus did not infringe their right of self-determination. In her response, Rosalyn Higgins criticised Australia's perception of the law of self-determination, describing it as 'at once mechanistic and minimalist'.[91] She observed:

The Australian perspective on self-determination is this: its substantive requirements are very little, and they may be fulfilled in two ways: by periodically intoning that one recognises the right and by complying with United Nations sanctions. That's it. There is nothing else that States (at least those who are not administering Powers or trusteeship authorities) have to do...The policy implications of this view of self-determination are obvious and we do not need to dwell on them. It is a view which leaves peoples awaiting self-determination at the

---

[87] Catriona Drew, 'The East Timor Story: International Law on Trial' (2001) 12 *European Journal of International Law* 627 at 663.

[88] 1960 Declaration on the Granting of Independence to Colonial Countries and Peoples adopted by the UN General Assembly, 14 December 1960. GA Res 1514, UN GAOR 15th Sess., Supp. No. 16, at 66, UN Doc A14684 (1961), para. 2; International Covenant on Civil and Political Rights, opened for Signature at New York, 16 December 1966 (in force 23 March 1976), 999 UNTS 171 Article 1(1); International Covenant on Economic, Social and Cultural Rights, New York, 16 December 1966, in force 3 January 1976, 999 UNTS 3, Article 1(1).

[89] R. Higgins, Final Oral Argument, paras. 59–98, http://www.icj-cij.org/icjwww/icases/ipa/ipa cr/iPA icr9513 19950213.PDF (accessed 6 March 2002).

[90] Australia and Indonesia: Treaty on the Zone of Cooperation in an Area between the Indonesian Province of East Timor and Northern Australia (with Annexes), signed over the Zone of Cooperation, above the Timor Sea, 11 December 1989, in force 9 February 1991, reprinted in (1990) 29 ILM 469.

[91] Higgins, 'Final Oral Argument' para. 69.

very margin of international law, as a 'left-over' in the robust world of sovereign freedoms...That effectively guarantees that if a certain people awaiting self-determination is not in the middle of an ongoing war-and-peace environment, nothing will be done for them.[92]

If this 'minimalist' view of self-determination is successfully named as the law, it offers little to those who fought for independence in East Timor.

A second view of the meaning of self-determination is couched in terms of guaranteeing to people the right to freedom from alien subjugation, domination and exploitation. This formulation of a right to political and economic independence appears in the language of the 1960 Declaration on Colonial Independence, which declares that the 'subjection of peoples to alien subjugation, domination and exploitation constitutes a denial of fundamental human rights' and speaks of the right of all peoples 'to complete independence'.[93] Similarly, the 1970 Declaration on Friendly Relations proclaims that by virtue of the principle of self-determination enshrined in the UN Charter, 'all peoples have the right freely to determine, without external interference, their political status and to pursue their economic, social and cultural development'.[94] The common Articles 1 of the International Covenant on Civil and Political Rights and the International Covenant on Economic, Social and Cultural Rights also describe self-determination as both the right of a people 'freely [to] pursue their economic, social and cultural development' and the right to control over territory and resources. It states 'all peoples may, for their own ends, freely dispose of their natural wealth and resources...In no case may a people be deprived of its own means of subsistence.'[95]

Commentators writing in the 1990s have advocated a renewed focus on this economic aspect of self-determination. For example,

---

[92] *Ibid.*, paras. 61–3.   [93] 1960 Declaration on Colonial Independence, paras. 1 and 4.

[94] 1970 Declaration on the Principles of International Law Concerning Friendly Relations and Cooperation among States in Accordance with the Charter of the United Nations, adopted by the UN General Assembly, 24 October 1970. GA Res. 2625, UN GAOR, 25th Sess., Supp. No. 28, at 121, UN DOC A/8028 (1971), reprinted in (1970) 9 ILM 1292, para. 1.

[95] International Covenant on Civil and Political Rights, 1966; International Covenant on Economic, Social and Cultural Rights, 1966. The 1986 Declaration on the Right to Development also makes clear that full realisation of the right of peoples to self-determination includes 'the exercise of their inalienable right to full sovereignty over all their natural wealth and resources'. Adopted by the UN General Assembly, 4 December 1986. GA Res. 41/128 (Annex), UN GAOR, 41st Sess., Supp. No. 53, at 186, UN Doc. A/41/53 (1987).

J. Oloka-Onyango argues that by 'primarily focusing on the political aspects of colonialism (i.e. on the political domination exercised over their
territories), the anti-colonial nationalists left out of the paradigm the extensive linkages that the system (as an economic phenomenon) had created between colony and colonized'.[96] For Oloka-Onyango, economic self-
determination as enshrined in international law is of utility for those
seeking to challenge the exploitative international political economy
that is a legacy of classical colonialism. Christine Chinkin and Shelley
Wright note that while the right of self-determination has been largely
viewed as 'a political right of fairly narrow interpretation', the final
limb of common Article 1 of the international human rights covenants
states that 'in no case may a people be deprived of its own means of
subsistence'.[97] Chinkin and Wright suggest that while the right to subsistence has received little attention, it is the most important aspect of
common Article 1.[98] For Catriona Drew: 'Implicit in any recognition of
a people's right to self-determination is recognition of the legitimacy of
that people's claim to a particular territory and/or set of resources...To
confer on a people a right of 'free choice' in the absence of a more substantive entitlement – to territory, natural resources etc – would simply
be meaningless.'[99]

The Human Rights Committee's General Comment on Article 1 notes
that this economic aspect of the right of self-determination entails corresponding duties for all states and for the international community.[100]
Thus this reading of self-determination does allow a focus on the role
of the international community and a return to the question of control
over territory and resources. This interpretation of self-determination
provides a legal framework for addressing the ways in which power and
profit operate in the postcolonial context, and can help to make visible the economic exploitation that is enabled through the practice of
humanitarian intervention and post-conflict reconstruction.

Yet I am uneasy about the vision of the state and its relationship to
the international community that such readings of self-determination
assume. I want to explore that uneasiness now through an examination

---

[96] J. Oloka-Onyango, 'Heretical Reflections on the Right to Self-Determination: Prospects
and Problems for a Democratic Global Future in the New Millennium' (1999) 15
American University International Law Review 151 at 171.

[97] Christine Chinkin and Shelley Wright, 'The Hunger Trap: Women, Food and
Self-Determination' (1993) 14 *Michigan Journal of International Law* 262 at 301, 307.

[98] *Ibid.*, 307.   [99] Drew, 'East Timor Story', 663.

[100] Human Rights Committee, *General Comment 12: The Right to Self-Determination of Peoples,
Article 1, Twenty-First Session*, 1984, http://www.unhchr.ch/tbs/doc.nsf/(symbol)/CCPR+
General+comment+12.En?OpenDocument (accessed 8 March 2002).

of the two concepts of 'self' and 'determination' underpinning this discourse.

The autonomous self

Both the political and the economic formulations of self-determination as a right to freedom from foreign domination and exploitation are concerned with questions of autonomy and freedom from foreign intervention. The powerful appeal of this notion can be seen in the case of East Timor, a nation which on 20 May 2002 was declared independent after three centuries of Portuguese colonial rule, twenty-four years of Indonesian occupation and two-and-a-half years of UN administration. It is moving to read Secretary-General Kofi Annan's welcome to the East Timorese nation, and his invocation of the moral and legal legitimacy of independent statehood: 'Your identity as an independent people will be recognised by the whole world...At this moment, we honour every citizen of East Timor who persisted in the struggle for independence... We also remember the many who are no longer with us, but who dreamed of this moment.'[101]

Yet such language affirms the image of the ideal state as separate, secure and autonomous. It reinforces a vision of international order as essentially consisting of an 'aggregate of independent, private spaces, socialised and connected through contractual relations'.[102] As Martti Koskienniemi has argued, this sense of self-determination both explains and justifies the existing state-centred international order: 'Without a principle that entitles – or perhaps even requires – groups of people to start minding their own business within separately organised 'States', it is difficult to think how statehood and everything we connect with it – political independence, territorial integrity and legal sovereignty – can be legitimate.'[103]

---

[101] 'New Country, East Timor, Is Born: UN, which Aided Transition, Vows Continued Help', http://www.un.org/apps/news/story.asp?NewsID=3714&Cr=timor&Cr1= (accessed 20 May 2002).

[102] Kane Race, 'The Beast with Two Backs: Bodies/Selves/Integrity' (1997) 9 *Australian Feminist Law Journal* 24 at 25, 29, discussing the 'ideal phallic body'. As Race notes, 'no body conforms to such an ideal', just as no state is as impermeable and isolated as this account would have us believe. On the parallels between the constitution of the phallic, masculine body and the sovereign body of the state, see Anne Orford, 'The Uses of Sovereignty in the New Imperial Order' (1996) 6 *Australian Feminist Law Journal* 63; Hilary Charlesworth and Christine Chinkin, *The Boundaries of International Law: a Feminist Analysis* (Manchester, 2000), pp. 137–8.

[103] Martti Koskenniemi, 'National Self-Determination Today: Problems of Legal Theory and Practice' (1994) 43 *International and Comparative Law Quarterly* 241 at 245.

I am reluctant to deploy this notion of the state and the international for a number of reasons. First, the use of the right of self-determination imagined in terms of a right to autonomy has strategic limitations, for reasons that parallel the problems faced by feminists attempting to rewrite the feminine body as autonomous, rather than lacking and partial. As Moira Gatens has argued, to do so essentially reproduces the masculine fantasy of an impossible, ideal body that is separate and isolated from all other bodies.[104] A similar notion emerges in international legal texts, which present the ideal sovereign state as impermeable, bounded, independent and separate from the chaotic world that surrounds it. This notion developed in part as a response to the anxieties about who should count as international legal subjects generated by the colonial enterprise.[105] The doctrinal attempt to define the 'proper subjects of international law' was fuelled by the political imperative of European lawyers seeking to find a way to distinguish 'sovereigns proper from other entities that also seemed to possess the attributes of sovereignty, such as pirates, non-European states, and nomads'.[106] The answer for positivists such as Thomas Lawrence was to create a distinction based on cultural differences between sovereigns and others.[107] Sovereignty was based on independence from external authority, and effective control over a territory and its inhabitants.

Of course, no sovereign state existed, or exists, in the splendid autonomy dreamt of by positivist international lawyers. All states are creatures of law, situated in a network of legally defined rights and obligations. The subjects of international law are themselves always constituted by that law. Yet the notion of the sovereign state as an autonomous entity, and of international law as emanating from the will of such states, justified the dispossession of those people who were characterised as non-sovereign. To reaffirm this notion of the ideal state is to risk branding as less than sovereign any state that 'receives the international',[108] in the sense of

---

[104] Moira Gatens, *Imaginary Bodies: Ethics, Power and Corporeality* (London, 1996), pp. 29–45.

[105] Antony Anghie, 'Finding the Peripheries: Sovereignty and Colonialism in Nineteenth-Century International Law' (1999) 40 *Harvard International Law Journal* 1 at 17.

[106] *Ibid.*, 26.

[107] Thomas Lawrence, *The Principles of International Law* (London, 1895), pp. 1–25.

[108] This phrase is taken from David Kennedy, 'Receiving the International: What's the Public/Private Distinction Got to Do with It?', paper presented at the New York University Institute for Law and Society, 3 March 1995. I am inspired here by Kane Race's arguments about ways 'to imagine positions of receptivity that need not suppose violence': Race, 'The Beast', 44.

being represented as the objects of aid or intervention. Indeed, just such a use of independence as an ideal can be seen in the statements made by those Indonesians and pro-Indonesian East Timorese who resent the end of Indonesian rule and want to characterise East Timor as too immature for statehood. For example, Mario Viegas Carrascalao, former governor of East Timor under Indonesian occupation and leader of the opposition Social Democratic Party in East Timor, argues 'independence represents a victory for everybody, but it's a very dependent independence...It's been done too quickly and we're not ready for the day after. We are becoming a nation with our hand held out.'[109]

Equally, the deployment of a notion of self-determination as a right to autonomy reinforces the sense of the foreign as a threat. It fits too easily into the terms of a debate premised on the need to protect a boundary between self and other, national and international, sovereign autonomy and foreign control. That which threatens to cross state borders – such as flows of refugees, introduced diseases, foreign capital or environmental pollution – is presented as a threat to the integrity of the nation or the health of the body-politic. There is today a disturbing, at times paranoid, side to the discussion of the threat posed to the nation by foreign influences.[110] We can see this illustrated in the increased racist attacks on refugees and migrants in many industrialised states, and in the re-emergence of xenophobic, far-Right nationalist parties in many parts of the world. In Australia, this trend is also evidenced by the hostility of responses to adverse findings by UN human rights bodies about issues ranging from Australia's anti-gay laws in Tasmania to the detention of refugees and to mandatory sentencing laws.[111]

---

[109] Tom Hyland and Lindsay Murdoch, 'The Future Begins Here', *The Age*, 18 May 2002, Insight, p. 3.

[110] On the emergence of a paranoid form of politics as a response to the vacuum created by the ending of the Cold War and its narratives about otherness and danger, see Eric L. Santner, *My Own Private Germany: Daniel Paul Schreber's Secret History of Modernity* (Princeton, 1996), p. xiii.

[111] For a discussion of media reactions to the *Toonen* decision of the Human Rights Committee in such terms, see Philip Alston, 'Reform of Treaty-Making Processes: Form over Substance?' in Philip Alston and Madelaine Chiam (eds.), *Treaty-Making and Australia: Globalisation versus Sovereignty?* (Canberra, 1995), pp. 1–26 at p. 5. The issue arose again in Australia in 2000, when the federal Attorney-General responded to an adverse report by the UN Committee on the Elimination of Racial Discrimination, rejecting it as 'an unbalanced and wide-ranging attack that intrudes unreasonably into Australia's domestic affairs': The Australian Attorney-General, the Hon. Daryl Williams, *CERD Report Unbalanced*, Press Release, 26 March 2000, http://law.gov.au/aghome/agnews/2000newsag/71700.htm (accessed 16 October 2001). The Foreign

Indeed, international intervention legitimised in the name of self-determination as a right to autonomy shares underlying assumptions with the use of force in the name of self-defence. In each case, the ideal 'self' to be determined or defended is one that is free from foreign interference. The argument that the use of force by the USA against Afghanistan is lawful as an act of self-defence, or 'defensive self-preservation', can be understood as part of this tradition.[112] The USA *is* engaged in 'self-defence' in its war on terror. The self it is defending is an imaginary one, defined by a belief in its capacity to achieve closure against that which is perceived as foreign. As Shelley Wright argues, the responses of the USA and some American international lawyers to the events of September 11 represent an 'anxious grab for certainty', a re-action to the anxiety produced by the failure of law or the nation-state ever to achieve absolute mastery over itself and its others.[113]

How then to affirm the right of self-determination, without reifying the autonomous state as the end of intervention? One strategy may be to reimagine the 'self' of self-determination, so that the integrity of the sovereign state and the right of a people to control their own territory is not dependent upon closure or separateness. The challenge then becomes to find ways to affirm and extend this sovereign state through interaction and connection, or through monitoring and controlling exchanges across its borders. The aim of such control is not to achieve perfect independence, but to reject those relations and flows that are exploitative, while welcoming those that are life-affirming and life-enhancing.

This is, after all, what the East Timorese people sought in the aftermath of the violent response to the announcement on 4 September 1999 that an overwhelming majority had voted for independence from Indonesia in the UN-sponsored referendum. When East Timorese leaders such as Xanana Gusmao and Jose Ramos Horta called for Indonesia to leave and for UN peace-keepers to take their place in East Timor, they were not demanding complete autonomy for that territory and its people. Rather, at stake was the right of the East Timorese people to

Minister Mr Downer, said that the Federal Government would not allow Australia 'to be run by people in UN committee meetings in Geneva': Debra Jopson, Simon Mann and Mike Seccombe, 'Ministers Tell UN Lobbyists: Stop Meddling', *Sydney Morning Herald*, 21 July 2000.

[112] See, for example, Thomas M. Franck, 'Terrorism and the Right of Self-Defence' (2001) 95 *American Journal of International Law* 839.

[113] Shelley Wright, 'The Horizon of Becoming: Culture, Gender and History after September 11' (2002) *Nordic Journal of International Law* (forthcoming).

control over the terms on which their borders were breached and intercourse conducted. A right of self-determination understood in these terms suggests that reconstruction as currently practised is unjust, not because it poses a foreign threat to sovereign autonomy, but rather because it represents a denial of the right of the peoples of Bosnia-Herzegovina and East Timor to control the terms on which they receive globalisation and the international community.[114]

The act of determination

Luce Irigaray begins her essay 'The Looking Glass, from the Other Side', with the following quote from *Through the Looking Glass*:

she suddenly began again. 'Then it really *has* happened, after all! And now, who am I? I *will* remember, if I can! I'm determined to do it!' But being determined didn't help her much, and all she could say, after a great deal of puzzling, was: 'L, I *know* it begins with L.'[115]

This text provides a useful starting point for exploring a related concern about the use of 'self-determination' as a concept. As this quote suggests, the notion of 'determination' carries with it a sense of a subject that is in control of its identity, capable of willing a particular version of that identity to carry the day. The etymology of the verb to 'determine', from the Latin *determinare* (to bound, limit or fix) evokes a subject capable of fixing its boundaries and limits. To determine something may mean to make an authoritative or judicial decision (as in the legal determination of a question), to fix or locate something in space (in the mathematical usage), or to identify the nature of something conclusively. 'Determination' also connotes the action of coming to a reasoned decision or directing the will towards an end or goal (as in Alice's determination to remember who she is). The action of self-determination, determination *of* the self *by* the self, suggests a subject capable of making authoritative decisions, using reason, directing its will, achieving its ends and establishing the location, boundaries and identity of its self.

Yet the work on subject-formation in the psychoanalytic field unsettles that conception of identity at the level of the individual subject. Irigaray's inclusion of the Alice passage at the beginning of her essay

---

[114] See generally Leela Gandhi, 'The Dialectics of Globalisation' in Christopher Palmer and Iain Topliss (eds.), *Globalising Australia* (Melbourne, 2000), pp. 133–9 at p. 139.

[115] Luce Irigaray, *This Sex Which Is Not One* (trans. Catherine Porter, Ithaca, 1985), p. 9 (emphasis in original).

on the looking glass (or mirror) hints at one way of reading the limits of determination in the field of identity, as it points us towards the Lacanian theory of the 'mirror stage' and its role in the creation of the self. According to this theory, in the beginning there is primal union between the mother and the child.[116] This is the time of the Real, of the child's sense that it is one with nature and the maternal body, a time of blissful unity. At the time of Lacan's mirror stage, which he posits as lasting from about the ages of six to eighteen months, the child begins to be aware that it is not one with the mother.[117] This is accompanied by a sense of loss or lack, as if the mother is suddenly perceived as completely absent or separate from the child.

The child addresses this sense of loss or lack because fortuitously, at about this time, the child begins to be able to perceive visual images although it is not yet able to control its motor functions. The child identifies with the coherent, whole, unified image of itself it sees in the mirror (the other), and/or with the whole body of the mother, who in turn appears to the child to be coherent and unified.[118] The child's subjectivity or sense of itself as being a coherent and unified totality is based on this incorporation of the specular image, as opposed to the fragmented and chaotic sense of self produced through its perceptions. Lacan describes this as a tension between the 'turbulent' and 'fragmented' body which the child perceives, and the unified, specular body which the child jubilantly assumes.[119] 'The child *sees* its wholeness before it *feels* its wholeness, and this seeing is actually constituent of its future identity as a distinct and whole being.'[120] Thus for Lacan, the child's gestalt or body image 'is certainly more constituent than constituted'.[121] At heart the subject is split, and incorporated within this split subject is the other. As Elizabeth Grosz describes it:

From this time on, lack, gap, splitting will be its mode of being. It will attempt to fill its (impossible, unfillable) lack. Its recognition of lack signals an ontological rift with nature or the Real. This gap will propel it into seeking an identificatory image of its own stability or permanence (the imaginary), and eventually language (the symbolic) by which it hopes to fill the lack. The child... is now constituted within the imaginary (i.e. the order of images, representations, doubles, and others) in its specular identifications.[122]

[116] Elizabeth Grosz, *Jacques Lacan: a Feminist Introduction* (Sydney, 1990), p. 34.
[117] Jacques Lacan, *Ecrits: a Selection* (trans. Alan Sheridan, London, 1977), pp. 1–7.
[118] Gatens, *Imaginary Bodies*, p. 33.   [119] Lacan, *Ecrits*, pp. 2, 4.
[120] Gatens, *Imaginary Bodies*, p. 33 (emphasis in original).   [121] Lacan, *Ecrits*, p. 2.
[122] Grosz, *Jacques Lacan*, p. 35.

Central to the subject is the sense of identifying with a unitary image which is at once alien and yet familiar. The child is now 'enmeshed in a system of confused recognition/misrecognition', involved in a 'dual, ambivalent relation to its own image'.[123] The image with which it identifies is accurate in that it is 'an inverted reflection, the presence of light rays emanating from the child: the image as icon'.[124] Yet it is also a delusion, in that 'the image prefigures a unity and mastery that the child still lacks'.[125] In other words, the image of the self as coherent and unified is dependent upon a split or fragmented relation between self and other at the heart of (masculine) subjectivity. The subject is formed through identification with a misrecognised, imagined other, so that otherness is paradoxically at the heart of the subject's sense of itself as unified and coherent.

Homi Bhabha argues that this scene of Lacanian Imaginary is the location of the colonial stereotype, a mode of representation which he sees as central to colonial discourse. For Bhabha:

The Imaginary is the transformation that takes place in the subject at the formative mirror phase, when it assumes a *discrete* image which allows it to postulate a series of equivalences, samenesses, identities, between the objects of the surrounding world. However, this positioning is itself problematic, for the subject finds or recognizes itself through an image which is simultaneously alienating and hence potentially confrontational. This is the basis of the close relation between the two forms of identification complicit with the Imaginary – narcissism and aggressivity. It is precisely these two forms of identification that constitute the dominant strategy of colonial power exercised in relation to the stereotype which, as a form of multiple and contradictory belief, gives knowledge of difference and simultaneously disavows or masks it.[126]

I will return in the next chapter to consider some of the implications of Bhabha's argument that colonial stereotypes are essentially unstable and thus productive. Here, I want to explore further his suggestion that the Imaginary is the location of the colonial stereotype – that the colonised is imagined as a double of the coloniser. International texts about intervention share the form of this doubling. The Third World has long been imagined as the double or other of 'the West', now the international community. Jennifer Beard has argued that we can read European texts dealing with the 'discovery' of the New World as attempts to master an encounter that took place, for explorers like

---

[123] *Ibid.*, p. 39.   [124] *Ibid.*   [125] *Ibid.*
[126] Bhabha, *Location of Culture*, p. 77 (emphasis in original).

Christopher Columbus, largely in the realm of the Imaginary.[127] The barbaric, primitive, innocent New World of early internationalist texts can be understood as Europe's double – essential to the self-image of Europeans and European states as rational, scientific, developed and civilised. In the texts of international administration that I have discussed in this chapter, it is Bosnia-Herzegovina and East Timor that are the doubles around which the constitution of the international community takes place. The relationship of the subjects of international law to these doubles is defined by a movement between the 'affirmation of wholeness/similarity' and 'the anxiety associated with lack and difference'.[128] International law recognises the people of Bosnia-Herzegovina and East Timor as equal subjects (all peoples have the right of self-determination), while at the same time treating them as different and lacking (some peoples are not yet capable of exercising the right of self-determination). As we will see in Chapter 5, the ambivalence of this response gives the narrative of humanitarian intervention its productivity.

To conclude, how then might the work of reimagining the subjects of international administration be approached? One answer is suggested by those feminist theorists who understand the Imaginary as the scene of the recognition and disavowal of gender difference. For Elizabeth Grosz, the relationship of the child's identity to its specular image can be understood as prefiguring the form of phallocentrism:

The child identifies with an image that is manifestly different from itself, though it also clearly resembles it in many respects. It takes as its own an image which is other, an image which remains out of the ego's control. The subject, in other words, recognizes itself at the moment it loses itself in/as the other. This other is the foundation and support of its identity, as well as what destabilizes or annihilates it. The subject's 'identity' is based on a (false) recognition of an other as the same. (Is this the 'origin' of phallocentrism?)[129]

Moira Gatens also suggests that a mechanism similar to that of doubling is at work in the relations between genders. 'Each gender is at once the antithesis of, and the complement to, the other...Each is deeply complicit in maintaining not only her or his *own* body image, but also that which it assumes: the body image *of the other*.'[130]

---

[127] Jennifer Beard, 'The Art of Development: Law and Ordering in the First World' (2002, unpublished doctoral thesis, copy on file with author).

[128] Bhabha, *Location of Culture*, p. 75.   [129] Grosz, *Jacques Lacan*, p. 41.

[130] Gatens, *Imaginary Bodies*, p. 36 (emphasis in original).

It is the implications of this insight for rewriting the relations between self and other that I want to develop here. Gatens argues that any
change in body image calls for a corresponding change in the body image of others, as 'our bodies are lived and constituted as part of a *network
of bodies*'.[131] As a result, a woman who does not perform her sexuality in
the authorised way is a challenge to patriarchal men – the masculine
body image depends on not being confronted by women who refuse
the feminine position: 'the full, phallic, masculine body *necessarily assumes* its antithesis: the lacking, castrated feminine body, which is its
complement, its body double'.[132]

Any change to the writing of the feminine body is therefore a threat,
because 'no change can take place in any part of this web of intersex-
uality without reverberations being felt throughout the whole web'.[133]
So the problem, and the promise, remains that feminists must address
the morphology of the male body. As Gatens writes:

> The feminist project of articulating, constructing or 'inventing' a full female
> form cannot amount to a 'separatist strategy'. Those who understand the posit-
> ing of this full female morphology as working toward an *autonomous* feminine
> sexuality or feminine subjectivity are clearly mistaken. This would involve a
> regression to the mirror-phase child's fantasy of autonomy, which can only be
> maintained by disavowal of one's counterpart...To posit a full female morphol-
> ogy inevitably involves *addressing* the phallic morphology of the male form.[134]

The two bodies we imagine 'are in fact one body and its lack or
complement'.[135] The act of determining the self can thus never be a separatist project, because the mapping or determination of our selves and
our bodies is always a project we undertake in concert with the bodies of
others. To return to Irigaray's image, once Alice passes to the other side
of the looking-glass, she can no longer remember who she was when
she was facing her reflection (despite her determination to do so). The
mirror, and all our imaginary doubles, are essential to the constitution
of our selves.

The strategic questions discussed by Gatens have strategic implications
if we read the texts of international law as involving a similar staging
of the autonomous, sovereign, Western state against the lacking, castrated, femininised Third World state – a staging which grounds the
constitution of the international community in the post-Cold War era.
It is not possible simply to rewrite Bosnia-Herzegovina or East Timor as

---

[131] *Ibid.*, p. 41 (emphasis in original).   [132] *Ibid.*, p. 38 (emphasis in original).
[133] *Ibid.*   [134] *Ibid.* (emphasis in original).   [135] *Ibid.*

autonomous subjects of international law, without addressing the morphology of the body of the Western state (as impermeable and bounded) and the related self-image of the international community. This suggests limits to the uses of the law of self-determination in the aftermath of intervention. The criticism that East Timor or Bosnia-Herzegovina have not yet achieved self-determination in substance can simply be used to shore up the self-image of the international community and found a call for further design projects on the part of international actors. Without more, the international community will simply take the failure to achieve self-determination in post-intervention territories as yet another problem for it to solve. The 'problem' of the failure of intervention to achieve its goals becomes the engine for a new set of legal design projects. As Gilles Deleuze and Félix Guattari comment with respect to the social machine more generally, 'it is in order to function that a social machine must not function well'.[136] International society 'is always destined to reconstitute itself on its own ruins'.[137]

The case of East Timor illustrates this well. On the eve of independence, IMF official Stephen Schwartz stated that 'the toughest challenges of nation-building and economic management are still to come' in East Timor, thus explaining the need for continued IMF management of the East Timorese economy.[138] The UN Secretary-General reported that independence brings new problems to be solved by the international community.[139] While the people of East Timor 'are now in a position to determine their own fate', they are 'desperately poor', and their self-government and independence 'are at risk if they are not reinforced through a continued international presence and commitment'.[140] The failure of UNTAET to develop an East Timorese public service, to recruit and train personnel in the justice sector, to establish an effective administrative support structure in that sector, to establish a fully functioning East Timorese police service or defence force, or to fill teaching posts, is not a failure of self-determination. Rather, it is a reason for the international community to remain in East Timor with the aim of

---

[136] Gilles Deleuze and Félix Guattari, *Anti-Oedipus: Capitalism and Schizophrenia*, (trans. Robert Hurley, Mark Seem and Helen R. Lane, Minneapolis, 1983), p. 151.

[137] *Ibid.*

[138] Donors' Meeting on East Timor, Staff Statement by Stephen Schwartz, Deputy Division Chief, IMF Asia and Pacific Department, Dili, 14–15 May 2002, http://www.imf.org/external/np/dm/2002/051402.htm (accessed 28 June 2002).

[139] Report of the Secretary-General on the United Nations Transitional Administration in East Timor, S/2002/432.

[140] *Ibid.*, p. 15.

eventually contributing to self-sufficiency in these areas.[141] The UN must stay in East Timor after independence 'to ensure the security and stability of the nascent State', and to support the post-independence administration, moving towards 'ownership by the East Timorese government' of the civilian administration 'while taking into account the need for accountability by the United Nations for the use of assessed funds'.[142] In each case, the involvement of the international community is represented as a response to the problems of an absence of readiness for self-government and independence.

Without taking on the sense of self of the international community, and its intimate relationship with its representation of law's others, it is not possible to address the effects of intervention and reconstruction projects. Instead, the very act of critique simply fuels the fantasies of modernist law. At stake in any representation of the 'self' of Bosnia-Herzegovina or East Timor is the self-image of the Western state, and now the international community. In the next chapter, I want to tease out the relationship between these two opposed images of self and other/double as they are imagined in the narratives of humanitarian intervention.

[141] *Ibid.*, pp. 2–10.   [142] *Ibid.*, p. 11.

5　The constitution of the international community: colonial stereotypes and humanitarian narratives

In his discussion of the relationship between law and narrative, Robert Cover argues that 'no set of legal institutions or prescriptions exists apart from the narratives that locate it and give it meaning'.[1] Once law is located within the context of such narratives, it can be understood as 'not merely a system of rules to be observed, but a world in which we live'.[2] This chapter suggests that humanitarian intervention is located firmly within a familiar heroic narrative. The world created by the narrative of humanitarian intervention is one in which international institutions are the bearers of progressive human rights and democratic values to local peoples in need of those rights and values in the post-Cold War era. As I will show, the characters and plot of this narrative serve to make plausible a conservative ending to the serial humanitarian and security crises for which military intervention is proposed as a solution. Yet the figure of the human rights victim around which this narrative turns promises to unsettle the conservative ends of intervention that are named as the law.

This book has so far focused on the meanings that are made about the causes and effects of intervention. I have suggested that internationalist accounts of military intervention and post-conflict reconstruction too often serve to obscure the power relations that intervention produces, and the exploitation that it enables. As a result, such accounts limit the opportunity to make use of the radical potential of human rights. This chapter builds on that argument, to suggest that the heroic narratives of humanitarian intervention make it possible for practices of economic

[1] Robert M. Cover, 'Foreword: Nomos and Narrative' (1983) 97 *Harvard Law Review* 4, at 4–5.
[2] *Ibid.*

exploitation to take place alongside military intervention, and for both to be coded as humanitarian on the part of the international community. The narratives of humanitarian intervention play a part in obscuring the relationship between militarism, governance and exploitation. Legal texts make sense of the relations between military intervention and developing states in terms of a deeper narrative and flow of meaning within which intervention stories are inserted. Whether through arguments about the need to control state aggression and increasing disorder, or through appeals to the need to protect human rights, democracy and humanitarianism, international lawyers justifying the use of force paint a picture of a world in which increased military intervention by international organisations is desirable. The legal stories that explain international intervention have increasingly informed everyday language through media reports and political soundbites. As a result, these highly technical, strategic accounts of the world become more and more a part of 'the stories that we are all inside, that we live daily'.[3] These stories create worlds inhabited by characters such as states, foreign capital and international organisations, with whom the readers of these stories are invited to identify.[4]

The first part of this chapter draws on feminist, Marxist and postcolonial theories of subjectivity and identification to explore the appeal of intervention narratives. I argue that legal texts about intervention create a powerful sense of self for those who identify with the hero of the story, be that the international community, the Security Council, the UN, NATO or the USA.[5] Intervention narratives operate not only or even principally in the realm of state systems, rationality and facts, but also in the realm of identification, imagination, subjectivity and emotion. The second part of the chapter explores the possibility for rejecting or resisting the forms of identification and closure that the heroic narrative offers.

[3] Terry Threadgold, 'Introduction' in Terry Threadgold and Anne Cranny-Francis (eds.), *Feminine, Masculine and Representation* (Sydney, 1990), pp. 1–35 at p. 27.

[4] Judith Grbich, 'Taxation Narratives of Economic Gain: Reading Bodies Transgressively' (1997) 5 *Feminist Legal Studies* 131 (arguing that narratives of taxation law create worlds inhabited by characters such as Capital).

[5] For a reading of the equally productive and horrific narratives that operated within Serbian political discourse to justify ethnic cleansing and war see Renata Salecl, *The Spoils of Freedom: Psychoanalysis and Feminism after the Fall of Socialism* (London, 1994), pp. 58–73.

Reading heroic narratives

While feminist and critical work in areas such as film theory, literary theory and cultural studies has developed sophisticated analyses of the nature of identification,[6] less work has been done by feminists and critical scholars to explore the ways in which a process of identification operates as part of international relations.[7] In turn, those mainstream scholars writing within the disciplines of international relations and international law have tended to focus on a public sphere of states, corporations and international organisations, avoiding any analysis of the relationship of issues of fantasy, desire and identity to internationalism.[8] Yet a focus on such questions is essential to a consideration of the power of intervention narratives.

In particular, the work of feminist, Marxist and postcolonial theorists interested in questions of subjectivity and identification provides useful tools for exploring the force of intervention stories. According to theorists writing in those traditions, our sense of self, or subjectivity, is not fixed, but is 'constantly being reconstituted in discourse each time we think or speak'.[9] Many such theories of subjectivity build on Louis Althusser's thesis that the individual becomes a subject of ideology through the process of interpellation.[10] For Althusser, interpellation refers to the role played by ideology or cultural representation in the creation of subjects. Ideology functions by 'interpellating' or 'hailing'

---

[6] See, for example, Judith Butler, *Gender Trouble: Feminism and the Subversion of Identity* (New York, 1990); Diana Fuss, *Identification Papers* (New York, 1995); E. Ann Kaplan, *Looking for the Other: Feminism, Film, and the Imperial Gaze* (New York, 1997); Kaja Silverman, *The Subject of Semiotics* (New York, 1983).

[7] For some exceptions, see Lynda Boose, 'Techno-Muscularity and the "Boy Eternal": from the Quagmire to the Gulf' in Amy Kaplan and Donald E. Pease (eds.), *Cultures of United States Imperialism* (Durham and London, 1993), pp. 581–616; David Campbell, *Writing Security: United States Foreign Policy and the Politics of Identity* (Durham, 1992); David Kennedy, 'Spring Break' (1985) 63 *Texas Law Review* 1377; Michael Rogin, ' "Make My Day!": Spectacle as Amnesia in Imperial Politics [and] the Sequel' in Amy Kaplan and Donald E. Pease (eds.), *Cultures*, p. 499; Salecl, *Spoils of Freedom*.

[8] V. Spike Peterson, 'The Politics of Identity and Gendered Nationalism' in Laura Neack, Patrick J. Haney and Jeanne A. K. Hey (eds.), *Foreign Policy Analysis in its Second Generation: Continuity and Change* (New Jersey, 1995), pp. 167–186 at p. 183 (arguing that the 'gendered dichotomy of public–private structures the study and practice of international relations and foreign policy' and that one result is the 'discipline's neglect of activities associated with the private sphere').

[9] Chris Weedon, *Feminist Practice and Poststructuralist Theory* (Cambridge, 1987), p. 33.

[10] Louis Althusser, *Lenin and Philosophy and Other Essays* (trans. Ben Brewster, London, 1971), p. 127.

the individual.[11] Through the process of interpellation, individuals recognise themselves as the subjects of cultural representations.[12] Such an approach provides a starting point for thinking about the relationship between particular representations, such as legal texts about international intervention, and the sense of self of those individuals who engage with such stories. Stories such as those told by international lawyers can be understood as one of the means by which a reader of such stories gains a sense of self and a way of understanding his or her relation to the world.

Feminist and postcolonial theorists suggest that this process of interpellation is an ongoing one, and that central to its success is the operation of narrative. For example, Kaja Silverman argues that the ways in which narrative operates to shape the subjectivity of the members of the audience is at the heart of the appeal of mainstream films.[13] The subjectivity of viewers is produced through the process of identification with characters within the narrative, an identification which is organised along gendered lines, producing a sexually differentiated subject.[14] This operation of narrative, and the invitation to identify with particular characters in a film, serve to reinforce an individual's interpellation into ideology, or insertion into the symbolic order.[15]

Postcolonial scholars have shown that the production of subjectivity through narrative is dependent not only upon sexual differentiation, but also upon racial differentiation. The deployment of heroic narratives governed encounters between Europe, later the 'West' or the 'international community', and those colonised or enslaved by Europeans. According to Edward Said:

The main battle in imperialism is over land, of course: but when it came to who owned the land, who had the right to settle and work on it, who kept it going, who won it back, and who now plans its future – these issues were reflected, contested, and even for a time decided in narrative...The power to narrate, or to block other narratives from forming and emerging, is very important to culture and imperialism, and constitutes one of the main connections between them.[16]

Law in general, and international law in particular, is one site for the forming, and blocking, of such narratives about property, personality

---

[11] Ibid., p. 162. In Althusser's formulation, ideology 'represents the imaginary relationship of individuals to their real conditions of existence'.
[12] Silverman, The Subject, p. 220.   [13] Ibid., pp. 215–36.   [14] Ibid., p. 221.
[15] Ibid., p. 221.
[16] Edward W. Said, Culture and Imperialism (London, 1993), p. xiii.

and power. Law operates not only in the realm of sovereignty, but also in the realm of subjectivity, where meanings are created and where we are invited to see ourselves and the world in certain ways. Intervention stories become part of lived experience through the practices of those reading these texts. The reader provides the links of subjectivity between particular narratives and the experience of the gendered and racialised metaphors upon which they depend as 'aspects of a private and sexualized sense of one's self'.[17] Models of the relationship between narrative, cultural representations and subjectivity developed in film and postcolonial theory enable an exploration of the pleasures, and the forms of identification, offered by post-Cold War intervention narratives. The elements of narrative that have been outlined by feminist and postcolonial theorists can be traced through stories about the need for humanitarian intervention in the post-Cold War era.

Disruption of the established order

Kaja Silverman points out that a classic narrative begins by disrupting the established symbolic order, 'dislocating the subject-positions within it, and challenging its ideals of coherence and fullness only in order subsequently to re-affirm that order, those positions, and those ideals'.[18] The narrative operates to 're-interpellate' the subject into the same subject positions with which they had already identified, thus 'giving that subject the illusion of a stable and continuous identity'.[19] Although the crisis to the symbolic order has the potential to be disruptive, the narrative operates to reaffirm that order in 'ideologically orthodox ways'.[20] As a result, it has a profoundly conservative effect on the subject.

The narrative of most intervention stories follows such a pattern. The call to arms is signalled by a crisis to the international order, whether that be an armed conflict or civil war that requires military intervention, or an economic crisis that requires monetary intervention. Intervention narratives create a sense of crisis by describing an increased likelihood of violence and disorder in the post-Cold War era. In the early 1990s, the power vacuum caused by the two superpowers ceasing to order and discipline destabilising forces in 'Third World' states began to be portrayed

---

[17] Grbich, 'Taxation Narratives', 134.   [18] Silverman, *The Subject*, p. 221.
[19] *Ibid.*   [20] *Ibid.*

as the cause of the crisis facing the new world order.[21] The apocalyptic vision with which such narratives begin is well illustrated in the following passage by Brian Urquhart:

The world is entering a period of great instability, characterised by long-standing international rivalries and resentments, intense ethnic and religious turmoil, a vast flow of arms and military technology, domestic disintegration, poverty and deep economic inequalities, instantaneous communication throughout the world, population pressures, natural and ecological disasters, the scarcity of vital resources, and huge movements of population.[22]

Similar images of crises or threats to security are used as justifications for particular interventions. The Gulf War, for example, is used to demonstrate 'the already conventional wisdom that the disappearance of the inhibiting shadow of potential nuclear war between the superpowers will permit bloodier and more intractable international disputes to emerge'.[23] The crisis in the former Yugoslavia illustrates the premodern ethnic tension that erupted in the post-Cold War era. The 'grim story of Yugoslavia's breakup and the ensuing ethnic conflict seems all the more disturbing because it has shattered the hope that the Cold War's end might herald a new era of peace'.[24] The ruins of the former Yugoslavia represent 'the crumpled dreams of a new cooperative security order in Europe'.[25] The cause of such crises is systematically linked to the political destabilisation resulting from the ending of the Cold War.[26]

The picture of the post-Cold War world that emerges from security texts is one in which 'struggles for national identity and self-determination have disintegrated into ethnic, religious, and political

---

[21] Leon Gordenker and Thomas G. Weiss, 'The Collective Security Idea and Changing World Politics' in Thomas G. Weiss (ed.), *Collective Security in a Changing World* (Boulder and London, 1993), pp. 3–18 at p. 14.

[22] Brian Urquhart, 'Learning from the Gulf' in Mara R. Bustelo and Philip Alston (eds.), *Whose New World Order? What Role for the United Nations?* (Leichhardt, 1991), p. 11 at p. 17.

[23] Abram Chayes, 'The Use of Force in the Persian Gulf' in Lori F. Damrosch and David J. Scheffer (eds.), *Law and Force in the New International Order* (Boulder, 1991), p. 4 at p. 11.

[24] James B. Steinberg, 'International Involvement in the Yugoslavia Conflict' in Lori Fisler Damrosch, *Enforcing Restraint: Collective Intervention in Internal Conflicts* (New York, 1993), p. 27.

[25] *Ibid.*

[26] See, for example, Lincoln P. Bloomfield, 'Collective Security and US Interests' in Thomas G. Weiss (ed.), *Collective Security*, p. 189 at p. 200, arguing that: 'Murderous civil war in the Balkans, the overthrow of democracy in Haiti, and spreading battles in parts of central Eurasia long smothered under the stabilizing blanket of Soviet imperial rule have all exposed a dangerous vacuum in Western decision centers.'

fragmentation'.[27] Far from leading to global peace, 'the passing of the Cold War has led to a new generation of conflicts: internal rather than international, driven by ethnic and communal differences rather than by political ideology, and of unprecedented levels of brutality'.[28] Despite initial optimism, it now appears that 'the conclusion of the Cold War does not mean an end to savagery and violence in international politics…that yearned-for day of beating swords into plowshares must be deferred once again'.[29]

These narratives present rogue states, ruthless dictators and ethnic tensions as threats to the established liberal international order. The argument made by those in favour of humanitarian intervention during the 1990s was that the use of force is necessary to address the problems of racist and ruthless dictators, tribalism, ethnic tension, civil war and religious fundamentalism thrown up in the post-Cold War era.[30] The need to halt the horrors of genocide or ethnic cleansing, or to address the effects of internal armed conflict on civilians, is sufficient justification for military intervention. A commitment to humanitarian ideals demands military action from the international community, increasingly in the form of aerial bombardment. The failure to take such action amounts to 'abstention from the foreign policy debate',[31] and any challenge to interventionism 'rewards tyrants' and 'betrays the very purposes of the international order'.[32]

In the case of Kosovo, legal commentators argue that intervention was required in order to promote justice and morality, despite the illegality of such intervention. According to Bruno Simma: 'The lesson which can be drawn from [the use of force by NATO] is that unfortunately there do occur "hard cases" in which terrible dilemmas must be faced, and imperative political and moral considerations may appear to leave no choice but to act outside the law.'[33]

---

[27] Thomas G. Weiss, 'On the Brink of a New Era? Humanitarian Interventions, 1991–94' in Donald C. F. Daniel and Bradd C. Hayes (eds.), *Beyond Traditional Peacekeeping* (New York, 1995), pp. 3–19.

[28] Larry Minear and Philippe Guillot, *Soldiers to the Rescue: Humanitarian Lessons from Rwanda* (Paris, 1996), p. 17.

[29] W. Michael Reisman, 'Some Lessons from Iraq: International Law and Democratic Politics' (1991) 16 *Yale Journal of International Law* 203 at 213.

[30] Arguments to that effect are explored in detail in Anne Orford, 'The Politics of Collective Security' (1996) 17 *Michigan Journal of International Law* 373.

[31] Weiss, 'On the Brink', p. 8.

[32] Fernando R. Tesón, 'Collective Humanitarian Intervention' (1996) 17 *Michigan Journal of International Law* 323 at 342.

[33] Bruno Simma, 'NATO, the UN and the Use of Force: Legal Aspects' (1999) 10 *European Journal of International Law* 1 at 22.

This view is also adopted by Michael Glennon. While acknowledging that the NATO air strikes against Serbia were not 'technically legal under the old regime', Glennon suggests that the 'death of the restrictive old rules on peacekeeping and peacemaking...should not be mourned'.[34] According to Glennon, 'in Kosovo, justice (as it is now understood) and the UN Charter seemed to collide'.[35] In this narrative, the international order, which represents values such as humanitarianism and justice, is threatened by states and leaders who have no commitment to human rights or peace.[36]

The implication of these arguments is that the international community is the guarantor of core values such as peace, security, human rights, justice and freedom. The constant representation of the international community as the guarantor of progressive values operates to perform the narrative function described by Silverman – 'to re-articulate the existing symbolic order in ideologically orthodox ways'.[37] As I have shown in earlier chapters, this ignores the ways in which domination and exploitation are maintained through military and economic intervention. Intervention discourse ignores almost completely the current historical context of rapid and massive global economic change within which security and humanitarian crises emerge and security actions take place. It constructs the identity of the international community as an active, humane saviour intervening to help people in trouble spots, obscuring other sets of relations between those who identify with the international community and those targeted for intervention.

'Knights in White Armour'[38]

According to feminist film theory, both male and female viewers are invited to identify with a masculine character associated with qualities such as potency and authority.[39] The narrative is structured around the actions of that main controlling figure with whom the spectator is invited to identify.[40] As Laura Mulvey argues, identification with the

---

[34] Michael J. Glennon, 'The New Interventionism: the Search for a Just International Law' (1999) 78 *Foreign Affairs* 2.

[35] *Ibid.*   [36] *Ibid.*, 4.   [37] Silverman, *The Subject*, p. 221.

[38] 'Knights in White Armour' is the title of a celebratory analysis of the role of UN peace-keepers in the new world order. See Christopher Bellamy, *Knights in White Armour: the New Art of War and Peace* (London, 1997).

[39] Silverman, *The Subject*, p. 223.

[40] Laura Mulvey, *Visual and Other Pleasures* (Bloomington, 1989), p. 14. Mulvey argues that this invitation to identify is structured by 'ways of seeing and pleasure in looking' (*Visual and Other Pleasures*, p. 15). A visual economy governs the sexual differentiation

masculine character leads to the '"masculinisation'" of the spectator position, regardless of the actual sex (or possible deviance) of any real live movie-goer'.[41] The female spectator may not be able to identify with the masculinity of the subject position on offer. On the other hand, Laura Mulvey points out, 'she may find herself secretly, unconsciously almost, enjoying the freedom of action and control over the...world that identification with a hero provides'.[42]

Postcolonial theorists have argued that in the narratives produced in colonial or imperial contexts, the hero with whom the reader or spectator is invited to identify is not only masculine, but also 'white'.[43] Colonial narratives produce a racially differentiated subject, through the same processes of identification and subjectivity discussed by feminist film theorists.[44] In cinematic terms, the imperial gaze, like the male gaze, invites the viewer's identification with the powerful, white character.[45] That imperialist character is associated with attributes including freedom, creativity, authority, civilisation, power, democracy, sovereignty and wealth. The world of the colonies, or of developing states in the post-World War II context, is a space in which the white man is imagined as having an enormous freedom to act and to create ideal worlds.

Intervention stories invite the reader to identify with a central figure with whom the qualities of agency and potency are associated. The characters given agency, and with whom identification is invited, include the UN, the Security Council, the 'international community', NATO and the USA. Those largely interchangeable characters are portrayed as the heroic agents of progress, democratic values, peace and security, who shape target states through their interventions. The images of new threats of violence and instability serve to announce the attractiveness of such heroes as guarantors of stability, bearers of democracy and protectors of human rights and of the oppressed.

While those heroes are not human, they are nevertheless imagined as having the characteristics attributed to white men. A series of related images of masculinity dominate the narratives of the new interventionism.

produced by watching films. This book does not explore the ways in which identification with characters in narratives of intervention is structured by a similar visual economy, but that process is clearly part of the CNN effect produced by filming on location in (always Third World) trouble-spots.

[41] Ibid., p. 29.   [42] Ibid.

[43] Toni Morrison, *Playing in the Dark: Whiteness and the Literary Imagination* (London, 1992), p. 38.

[44] Diana Fuss, *Identification Papers*, p. 141.   [45] See generally Kaplan, *Looking for the Other*.

Stories about the need for the Security Council to restore order in the post-Cold War era, for example, draw on the image of white masculinity as tough, aggressive and decisive. When still US Ambassador to the UN, Madeleine Albright used the notion of new threats and conflicts in the post-Cold War era to justify increased military intervention under Security Council auspices.

We are privileged to live at a time when the enforcement of international standards of behaviour through the actions of the Security Council is more possible, widespread, and varied than it has ever been. It is also perhaps more necessary than it has ever been. Although we are opposed by no superpower, threats and conflicts continue to arise that engage our interests, even when they do not endanger directly our territory or citizens. We live in an unsettled age, beset by squabbles, wars, unsatisfied ambitions, and weapons that are more deadly and more widely available than ever in history.[46]

Such paternalistic descriptions of the need for international intervention have relied upon images of the Security Council as a benevolent patriarch. Jeffrey Clark argues that the 'vision of a pacified Somalia capable of again feeding its population is now possible' due to actions of the international military forces.[47] Similarly, Tom Farer paints a picture of the Security Council as a tough but fair figure, intervening in 'defense of humanitarian values or, less grandly, a modest degree of law and order'.[48] Farer suggests that the need for intervention in Somalia 'arose from the tribal wars unleashed by the collapse of public authority'. To create order in 'such places', 'the cops may first have to occupy them'.[49] The role of the international community, represented by its 'cops', is to bring calm professionalism, order, peace and security to emotional, fearful and hysterical peoples.

In order to create order in 'such places', a certain amount of pragmatic leadership is necessary. Many legal commentators suggest that such leadership must be provided by the actions of the USA, and where necessary by tough military leaders. 'Everyone likes to criticize US pretensions to being the constable of the world. But when people need the

---

[46] Ambassador Madeleine K. Albright, 'International Law Approaches the Twenty-First Century: a US Perspective on Enforcement' (1995) 18 *Fordham International Law Journal* 1595 at 1597.

[47] Jeffrey Clark, 'Debacle in Somalia: Failure of the Collective Response' in Damrosch, *Enforcing Restraint*, p. 231.

[48] Tom J. Farer, 'Intervention in Unnatural Humanitarian Emergencies: Lessons of the First Phase' (1996) 18 *Human Rights Quarterly* 1.

[49] *Ibid.*, p. 16.

cops, guess who they call? The international security system depends centrally on the United States.'[50]

The narration of international intervention also draws upon a less militaristic and more family-oriented version of masculinity. Cultural theorists have commented that in films of the late 1980s and early 1990s, the white male hero began to be portrayed as a 'sensitive family man', an 'emotional domestic hero', able to signify a new model of masculine strength and power, derived from a commitment to personal and family-oriented values.[51] While that later version of masculinity appears to offer a critique of the earlier, more violent and militaristic version, in fact it is based upon many of the same images and assumptions. Militarism, dominance, nationalism, individualism and violence continue to be at the heart of this image of masculinity.[52] In the second model, however, violence is resorted to in the service of family, home and nation, or to guard against abusive fathers, rather than more overtly in the interests of competition and machismo.[53]

Using similar images, texts about humanitarian intervention represent the international community as the guarantor of the values of human rights and democracy, and as the protector of suffering peoples. The Gulf War, we are told, 'finally consummated the marriage between the UN and the one power whose backing is a precondition for any collective security system'.[54] Through that image of the USA and the UN as man and wife, the USA is portrayed as a sensitive family man, willing to defend the international values of humanitarianism, human rights, democracy and security. Representations of military interventions in the former Yugoslavia, Haiti and Somalia portray the UN as the figure capable of ensuring that the peoples of failed states or corrupt regimes receive aid and are guaranteed survival.[55]

Through such images, the international community is systematically allied with the values of human rights and democracy. Intervention by the international community is justified by reference to a history beginning with the framers of the UN Charter of 1945, who 'understood the linkage between the protection of basic human dignity and the preservation of peace and security'.[56] The international community is the source

---

[50] Reisman, 'Some Lessons', 206.
[51] Susan Jeffords, *Hard Bodies: Hollywood Masculinity in the Reagan Era* (New Brunswick, 1994), p. 118.
[52] *Ibid.*, pp. 91–2.   [53] *Ibid.*, pp. 42–3.   [54] Bloomfield, 'Collective Security', p. 190.
[55] See, for example, Gordenker and Weiss, 'Collective Security Idea', p. 15; Clark, 'Debacle', p. 205.
[56] Max M. Kampelman, 'Foreword' in Damrosch, *Enforcing Restraint*, p. vii.

and necessary provider of these values to people in need of saving.[57] It is 'the responsibility of the international community to intervene in order to preserve peace and important human values'.[58] That sense of responsibility underpins growing support for the notion of a 'global humanitarian imperative', requiring a 'duty to interfere' in countries 'in which there is widespread suffering or abuse'.[59] As a result of such links between the international community and desirable values, Tom Farer can argue that 'the threat to a humane international order consists not of [Security] Council hyperactivity, but rather of no action at all'.[60]

The NATO intervention in Kosovo drew upon these images of the international community as hero. Media reports widely promoted the softer image of NATO acting to protect Kosovar Albanians from ethnic cleansing and to guarantee the values of humanitarianism and human rights. Similar representations dominate legal analyses. Antonio Cassese, for example, while arguing that the NATO action represents a significant breach of UN standards, nevertheless comments:

Any person of common sense is justified in asking him or herself the following dramatic question: Faced with such an enormous human-made tragedy and given the inaction of the UN Security Council due to the refusal of Russia and China to countenance any significant involvement of the international community to stop the massacres and expulsions, should one sit idly by and watch thousands of human beings being slaughtered or brutally persecuted? Should one remain silent and inactive only because the existing body of international law rules proves incapable of remedying such a situation? Or, rather, should respect for the Rule of Law be sacrificed on the altar of human compassion?[61]

Cassese concludes that while NATO armed intervention is contrary to current international law, 'from an ethical viewpoint resort to armed force was justified'.[62] At the same time, US leadership was able to appear resolute and tough in its support for NATO action. Media images of the widespread devastation and destruction wrought by NATO's aerial bombardment served to remind the world of the power and ruthlessness of NATO member states, particularly the USA.[63]

---

[57] Ibid.   [58] Ibid., p. viii–ix.
[59] Minear and Guillot, Soldiers, p. 19.
[60] Tom Farer, 'A Paradigm of Legitimate Intervention' in Damrosch, Enforcing Restraint, p. 316 at p. 330.
[61] Antonio Cassese, 'Ex Iniuria Ius Oritur: Are We Moving towards International Legitimation of Forcible Humanitarian Countermeasures in the World Community?' (1999) 10 European Journal of International Law 23 at 25.
[62] Ibid.
[63] Edward Said, 'Protecting the Kosovars?' (1999) 234 New Left Review 73.

Intervention narratives are premised on the notion of an international community facing new dangers, acting to save the oppressed and to protect values such as democracy and human rights. The reader of intervention literature is asked to identify with the active hero of the story, be that the international community, the UN or the USA, at the cost of the violence done to the imagined objects who form the matter of the hero's quest. This is a dream of heroic masculinity, where the colonial subject as coloniser recognises itself as a white knight riding to the rescue of beleaguered victims, across devastated landscapes of destruction and death. The hero possesses the attributes of that version of aggressive white masculinity produced in late twentieth-century US culture, a white masculinity obsessed with competitive militarism and the protection of universal (read imperial) values.[64]

The subject of intervention narratives, the muscular hero, is portrayed as the character able to act in the world, and to imagine, create and bring about new worlds in his own image.[65] Agency is only held by the international community, international organisations or the USA. The governments or elites of target states are portrayed as corrupt and exercising only deviant agency, if any. Missing is any sense of the agency of the peoples of the states where intervention is to be conducted. There is no sense in which these peoples are understood to be themselves actively working to shape their communities and their world, except to the extent of seeking the protection of the international community. Only the hero of the story, the international community, has any capacity to animate or shape the peoples of target states, bringing them order, human rights, democracy and stability. By identifying with the humanitarian 'knights in white armour' of intervention stories, readers

---

[64] For a discussion of the relationship between colonialism and universality, in which 'European practices are posited as universally applicable norms with which the colonial peoples must conform', see further Antony Anghie, 'Francisco de Vitoria and the Colonial Origins of International Law' (1996) 5 *Social and Legal Studies* 321 at 332–3.

[65] Feminists in many areas have argued that this heroic narrative gives meaning to their disciplines. See, for example, Judith Grbich, 'Taxation Narratives' (arguing that the narratives of economic progress and growth that underlie taxation law are dependent upon such a story about the activity of the masculine subject – in that case Capital); Donna Haraway, *Primate Visions: Gender, Race, and Nature in the World of Modern Science* (New York, 1989), pp. 231–43 (showing that a similar narrative of heroic adventure underlies the scientific discourse of primatology); Carol Cohn, 'Sex and Death in the Rational World of Defense Intellectuals' (1987) 12 *Signs* 687 at 699–702 (arguing that a similar story is told in the area of nuclear deterrence. Images of 'male birth and creation' are central to the ways in which defence experts imagine their role in the world).

experience a pleasurable sense of expanded freedom to be and act in the world.

Symbols of helplessness

The third element of narrative that can be traced in intervention stories is the constitution of racialised or feminised characters who serve as a background and foil to the actions of the hero. The spectator's pleasurable identification with the white, masculine character is further facilitated through the creation of a secondary, passive character who lacks the characteristics of power, agency and authority. While the heroic central character is structurally male, the second character, representing the 'space for and the resistance to' the actions of the hero, is coded as female.[66] In colonial discourse, this second character in the narrative is the black, native or colonised subject. The black subject is a resource that allows the white man to imagine himself as civilised and free against a background of savagery and slavery.[67] As Frantz Fanon argues, 'not only must the black man be black; he must be black in relation to the white man'.[68] The creation of that second character is thus essential, both to the constitution of the white hero, and to the process by which identification with that heroic character is invited.

The plot of the narrative of colonialism derives from imagining the colonised subject as 'a reformed, recognizable Other, *as a subject of a difference that is almost the same, but not quite*'.[69] The hero's journey is about the civilisation, progress or development of that colonised subject. Intervention by white men is justified in order first to civilise the natives of subject colonies, and later, in the era of decolonisation, to assist the development of those former colonies. The notion of progress continues to provide the imaginative framework for intervention stories in the era of decolonisation. According to the 'fantasy of timeless, even, and limitless development', 'all societies will come to look like us, all will arrive eventually at the same stage or level, all the possibilities for the future are being lived now'.[70] The plot of such narratives, however, always ensures that the black subject is never truly able to claim the full subjectivity or agency reserved for the heroic character.[71] As Homi Bhabha notes in

---

[66] Haraway, *Primate Visions*, p. 234.   [67] Morrison, *Playing in the Dark*, p. 44.
[68] Frantz Fanon, *Black Skin, White Masks* (New York, 1967), p. 110.
[69] Homi K. Bhabha, *The Location of Culture* (London, 1994), p. 86 (emphasis in original).
[70] Kristin Ross, *Fast Cars, Clean Bodies: Decolonization and the Reordering of French Culture* (Cambridge, 1996), p. 10.
[71] *Ibid.*, p. 90.

the context of debates about governing India, 'to be Anglicized is *emphatically* not to be English'.[72] While the hero is free to act in the world to shape it in his image, the object he creates can never quite become him. The aim is not to make further heroes, of equal status to the hero. Rather, the colonial narrative involves making objects in the image of the white subject, who reflect his desires and ambitions but do not quite achieve them.

Thus heroic narratives operate to structure the subjectivity of readers or viewers by inviting identification with the white male hero, who is defined in opposition to characters who lack his potency and authority, as a result of sexual and racial differentiation. Although the white man is at the centre of such narratives, the meanings attributed to white masculinity in cultural narratives about heroism are not constant. Those meanings vary according to the challenges or crises that white masculinity is imagined as facing in a particular period. So, for example, as Toni Morrison has shown, the sense of freedom, autonomy, authority and absolute power attributed to the white subject in early American novels was formed against the backdrop of slavery and colonisation – 'nothing highlighted freedom – if it did not in fact create it – like slavery'.[73]

The values of the new world order are defined through actions taken against just such secondary characters – those disordered or evil rogue states, whose leaders need to be taught that the hard body of the international community can impose its will on them. Identification with the potent character of NATO or the Security Council is facilitated through the creation of a character lacking power and authority. The heroic narrative depends upon the constitution of that second passive character, which the hero is able to shape or act upon in order to make his mark upon the world. International organisations and major powers are imagined as the bearers of human rights and democracy, while local peoples are presented as victims of abuses conducted by agents of local interests. The people of states in Africa, Asia, South America and Eastern Europe are portrayed as childlike, primitive, barbaric or unable to govern themselves.[74] Those peoples are to be refashioned as an extension

---

[72] Bhabha, *Location of Culture*, pp. 85–92 (emphasis in original).

[73] Morrison, *Playing in the Dark*, pp. 37–8. Morrison argues that the 'unfree' (slaves, the colonised) were always present 'within the heart of the democratic experiment – the critical absence of democracy, its echo, shadow, and silent force' (p. 48).

[74] Patricia J. Williams, *The Rooster's Egg: on the Persistence of Prejudice* (Cambridge, 1995), pp. 204–5. Patricia Williams argues that discussions of the need for Security Council intervention in Somalia were based on the premise that 'some people just aren't able to govern themselves and it's about time the wise strong hand of greater minds intervened. Surprise, surprise, most of those unruly masses happen to live in Africa.'

of the self of the hero. Through the deployment of such colonial stereo-types, the international community is 'defined in and through the white male body and against the racially marked male body'.[75]

The reader's identification with or as an active, autonomous self who can act in the world as a rescuer or saviour depends upon imagining those who live in states like Haiti or Somalia or Yugoslavia in racialised terms. Security texts regularly portray the leaders or elites of states like Iraq or Somalia as oppressors, criminals or primitive barbarians, requiring disciplining and controlling. The leaders of target states are described as 'tinhorn dictators' or 'contemporary tyrants',[76] while the people are engaged in childlike 'squabbles', motivated by 'unsatisfied ambitions'.[77] According to Farer, intervention on the basis of 'feed and leave' could not have succeeded in Somalia, as the people of Somalia could not be expected to govern themselves.[78] Many security texts suggest that irrational 'ethnic particularism' or religious tensions are emerging as major threats to peace and security.[79] Farer, for example, suggests that the international community needs to intervene to con-trol the hysterical urges of those engaged in conflicts motivated by reli-gious or ethnic tension: 'peoples in a state of ecstatic mutual fear' are 'likely to go on clawing at each other unless external actors can either club them into submission, break the stalemate... and/or guarantee the safety of those willing to assume a defensive posture'.[80] The hierarchy of race underpinning such representations of the need for intervention is illustrated by Max Kampelman in his comments on the break-up of the former Yugoslavia: 'Are we entering a new form of Dark Age? Is the defeat of order and decency that is now so evident in Europe only a temporary barrier on the path to a new civilized order? If Europe fails, how can we expect Asia and Africa to succeed?'[81]

[75] Jeffords, *Hard Bodies*, p. 148.
[76] Reisman, 'Some Lessons', 213 (arguing that 'tinhorn dictators' and 'contemporary tyrants' threaten post-Cold War peace and security).
[77] Albright, 'International Law Approaches', 1597.
[78] Farer, 'Intervention', 16. See the discussion of the racial stereotypes underlying media coverage of Security Council intervention in Somalia in Williams, *The Rooster's Egg*, p. 202. Williams notes that 'the Somalis, all Somalis, were described as "undisciplined", "criminal elements", whose criminality involved "stealing from their own"'.
[79] Gordenker and Weiss, 'Collective Security Idea', p. 14 (treating 'ethnic particularism' as a threat to peace and security); Michael Stopford, 'Locating the Balance: the United Nations and the New World Disorder' (1994) 34 *Virginia Journal of International Law* 685 at 686, 698 (suggesting that the breakdown of internal state structures and ancient ethnic and religious tensions are the major challenges to peace and security).
[80] Farer, 'Intervention', 15.   [81] Kampelman, 'Foreword', p. viii.

Humanitarian intervention narratives also regularly produce images of the people who live in states targeted for intervention as starving, powerless, suffering, abused or helpless victims, often women and children, in need of rescue or salvation. The capacity to imagine that a heroic international community is needed to rescue huge numbers of the world's peoples is made possible against the background of other, similar stories. As Arturo Escobar has argued, the familiar image of a helpless and underdeveloped 'Third World' has been produced as a symbol of poverty and helplessness since the end of World War II, through the dominant discourse of development.[82] That discourse has both constituted and disciplined the people of developing countries. The image of the 'starving African' portrayed in so many media stories symbolises the way in which developmentalism produces the 'Third World' as a problem in need of a ready solution: international intervention.[83]

The nature of the self created through identification with the role of saviour depends upon the existence of such victims. David Kennedy has explored that relationship, through an analysis of the shifting meanings he made of his role as a human rights activist on a US delegation to Uruguayan prisons in 1984.[84] Kennedy draws attention to the way in which his identity as an active American lawyer on a mission for human rights depended upon imagining those in prison as passive victims. When he met with a female prisoner whom he characterised as a victim of human rights abuses, Kennedy experienced a heightened sense of purpose and motivation. In contrast, when he met with two male prisoners visited by his delegation as equals and political activists engaged in struggle, he was left feeling solidarity but a lack of agency, connected but resigned.

Ramon and Francisco seemed to carry themselves as temporarily defeated warriors in a greater political struggle, and that is how they seemed to view their own stories of capture, torture, and imprisonment. Imprisoned warriors like Ramon and Francisco seemed our equals; they needed no rescue. To them we were comrades, coparticipants in a political struggle. The connection we had felt when in their presence...diminished my sense of purpose...The passive victim awakens my indignation and motivates me to act....We might be able to do something.[85]

[82] Arturo Escobar, *Encountering Development: the Making and Unmaking of the Third World* (Princeton, 1995).
[83] *Ibid.*, pp. 103–4.   [84] David Kennedy, 'Spring Break' (1985) 63 *Texas Law Review* 1377.
[85] *Ibid.*, 402–5.

This gendered differentiation between active political equal and passive victim, between political person and abject object, between warrior body and violated body, structured Kennedy's 'sense of progress, of moving meaningfully forward with our mission...The incomprehensible violation of a woman's body kept something hidden and mysterious, so that something else, intentional knightly deployment, could seem familiar.'[86] Kennedy reveals that the sense of agency and movement he felt was dependent upon constructing those he met as 'victims'. The gendered distinction between responding to those prisoners as active warriors or passive victims shaped the meanings that his human rights team made of their experiences. Those distinctions between saviour and victim, between international and local, between avenger and abused, are at the heart of the fascination of intervention stories. These oppositions are necessary to sustain the feeling of progress, agency and freedom that such narratives engender.[87]

Kennedy's analysis stresses the importance of the second passive character to the subjectivity of those who identify with the heroic figure. The passive victim exists in these texts in order to constitute the hero or internationalist as the holder of those values which the victim lacks. In the same way, stories about humanitarian intervention involve detailed descriptions of powerless, victimised states and peoples, in order to facilitate the reader's identification with the heroes of intervention. The reader who identifies with those heroes comes to form his or her sense of self at least partly around that identification. That pleasurable process allows the reader to imagine himself or herself to be on the side of the good and the just, part of a state or international community actively able to shape the world in the image of the ideals of freedom, democracy and order.

Fear of powerlessness

The fourth aspect of theories of subjectivity and narrative that applies to intervention stories is the analysis of the resolution of the threat posed by the introduction of the feminised or racialised character. In cinematic terms, the female subject has the additional function of diverting the attention of the viewer from his or her own passivity.[88] While the creation of a passive or powerless character is supposed to facilitate the identification by the viewer of the film with the subject having the attributes of

---

[86] Ibid., 404–5.   [87] Ibid., 402–5.   [88] Silverman, *The Subject*, p. 223.

power and control, the creation of such a character also carries risk. The viewer might feel increased anxiety at the risk of identifying as, or with, the character lacking the desirable attributes of potency or authority.[89] That rediscovery of the female subject's lack may induce in the male subject 'the fear of a similar depravation'.[90] One common technique for dealing with the anxiety produced by the discovery of her deficiency is to demonstrate that the female subject's weak or passive condition is her own fault, the result of her wrong-doing or inadequacy.[91] The narrative then operates to punish or save the guilty female object.[92] That method of resolving the problem posed by the female figure is pleasurable for the spectator identifying with the masculine character, and allows the spectator to escape the sense of anxiety produced by the revelation of the lack of the female subject.[93] As Laura Mulvey argues, 'pleasure lies in ascertaining guilt…, asserting control and subjugating the guilty person through punishment or forgiveness'.[94]

In intervention narratives, any anxiety about the possibility that the viewer or reader is in a position to suffer as a result of the crisis, or any sense that the viewer or reader is in fact powerless, is healed by the sacrifice or salvation of the target state and its people. This state is a character whose lack of power, authority or agency is attributable to its own mistakes, corruption or fault. The governments or elites of such states are portrayed as corrupt, nepotistic, overreaching and authoritarian, or the people of those states are portrayed as being engaged in savage ethnic or religious conflicts. The origins of crises lie with defective governance or an inability of peoples to govern themselves.

In addition, the assumption that international actors played no role in causing the crisis is central to establishing the fault of the target state. There is thus no suggestion in representations of heroic intervention by the international community that international actors may have had any role to play in contributing to the crisis.[95] Raising such considerations would threaten the progress of the narrative. The ferocity of the attack on states or groups who resist intervention operates to ensure that readers and viewers do not succumb to the temptation to identify with a particular target state, its leaders or its people. The sacrifice, punishment and salvation of that state are central to the successful

---

[89] See further Krysti Justine Guest, 'Exploitation under Erasure: Economic, Social and Cultural Rights Engage Economic Globalisation' (1997) 19 *Adelaide Law Review* 73, at 75.
[90] Silverman, *The Subject*, p. 223.   [91] *Ibid.*, p. 224.
[92] Mulvey, *Visual and Other Pleasures*, p. 21.   [93] *Ibid.*   [94] *Ibid.*, pp. 1–2.
[95] See further the analysis in Chapter 3 above.

resolution of the anxiety produced by the introduction of the passive character.

Reaffirmation of the existing order

The progress of the narrative, from crisis to resolution through the punishment, sacrifice or salvation of the target state, operates to reaffirm the order, position and ideals that were under threat at the start of the narrative.[96] Narratives of crisis and redemption operate to reinsert the viewer into a discourse or symbolic order which heals the crisis revealed at the start of the narrative. While the representation of a post-Cold War security crisis operates to disrupt 'the existing symbolic order, dislocating the subject-positions within it, and challenging its ideals of coherence and fullness', intervention by the international community serves 'subsequently to re-affirm that order, those positions, and those ideals'.[97]

The sense of a restoration of order and stability is well illustrated by statements made by Madeleine Albright. Albright argues that 'UN peacekeeping contributes to a world that is less violent, more stable, and more democratic than it would otherwise be.'[98] She uses as an example the intervention in Haiti, suggesting that it led to 'the effort to place the law on the side of the people of Haiti for perhaps the first time in that nation's history'.[99] According to Albright, the steps 'we' have taken in Haiti 'have honored our values, eased a humanitarian crisis, and enabled Haiti, in the words of the UN Charter, to pursue "social progress and better standards of life in larger freedom"'.[100] She sees as 'our mandate in this new era' the need to develop a 'framework of law, principle, power, and purpose' similar to that forged by the generation that drafted the UN Charter.

---

[96] See Anghie, 'Francisco de Vitoria', 333 (arguing that 'the construction of the barbarian as both within the reach of the law and yet outside its protection creates an object against which sovereignty may express its fullest powers by engaging in an unmediated and unqualified violence which is justified as leading to conversion, salvation, civilization').

[97] Silverman, The Subject, p. 221.   [98] Albright, 'International Law Approaches', 1599.

[99] Ibid. 1603. For a discussion of the amnesia at work in such representations of the history of Haiti, see Noam Chomsky, World Orders, Old and New (London, 1994), pp. 36–7; Said, Culture, p. 349 (arguing that 'almost from the moment Haiti gained its independence as a Black republic in 1803, Americans tended to imagine it as a void into which they could pour their own ideas'); Greg Chamberlain, 'Up by the Roots: Haitian History through 1987' in North American Congress on Latin America, Haiti: Dangerous Crossroads (Boston, 1995), p. 13.

[100] Albright, 'International Law Approaches', 1599.

We have a responsibility in our time, as our predecessors did in theirs, not to be prisoners of history, but to shape it: to build a world not without conflict, but in which conflict is effectively contained; a world not without repression, but in which the sway of freedom is enlarged; a world not without lawless behaviour, but in which the law-abiding are progressively more secure.[101]

Albright is able to draw on a long history in which Americans have used Haiti and its people to symbolise 'degeneracy' and 'racial inferiority'.[102] She can be confident that few amongst her audience will forgo the pleasure offered by the narrative of heroic intervention long enough to consider the extent to which the history of US intervention in Haiti has served to enshrine the rights of US corporations at the expense of the agency of the Haitian people.[103]

Analyses of the intervention in Kosovo also operate to reassure readers that the NATO action restored the values at the heart of the international order, while paradoxically breaching the rules underpinning that order. Michael Glennon, for example, establishes this by arguing that the old 'anti-interventionist regime' based on the UN Charter 'has fallen out of sync with modern notions of justice'.[104] In Glennon's view, while the NATO action was 'technically' a breach of international law, it did operate to guarantee core values central to a 'just world order'.[105] In fact, the world order prefigured by the new interventionism promises to be a better guarantor of the core values of human rights, order and stability than was the system premised upon the counter-interventionist norms of the UN Charter.[106] According to Glennon, 'achieving justice is the hard part; revising international law to reflect it can come afterward'.[107] This narrative redeems NATO's lawless intervention as an action that restores the order and ideals that were threatened by the crisis in Kosovo.

Violence and narrative pleasure

The operation of intervention narratives, and the pleasures offered to the reader by identifying with the hero's freedom of action and control over the world, depend upon the acceptance of gendered and

---

[101] Ibid., 1605–6.   [102] Said, Culture, p. 349.

[103] Chomsky, World Orders, pp. 36–7 (analysing the impact of US support for France's violent attempt to repress the Haitian slave rebellion of 1791 and of the nineteen-year US occupation of Haiti from 1915); Alex Dupuy, Haiti in the New World Order (Colorado,1997) (providing an analysis of the political economy of the 1993 intervention conducted under Security Council auspices).

[104] Glennon, 'The New Interventionism', 2.   [105] Ibid., 4.   [106] Ibid., 4–5.   [107] Ibid., 7.

racialised metaphors. While blackness represents ungovernability and inferiority,[108] femaleness represents lack of agency or potency. Those narratives describe a world in which a target state, as passive substance or matter, waits to be animated by some other imagined character, such as the international community or the Security Council. A culture that imagines itself in such heroic terms develops because of, not coincidentally with or in spite of, the presence of dispossessed, enslaved and exploited peoples. Difference, particularly 'racial' difference, becomes a way of making sense of exploitation.[109]

Debates about whether to intervene in Yugoslavia, Haiti or Somalia are shaped by and in turn shape ideas about race and gender, and more generally about belonging and entitlement.[110] The 'persistence of prejudice' limits the extent to which it is possible to address the requirements of a just world order. Intervention stories provide 'a powerful schema of thought justifying significant intrusions' into the lives of those in target states.[111] Assertions that a heroic subject – the UN, NATO or the international community – knows better than those in such states, and that the development of those peoples will save them, plays 'dangerously against a backdrop in which [the] history of paternalistic white protectionism still demands black loyalty to white people and their lifestyle as a powerful symbolic precedent for deeming black social organisation "successful"'.[112]

The horror of such narratives is that they can be, indeed must be, retold over and over, with the promised redemption involving 'an ever greater subordination to already existing scenarios'.[113] The creation or production of the self of the international community becomes an endlessly repetitive project. As the serial post-Cold War security crises reveal clearly, that project is always carried out over the bodies of others.[114] Intervention stories highlight the sadism of all heroic narratives, which depend upon the fantasy of 'reducing the other to a flawless, perfectly controlled mirror of the self'.[115] The appeal of the new world order, with its linked portrayals of masculinism, whiteness and internationalism,

---

[108] Williams, The Rooster's Egg, p. 105 (arguing that a 'stigma of inferiority' is 'embodied in black presence' – emphasis in original).

[109] Guest, 'Exploitation', 93.   [110] Williams, The Rooster's Egg, p. 8.

[111] Ibid., p. 177.   [112] Ibid., p. 221.   [113] Silverman, The Subject, p. 231.

[114] Elaine Scarry suggests that this sadistic project of making the self through marking the world is at the heart of the activities of not only torture and war, but all the ways in which Western cultures make artefacts and, through them, the world. See Elaine Scarry, The Body in Pain: the Making and Unmaking of the World (New York, 1985).

[115] Haraway, Primate Visions, p. 233.

depends 'on the successful reproduction of certain images and defini-
tions of masculinity'.[116] The problem facing all of those against whom
the subject of the new world order defines himself is that in order to
'keep the revolution going', the USA, and now the 'international community', must regularly set up, and win, military confrontations.[117]

The fact that the reader is invited to identify with a white, violent,
masculine hero limits the capacity of international law to address the
ways in which the hero's journey of action and self-validation affects
the lives of the human beings caught up in that quest. There is no
space within the dominant narrative of post-Cold War internationalism
to consider the effects of the hero's actions on the human targets of
intervention, or to treat the targets of intervention (whether states or
peoples) as having legitimate agency. Any attempt to act out or imagine
ways of being in the world that differ from those desired by the USA
or the international community is presented as a threat to the control,
virility and freedom of action of the hero. As a consequence, violence
becomes a logical form of self-defence. The self that is being defended
(when the Security Council authorises the use of sanctions that lead to
the deaths of hundreds of thousands of Iraqi children, or when NATO
carries out aerial bombardment) is the competitive, irresponsible and
brutal self of white, imperial masculinity, reproduced unendingly in
the heroic narratives of militarist internationalism.[118]

Insecure identification: the productivity of colonial stereotypes

I have argued in this chapter that the fascination of intervention stories is produced through the process of identification with, or as, the
heroes of intervention. Intervention stories 'work by interpellation, by
calling an audience into the story'.[119] They are successful to the extent
that people find themselves living inside those stories. The pleasures
that identification with a hero provides, and the images and myths that

---

[116] Jeffords, *Hard Bodies*, p. 156.   [117] *Ibid.*

[118] According to UNICEF, there would have been half a million fewer deaths of children
under five in Iraq between 1991 and 1998 were it not for the imposition of sanctions
by the Security Council. See UNICEF, 'Iraq Survey shows "Humanitarian Emergency"',
12 August 1999, http://www.unicef.org/newsline/99pr29.htm (accessed 16 August
2002). For a discussion of the NATO aerial bombardment in Kosovo, see
Chapter 6 below.

[119] Haraway, *Primate Visions*, p. 169.

underlie the appeal of the story of intervention, are vital to its success in becoming one of 'the stories that we are all inside, that we live daily'.[120] Only by thinking through the force of that appeal is it possible to begin to come to terms with the personal and political investment we have in the power relations that such stories engender.

International legal discourse about humanitarian intervention tries to tie those who engage with it to a narrow range of identities. To become 'internationalists' we are asked to abandon many identifications and alliances, and to make sacrifices of others in order to produce a valuable self.[121] Escaping that process is one of the challenges facing those who seek to contest the conservative ends of the heroic narrative. A starting point for thinking about ways of opposing or refusing this interpellation as hero can be found in the critique of Althusser developed by Terry Eagleton.[122] Eagleton suggests that Althusser's theory of ideology leaves little scope for disobeying or refusing the call to identify with a particular subject position, and that this follows from Althusser's mistaken attribution of coherence and unity both to the subject and to ideology. Eagleton argues that Althusser posits a subject that is 'a good deal more stable and coherent' than the Lacanian subject upon which Althussers's theory is based.[123] In particular, Althusser's subject corresponds only to the Lacanian ego, and thus appears unified and coherent, whereas for Lacan the subject ' "as a whole" is the split, lacking, desiring effect of the unconscious'.[124] Eagleton suggests that this leads to a 'certain political pessimism' on the part of Althusser:

> To expel desire from the subject is to mute its potentially rebellious clamour, ignoring the ways in which it may attain its allotted place in the social order only ambiguously and precariously... If Althusser's subject were as split, desirous and unstable as Lacan's, then the process of interpellation might figure as a more chancy, contradictory affair than it actually does.[125]

Similarly, Judith Butler argues that Althusser critically fails to 'consider the range of *disobedience* that such an interpellating law might produce',

---

[120] Threadgold, 'Introduction', p. 27.

[121] For a similar argument about the capacity of the media to 'create mainstream icons whose struggles and achievements we can identify with' while excluding identification with those people who are 'othered' by the media, see Roseanne Kennedy, 'Global Mourning, Local Politics' in Re:Public (ed.), *Planet Diana: Cultural Studies and Global Mourning* (Nepean, 1997), pp. 49–53 at p. 52.

[122] Terry Eagleton, 'Ideology and its Vicissitudes in Western Marxism' in Slavoj Zizek (ed.), *Mapping Ideology* (London, 1994), pp. 179–226.

[123] *Ibid.*, p. 216.   [124] *Ibid.*   [125] *Ibid.*, p. 216.

such as refusal, parody or rupture.[126] For Butler, there is a 'slippage between discursive command and its appropriated effect'. 'The call by the
law which seeks to produce a lawful subject, produces a set of consequences that exceed and confound what appears to be the disciplining
intention motivating the law.'[127] Thus while we are hailed as heroic muscular humanitarians, it may be that our response to that call, and thus
our identification with that position, is not stable and secure but rather
'a more chancy, contradictory affair'.

The chancy nature of interpellation is exacerbated because that which
hails us is, in Lacan's theory, the Other, 'which means something like the
whole field of language and the unconscious'.[128] This field is, for Lacan, 'a
notoriously elusive, treacherous, terrain in which nothing quite stays in
place'.[129] As a result, the relations between the subject and the Other are
'a good deal more fraught and fragile than Althusser's model would
imply'.[130] Interpellation is in part a result of the subject's desire for the
recognition of the Other, and 'the fact that there is desire at work here'
serves to unsettle the terms on which the subject responds to the call of
ideology. In turn, the Other 'can never quite know whether I have "truly"
responded to its invocation'.[131] Because I can never really be present as a
whole subject in my responses to that call, the Other can never be sure
that my response is authentic or reliable.

How then might we understand the possibilities for subverting the
forms of identification that are created through humanitarian narratives? I want to conclude by returning to the work of Homi Bhabha.
Bhabha suggests that the stereotype is the pivot around which the constitution of identity takes place in colonial societies.[132] In intervention
texts, as I have suggested, these stereotypes include the representation of
Yugoslavs, Rwandans, Somalis and East Timorese as childlike, unable to
govern themselves, barbaric and unruly. But Bhabha, like Eagleton, does
not portray power as unidirectional, nor does he attribute closure and
coherence to the colonial subject. For Bhabha, this is to pay inadequate
attention to 'fantasy (as the scene of desire) in the production of the
"political" effects of discourse'.[133] In contrast, Bhabha reads the colonial
stereotype as offering a form of identification 'that vacillates between
what is always "in place", already known, and something that must be
anxiously repeated'.[134] Such stereotypes are relentlessly repeated as if

---

[126] Judith Butler, *Bodies that Matter* (New York, 1993), pp. 122.
[127] *Ibid.*   [128] Eagleton, 'Ideology', p. 216.   [129] *Ibid.*, p. 216.   [130] *Ibid.*, p. 216.
[131] *Ibid.*, p. 217.   [132] Bhabha, *Location of Culture*, p. 66.
[133] *Ibid.*, p. 72.   [134] *Ibid.*, p. 66.

'the essential...that needs no proof, can never really, in discourse, be proved'.[135] The resulting ambivalence of colonial discourse – the movement between something which is always in place and something that must be anxiously repeated – is what 'gives the colonial stereotype its currency: ensures its repeatability in changing historical and discursive conjunctures'.[136]

Bhabha develops a reading of this ambivalence in terms of the Freudian fable of fetishism.[137] For Freud, fetishism is a defensive process set in train in response to a little boy's traumatic realisation of sexual difference.[138] The fetish simultaneously memorialises the horror of that recognition of difference, and disavows knowledge of it.[139] The resulting 'affection and hostility in the treatment of the fetish...run parallel with the disavowal and the acknowledgement' of sexual difference.[140] Bhabha argues that, as with the fetish, colonial discourse recognises difference (here racial) while disavowing that difference 'by the fixation on an object [the reformable native] that masks that difference and restores an original presence'.[141]

For fetishism is always a 'play' or vacillation between the archaic affirmation of wholeness/similarity – in Freud's terms: 'All men have penises'; in ours: "All men have the same skin/race/culture' – and the anxiety associated with lack and difference – again, for Freud "Some do not have penises"; for us "Some do not have the same skin/race/culture.[142]

We might rewrite this in the age of globalisation as 'All have the same rights/Some do not have rights'. The colonial stereotypes deployed in humanitarian intervention narratives can then be read as 'the scene of a similar fantasy and defence' as that which takes place in fetishism.[143] The colonial subject desires a wholeness which is always threatened by difference. Difference is brought into consciousness in the figure of the human rights victim, but then disavowed through the use of force in the name of bringing into being the reformed subject of difference that is almost the same, but not quite. This movement resembles that vacillation which Freud describes in responses to the fetish. The human rights victim represents at once resemblance or mimicry ('a difference that is almost nothing but not quite') and menace ('a difference that is

---

[135] Ibid.   [136] Ibid.   [137] Ibid., pp. 73–4.

[138] Sigmund Freud, 'Fetishism' in James Strachey (ed.), The Standard Edition of the Complete Psychological Works of Sigmund Freud, Volume XXI (London, 1961), pp. 152–7 at p. 152.

[139] Ibid., p. 154.   [140] Ibid., p. 157.   [141] Bhabha, Location of Culture, p. 74.

[142] Ibid.   [143] Ibid., p. 75.

almost total but not quite').[144] The use of these stereotypes gives access to a heroic identity premised on the recognition of difference and the simultaneous disavowal of that difference.

The political point generated by Bhabha's analysis is his argument that the stereotype does *not* offer '*at any one time, a secure* point of identification'.[145] Bhabha suggests instead that 'the stereotype is a complex, ambivalent, contradictory mode of representation, as anxious as it is assertive'.[146] The stereotype must be endlessly rehearsed and invited into consciousness so that the unstable colonial subject can be secured – 'the *same old* stories…*must* be told (compulsively) again and afresh, and are differently gratifying and terrifying each time'.[147] As we have seen, this is precisely the way in which humanitarian narratives operate. Each new situation in which the international community intervenes is described according to the same old stories, which are nonetheless 'differently gratifying and terrifying each time'.

Bhabha's reading of the productivity of colonial stereotype reveals 'the boundaries of colonial discourse and…enables a transgression of these limits from the space of that otherness'.[148] The human rights victim memorialises the splitting at the heart of colonial subjectivity, and thus can bring to consciousness the desire that is embodied in the imaginary world of colonial societies. As Bhabha suggests:

The stereotype is at once a substitute and a shadow. By acceding to the wildest fantasies (in the popular sense) of the colonizer, the stereotyped Other reveals something of the 'fantasy' (as desire, defence) of that position of mastery…it is in all cases a desire to return to the fullness of the mother, a desire for an unbroken and undifferentiated line of vision and origin.[149]

The fetish refers back 'through displacements of the signifier, to vulnerable or highly charged areas in the social fantasy that produced it'.[150] Because the fetish not only disavows the traumatic sight of the mother's body, but also commemorates or mourns that thing which is thought to be missing, Laura Mulvey stresses that 'a fetish still stays in touch with its original traumatic real and retains a potential access to its own historical story'.[151] As a result, if we read the glossy salvation story of humanitarian intervention as a colonial discourse, and the human rights victim as a 'fetish', it is this potential access to the original trauma that

[144] *Ibid.*, p. 90–1.   [145] *Ibid.*, p. 69 (emphasis in original).   [146] *Ibid.*, p. 70.
[147] *Ibid.*, p. 77 (emphasis in original).   [148] *Ibid.*, p. 67.   [149] *Ibid.*, p. 82.
[150] Laura Mulvey, *Fetishism and Curiosity* (London, 1996), p. 10.   [151] *Ibid.*, p. 5.

is the most productive element of that narrative. Humanitarian intervention, as it is currently performed, serves to recuperate that potentially
subversive recognition of difference. Yet the fact that this intervention
must constantly be repeated suggests that the position of mastery of the
international community is always contingent and unstable. In the next
chapter, I want to suggest that the dream of humanitarian intervention
holds out the promise of mourning this loss of unity, this separation
from the Real, in a manner far less deadly than that offered by declar-
ing a war on terror or other paranoid fantasies.

6　Dreams of human rights

To conclude a book about humanitarian intervention in the aftermath of the September 11, 2001 attacks on the United States feels a little like taking 'still the last train after the last train – and yet [being] late to an end of history'.[1] This sense of the end of an epoch was certainly the mood in which human rights warrior Michael Ignatieff wrote his widely circulated article entitled 'Is the Human Rights Era Ending?', published in the *New York Times* in February 2002.[2] For Ignatieff, 'the question after September 11 is whether the era of human rights has come and gone'.[3] In particular, Ignatieff fears that we are witnessing the end of 'the era of humanitarian intervention in Bosnia, Kosovo and East Timor'.[4] The attacks on the towers of the World Trade Centre and the Pentagon in the USA are treated by many other international lawyers as marking a turning point, the end of a humane and secure era in world affairs. In the words of Michael Reisman, 'with the end of the Cold War, many in America and throughout the industrialized world came to take national security for granted'.[5] For Reisman, the acts of September 11 'shattered the world view and, quite possibly, the emotional foundation on which that sense of security rested'.[6] They were an attack on 'all peoples who value freedom and human rights' and as a result we have all been 'forced into a war of self-defense'.[7] Similarly, Thomas Franck has argued that the

---

[1] Jacques Derrida, *Specters of Marx: the State of the Debt, the Work of Mourning, and the New International* (New York, 1992), p. 15.

[2] Michael Ignatieff, 'Is the Human Rights Era Ending?', *The New York Times*, 5 February 2002.

[3] *Ibid.*　[4] *Ibid.*

[5] W. Michael Reisman, 'In Defense of World Public Order' (2001) 95 *American Journal of International Law* 833.

[6] *Ibid.*　[7] *Ibid.*

186

use of force by the USA against Afghanistan was lawful as an act of self-defense, or 'defensive self-preservation'.[8]

Costas Douzinas argues that, in a quite different sense, the era of humanitarian intervention itself meant the end of human rights.[9] For Douzinas, a significant shift occurs when rights 'are turned from a discourse of rebellion and dissent into that of state legitimacy'.[10] While on the one hand the appeal to human rights is used to undermine the legitimacy of 'rogue', 'failed' or target states in the context of intervention, that appeal also serves at the same time to authorise or legitimise the actions of those powerful states who collectively act as the 'international community'. Thus the revolutionary potential of human rights is radically circumscribed when rights become an apology for state violence.

This chapter uses these disparate notions of the end of human rights as a point of departure, to reflect upon what, if anything, has been lost in the move from 'the era of humanitarian intervention' to an international relations dominated by a war on terror. I explore the possibilities offered by humanitarian intervention for achieving justice, possibilities that are foreclosed by an international relations ordered around the need to fight all-powerful enemies. While the narrative of humanitarian intervention attempts to secure the boundaries between the international community and its others, the figure of the human rights victim works to unsettle that imaginative geography. Intervention in the name of humanitarianism prohibits this figure from becoming the refugee, a claimant for justice and sanctuary in the name of humanity. Yet as we will see, this suffering figure haunts the texts of international lawyers – the demands made by her of the international community in the name of justice cannot be contained by the official narratives of intervention.

The end of the human rights era?

To what extent did the adoption of humanitarian intervention as a basis for justifying military action serve human rights ends? Certainly it is difficult to read detailed accounts of the slaughter and atrocities committed in Rwanda in 1994, Bosnia and Herzegovina during 1995, or East Timor in 1999, without being moved to support the use of force to protect human rights. In the language of the UN Secretary-General,

[8] Thomas M. Franck, 'Terrorism and the Right of Self-Defense' (2001) 95 *American Journal of International Law* 839.

[9] Costas Douzinas, *The End of Human Rights* (Oxford, 2000), pp. 129–41.

[10] *Ibid.*, p. 7.

'a deliberate and systematic attempt to terrorize, expel or murder an entire people must be met decisively with all necessary means, and with the political will to carry the policy through to its logical conclusion'.[11] Or as the Report of the Independent Inquiry into the Actions of the UN during the 1994 Genocide in Rwanda states, 'there can be no neutrality in the face of genocide'.[12] The use of force in response to violence and intimidation in places such as East Timor is in part an example of humanitarian impulses driving foreign policy and the actions of international organisations. Yet attention to the cultural and material effects of humanitarian intervention and post-intervention reconstruction suggests that we have not lost a human rights age with the emergence of a war on terror. As I have argued throughout this book, the performance of humanitarian intervention during the 1990s constrained any radical potential of human rights as the ends of intervention.

For instance, humanitarian intervention and post-conflict reconstruction has enabled continued material exploitation, and entrenched economic liberalisation. As I argued in Chapter 3, the narrative of intervention masks the involvement of international economic institutions and development agencies in shaping those societies that later erupt into humanitarian and security crises. The failure to explore the relationship between economic globalisation and insecurity means that the international community appears purely in the role of saviour and humanitarian when it intervenes militarily. Similarly, Chapter 4 showed that the post-intervention administration and reconstruction of territories by the international community in turn entrenches an unjust international economic order and a neocolonial mode of governance. Reading the texts of humanitarian intervention alongside those of post-conflict reconstruction reveals the dream of a world of sameness or, to adopt the language of free trade, harmonisation. In the 'Single Economic Space' of this imagined future, any national or indigenous differences, or technical barriers to trade, will be swept away by an all-powerful international community in its relentless march towards standardised regimes of privatisation, investment deregulation, intellectual property

[11] *Report of the Secretary-General Pursuant to General Assembly Resolution 53/35: the Fall of Srebrenica*, UN Doc A/54/549, 15 November 1999, para 502 (hereinafter Srebrenica report), http://www.unhchr.ch/Huridocda/Huridoca.nsf/TestFrame/ 4e8fe0c73ec7e4cc80256839003eeb04?Open document (accessed 24 July 2002).

[12] *Report of the Independent Inquiry into the Actions of the United Nations during the 1994 Genocide in Rwanda*, UN Doc S/1999/1257, 15 December 1999 (hereinafter Independent Inquiry Report), http://www.un.org/News/ossg/rwanda_report.htm (accessed 2 May 2002), p. 33.

protection, and limited health and safety regulations.[13] As with classical colonialism, the threatening underside of this dream of harmonisation is that, in its name, local or indigenous cultures are destroyed, resources are exploited and resistance is quashed. Thus while humanitarian intervention seems to promise a world in which self-determination and human rights will be privileged over national interests or imperial ambitions, we nonetheless see exploitation, domination, invasion and governance legitimised in its wake.

The narrating of humanitarian intervention has had conservative effects in another sense. This narrative involves the deployment of colonial stereotypes, according to which the native other is represented as in need of reform, protection, education and governance. The human rights victim is put on display for those who identify with the international community. As Rey Chow comments, 'the "Third World", as the site of the "raw" material that is "monstrosity", is produced for the surplus-value of spectacle, entertainment, and spiritual enrichment for the "First World".'[14] The narrative of humanitarian intervention relies upon colonial stereotypes of suffering natives or human rights victims as the pivot for establishing the identity of the heroic international community.[15] It exploits these victims as a resource with which to produce narratives about valuable selves and unified communities (national and international), and to make the relations underpinning the international order appear just and natural. The plot of these narratives masks the role played by international organisational priorities in contributing to humanitarian crises, the power relations that intervention effects and the exploitation enabled through the new regimes put in place post-intervention.

As I argued in Chapter 3, the performance of humanitarian intervention also operates to draw boundaries between 'us' and 'them' as a means of distancing the other, and locating suffering and violence elsewhere.

[13] The phrase 'Single Economic Space' has been adopted by officials of the Office of the High Representative of the international community in Bosnia-Herzegovina to describe their vision for the future of the country. See 'Speech by the High Representative, Paddy Ashdown at a workshop on the Single Economic Space', 14 June 2002, http://www.ohr.int/ohr-dept/presso/presssp/default.asp?content_id=8931 (accessed 30 July 2002); 'Statement by PDHR Don Nays on the Occasion of OHR Business Forum', 24 June 2002, http://www.ohr.int/ohr-dept/presso/presssp/default.asp?content_id=9145 (accessed 30 July 2002). See further the discussion in Chapter 4 above.

[14] Rey Chow, 'Violence in the Other Country: China as Crisis, Spectacle and Woman' in Chandra Talpade Mohanty, Ann Russo and Lourdes Torres (eds.), *Third World Women and the Politics of Feminism* (Bloomington, 1991), pp. 81–100, p. 81.

[15] See further the detailed argument in Chapter 5 above.

For example, Renata Salecl comments that Western media reporting of the war in Bosnia and Herzegovina focused on the image of women dressed in traditional, religious dress and wearing headscarves. Salecl comments that these photographs were often staged, and that women in traditional dress are not often seen on the streets of Bosnia. The function of such images was to re-establish racist cultural boundaries between 'us' (the civilised observers) and 'them' (the fighting savages).[16] For Salecl:

In this attitude of the observer, one encounters a desperate attempt to artificially create cultural differences: as if the most horrible thing for the observer is the recognition that the 'other' (the Muslim, for example) is too similar. It is similarity not difference that produces the need to distance oneself from the other.[17]

This attempt to draw distinctions between us and them works to erase the violence of practices authorised by the international community, such as aerial bombardment, economic sanctions or forced economic restructuring. In the texts of humanitarian intervention, the heroic subject is produced according to the logic of a narrative which legalises (or at least legitimises) the violence carried out in the name of the international community. This is not to condone the violent acts of those involved in committing rapes, murders, mutilations, torture and destruction in places subject to humanitarian intervention. Yet one of the effects of the ways in which the plot of intervention narratives develops is to condemn that violence, while legitimising or ignoring the violence conducted by the international community in the name of human rights.

The military strategies for conducting humanitarian warfare in the post-Cold War era contribute to this erasure of the violence of the international community. For instance, the refusal to provide official 'body counts' of those killed or injured during humanitarian intervention is a striking feature of many of those military actions.[18] As Margot Norris has argued, the censorship of activities of the Pentagon during the Gulf War (treated by at least some commentators as an early example of humanitarian intervention) made it impossible to specify the number of

[16] Renata Salecl, *The Spoils of Freedom: Psychoanalysis and Feminism after the Fall of Socialism* (London, 1994), p. 135.
[17] *Ibid.*
[18] Margot Norris, 'Military Censorship and the Body Count in the Persian Gulf War' (1991) *Cultural Critique* 223.

Iraqis killed in that conflict.[19] Instead, the Pentagon provided extremely detailed information about attacks on 'hard' targets such as weapons, machines and infrastructure, while refusing to provide or verify information about the damage done to Iraqi soldiers and civilians.[20] Norris argues that it was the desire to censor information about the wounded and dead bodies of Iraqis – 'the control of necrology' – that was behind the extraordinary degree of influence exercised by the Pentagon over media attempts to report the war.[21] Philip Knightley has argued that a similar degree of control by NATO commanders over the reporting of the military intervention in Kosovo meant that war correspondents effectively became part of the military propaganda machine in that conflict.[22] This was further enabled by the nature of the NATO intervention – since it was conducted 'entirely from the air by means of a high-altitude bombing campaign...no-one except the victims really knew what was happening on the ground'.[23] Knightley describes correspondents 'either gathering at NATO headquarters or clustered along the borders of those countries surrounding Kosovo [trying] to peer over'.[24] This censorship contributes to a form of 'technological utopianism', based on 'an illusion that a ludic substitute for war has already been discovered, and that technology has ushered in a new Enlightenment in which a set of rational and logical strategies designed to disarm the enemy...can be implemented with weapons that greatly minimize, if not totally eliminate, human killing'.[25] Humanitarian intervention conducted as 'virtual war' may contribute to this belief that our violence is clean and surgical, while their violence is cruel and destructive.[26] Indeed, our 'targets' are converted into something other than flesh and blood as part of the technologies that enable warfare to be conducted so apparently safely and efficiently. As Michael P. Clark suggests:

More traditional forms of censorship that simply suppressed disturbing images of the battlefield have been rendered obsolete by the military use of video images of targets that convert the object into information as a condition of the violence directed toward it. Sighting the target and censoring its reality become one with the technology that transmits its image...This technology, used so extensively

---

[19] *Ibid.*, 224.   [20] *Ibid.*

[21] See the discussion of complaints by war correspondents in Norris, 'Military Censorship', 228–30.

[22] Philip Knightley, 'Fighting Dirty', *Guardian Weekly*, 30 March–5 April 2000, p. 23.

[23] *Ibid.*   [24] *Ibid.*   [25] Norris, 'Military Censorship', 231.

[26] On the NATO intervention in Kosovo as 'virtual war', see Michael Ignatieff, *Virtual War: Kosovo and beyond* (London, 2001).

during the Gulf War (and now in the bombing of Yugoslavia), allows the viewer at home to participate in the sighting and elimination of the enemy target without conveying even the mediated sense of presence and context experienced by the soldiers viewing the same image in their cockpits and tanks.[27]

This sense that our military victories in the name of human rights are bloodless is reproduced through the partial nature of the accountability mechanisms established as part of the post-intervention environment. The logic of war crimes trials is that they establish a respect for authorised forms of violence, while questioning those forms of violence that are outlawed by the international community.[28] This logic has meant that the practices of warfare that are used by militarily powerful states, such as aerial bombardment, are not outlawed by the laws of war.[29] Bombing campaigns must instead be conducted according to norms of international humanitarian law. These norms of air war merely require attackers to direct their actions against broadly defined 'military objectives' rather than civilian objects, and to ensure that the risk of endangering civilians and civilian objects is not disproportionate to the military advantage to be gained by the attack.[30] The utilitarian language of this balancing test reveals that the lives of civilians can be sacrificed if the value of their existence is weighed against the importance of 'military objectives' and found wanting. The nature of this calculation is even more striking in cases of humanitarian intervention, where protection of these 'civilian objects' is the declared purpose of the military

---

[27] Michael P. Clark, 'The Work of War after the Age of Mechanical Reproduction' in Michael Bibby, *The Vietnam War and Postmodernity* (Amherst, 1999), pp. 17–47 at p. 28.

[28] Simon Chesterman, 'Never Again … and Again: Law, Order, and the Gender of War Crimes in Bosnia and beyond' (1997) 22 *Yale Journal of International Law* 299. This quarantining of 'our' actions from reflection is undergoing a challenge as a result of the move towards using humanitarian justifications as a basis for intervention. While major human rights NGOs such as Amnesty International and Human Rights Watch have not been willing to question the use of human rights rhetoric in justifications for intervention, both Amnesty International and Human Rights Watch have prepared detailed reports documenting the breaches of international humanitarian law by NATO during its bombing campaign. Amnesty International, *'Collateral Damage' or Unlawful Killings? Violations of the Laws of War by NATO during Operation Allied Force* (2000); Human Rights Watch, *Civilian Deaths in the NATO Air Campaign* (2000).

[29] For a history of the colonial fantasy that 'punishment from the air', 'bombing the savages' or 'control without occupation' has a moral purpose, see Sven Lindqvist, *A History of Bombing* (London, 2001). The book is constructed as a 'labyrinth', with twenty-two entrances to 'ways of reading' the book. See particularly the 'ways of reading' entitled 'Bombing the Savages' and 'The Bomb on Trial'.

[30] See further W. J. Fenrick, 'Targeting and Proportionality during the NATO Bombing Campaign against Yugoslavia' (2001) 12 *European Journal of International Law* 489.

action being undertaken.[31] Yet it has proved difficult for victims alleging violations of even these limited norms to bring those engaged in humanitarian intervention before war crimes tribunals or human rights courts.

To take one example, several human rights NGOs, legal teams and international bodies have criticised the conduct of the NATO bombing campaign, Operation Allied Force, carried out against the Federal Republic of Yugoslavia from 24 March to 10 June 1999. During that seventy-eight-day campaign, NATO dropped more than 25,000 bombs, killing an estimated 500 Yugoslav civilians. These deaths resulted partly from the use of cluster bombs, attacks on targets in densely populated urban areas, attacks on mobile targets, attacks on civilian targets and the practice of dropping bombs from extremely high altitudes to avoid pilot deaths.[32] Attempts to bring the issue of whether this conduct violated international humanitarian law before international judicial fora have been remarkably unsuccessful. The Office of the Prosecutor (OTP) at the International Criminal Tribunal for the Former Yugoslavia (ICTY) received 'numerous requests that she investigate allegations that senior political and military figures from NATO countries committed serious violations of international humanitarian law' during the bombing campaign.[33] On 2 June 2000, the Chief Prosecutor announced to the Security Council her decision not to initiate an investigation of the claims that NATO had engaged in serious violations of international humanitarian law in the former Yugoslavia, based upon the report of a committee she had established to investigate the matter.[34] Commentators have criticised this decision as one designed to 'legitimate NATO's war on Yugoslavia', and have unfavourably compared the reasoning in the OTP report with the careful case made substantiating the allegations by NGOs such as Amnesty International and Human Rights Watch.[35]

[31] Michael Bothe, 'The Protection of the Civilian Population and NATO Bombing on Yugoslavia: Comments on a Report to the Prosecutor of the ICTY' (2001) 12 *European Journal of International Law* 531 at 535.

[32] Human Rights Watch, *Civilian Deaths*.

[33] Final Report to the Prosecutor by the Committee Established to Review the NATO Bombing Campaign against the Federal Republic of Yugoslavia, para 1, available at http://www.un.org/icty/pressreal/nato061300.htm (accessed 20 July 2002).

[34] *Ibid.*, para 91 (recommendation by the Committee 'that no investigation be commenced by the OTP in relation to the NATO bombing campaign or incidents occurring during the campaign').

[35] Michael Mandel, 'Politics and Human Rights in International Criminal Law: our Case against NATO and the Lessons to Be Learned from It' (2001) 25 *Fordham International*

Similarly, the families of victims of the controversial NATO bombing of the television station Radio Televizije Srbije (RTS) in Belgrade, in which sixteen civilians were killed and sixteen more seriously injured, attempted to have that matter heard before the European Court of Human Rights. Their application was brought against the seventeen member states of NATO which are also Contracting States to the European Convention on Human Rights (ECHR).[36] It argued that the bombing of the RTS headquarters violated Articles 2 (right to life), 10 (freedom of expression) and 13 (right to an effective remedy) of the ECHR.[37] The Grand Chamber of the Court declared the case inadmissible, on the grounds that the impugned act did not take place within the territorial jurisdiction of the respondent states as required under Article 1. The Court distinguished this case from situations where a respondent State had invaded and occupied a territory, had effective control over its inhabitants and exercised all or some of the public powers normally exercised by the government.[38] It held that the Convention operates: 'in the legal space of the Contracting States. The FRY clearly does not fall within this legal space. The Convention was not designed to be applied throughout the world, even in respect of the conduct of Contracting States.'[39]

In this sense, those Contracting States that carry out their military campaigns through aerial bombardment are less accountable for human rights violations than are those Contracting States who have to rely upon military occupation to gain control over a territory and its inhabitants. This poses a serious limitation on the capacity of the European human rights system to constrain the abuses perpetrated by European states outside the territories over which those states exercise what the law recognises as 'effective control'. As the historian of bombing Sven Lindqvist has shown, European powers long ago realised that bombing allowed them to exercise 'control without occupation' to pacify 'restless

Law Journal 95 at 97. See also Andreas Laursen, 'NATO, the War over Kosovo, and the ICTY Investigation' (2002) 17 American University International Law Review 765. For the Human Rights Watch and Amnesty Reports, see above n. 28.

36 Bankovic, Stojanovic, Stoimenovski, Joksimovic and Sukovic v. Belgium, the Czech Republic, Denmark, France, Germany, Greece, Hungary, Iceland, Italy, Luxembourg, the Netherlands, Norway, Poland, Portugal, Spain, Turkey and the United Kingdom, Application no. 52207/99, Admissibility Decision, 12 December 2001, available at http://hudoc.echr.coe.int/ hudoc/ViewRoot.asp?Item=0&Action=Html&X=806064118&Notice= 0&Noticemode=&RelatedMode=0 (accessed 20 July 2002).

37 European Convention for the Protection of Human Rights and Fundamental Freedoms, opened for signature 4 November 1950, Rome, 213 UNTS 222 (entered into force 3 September 1953) ('ECHR').

38 Ibid., para 71.   39 Ibid., para 80.

natives' – for instance in the French and Spanish bombing of their re-
spective parts of Morocco in 1912, and in Britain's bombing of India's
northwest in 1915, Egypt in 1916, Afghanistan and Somalia in 1919,
Trans-Jordan in 1920, and Iraq in 1920.[40] It is only those seeking to resist this form of imperial control who are not yet able to translate into
international law the realisation that 'the point of political action is not
to seize space, but to transform it'.[41]

In addition, the gathering of evidence for war crimes trials in the aftermath of humanitarian intervention is a performance that generates
meanings and allocates guilt and innocence. The reproduction on television and in photographs of images of the mass exhumation of bodies
from unmarked graves in Rwanda, the former Yugoslavia and East Timor
is accompanied by texts that secure the meanings to be made of these
bodies. The scene of recovery of buried bodies is always one of European
experts in front of a freshly dug pit. It is often followed by an image
of unnamed people in mourning, sometimes carrying photographs of
their relatives or friends. Just as the bodies of dead soldiers operated to
secure national communities in Europe and its colonies following World
War 1, the bodies of those civilians slaughtered by our enemies operate
to secure the international community in the era of peace-keeping and
military intervention.[42] Those mass graves are one site of the constitution of the international community. The serial, regular, unidentified
bodies recovered from those graves are made to represent a failure of
law and an absence of rights.

This pattern can be traced back to the founding texts of international
law. Internationalists relate the story of the birth of international law in
Western Europe as a triumph of reason and order over barbarism and religious intolerance.[43] In particular, this ordering effect of humanitarian
intervention derives from the use of the language of human rights to justify the use of force. The natural law tradition from which human rights
derives has long been used as a means of resolving the central problem
that defines modern international law – how are 'we' (Europeans/the

---

[40] Lindqvist, A History, sections 74, pp. 100–2.

[41] Steve Pile, 'Freud, Dreams and Imaginative Geographies' in Anthony Elliott (ed.), Freud
2000 (Melbourne, 1998), pp. 204–34 at p. 207.

[42] On the 'commemorative fate of the obscure masses of the nation's war dead' in
Britain and France following World War 1, see Benedict Anderson, The Spectre of
Comparisons: Nationalism, Southeast Asia and the World (London, 1998), pp. 51–7.

[43] David Kennedy, 'Images of Religion in International Legal Theory' in Mark Janis (ed.),
The Influence of Religion on the Development of International Law (Dordrecht, 1991), p. 137 at
pp. 138–9.

West/the international community) to recognise difference while still maintaining legal authority to rule a colony and acquire land?[44]

As Antony Anghie has shown, the natural law of jurists such as the Spanish theologian Francisco de Vitoria proved useful in establishing an overarching legal system premised on the notion that all societies, whether European or 'barbarian', were bound by a universal law expressed in Christian doctrine and the Roman law of nations.[45] Vitoria portrays the Spaniards and the peoples of the Americas (referred to by Vitoria as Indians) as the same, to the extent that both are capable of reason and thus of discerning the universal, secular natural law which Vitoria posits as founding relations between sovereigns. In this regime, 'natural law' is no longer treated as deriving from divine law, but rather as representing a universal system of law that is accessible to any peoples capable of reason. For Vitoria, Spaniards and Indians are different to the extent that Indians do not comply with the universal norms of the system, norms which now require the Indians to treat the Spanish invaders as 'ambassadors of the Christian peoples' and thus inviolable. The Indians engage in illicit violence when they repel the friendly advances and proselytising of these Christian ambassadors, so that 'any Indian resistance to Spanish presence is a violation of the law of nations'.[46] The Spanish are justified in waging perpetual war against the Indians in response to these illicit acts of violence. Thus Anghie comments that 'violence originates within Vitoria's system through the deviance of the Indian'.[47] The international legal order founded on the work of Vitoria is thus premised upon respect for the lawful forms of violence exercised by European ambassadors against natives.

The patterns that Anghie has identified in Vitoria's writing are employed in current legal and political texts about humanitarian intervention 'in the supposedly post-imperial world'.[48] In those texts, as in the older texts of natural law, lawful forms of violence originate through the 'deviance' of those against whom the international community decides to use force, today in the name of human rights. At the heart of the establishment of international law was, and is, the legitimacy of the violence exercised as sacrifice or punishment of those constituted as law's savage, barbaric, others. In this sense, the international community shares something with those national or 'tribal' communities against which it constitutes itself – the wounding and killing of

---

[44] Antony Anghie, 'Francisco de Vitoria and the Colonial Origins of International Law' (1996) 5 *Social and Legal Studies* 321 at 322.
[45] *Ibid.*   [46] *Ibid.*, 328.   [47] *Ibid.*   [48] *Ibid.*, 332.

its others as an organic and necessary part of its foundation. As Elaine Scarry has argued in her extraordinary meditation on the meaning of war, this is an essential part of war's telos.[49] This helps to explain the vehemence with which those who identify with or as the international community come to dismiss the leaders of 'rogue' or 'failed' national or tribal communities as less than human. That characterisation is necessary precisely because these communities in fact share that which the international community rejects as illegitimate: an originary violence deployed against those who are marked out on the grounds of race, ethnicity and gender. As David Campbell argues, 'the intensification of so-called ethnic and nationalist conflict in places such as Bosnia, while clearly horrific, is an exacerbation rather than an aberration of the logic behind the constitution of political community'.[50] The narrative of humanitarian intervention authorises and thus erases the violent foundations of the international community. The absence of representations of the wounded or dead bodies of our enemies, particularly when juxtaposed against detailed reporting of the bodies wounded by more 'primitive' acts of vicious ethnic cleansing, reassures us of the civility of our society and the barbarity of those others upon whom we have inflicted violence.

Finally, the perception that the international community is present in conflict situations as a protector of civilians can itself pose a threat to human rights if it is relied upon. An example of the damage caused to those who put their faith in the international community as a humanitarian protector when it fails to perform that role can be seen in the case of the Rwandan genocide. As I discussed in Chapter 3, the UN Assistance Mission in Rwanda (UNAMIR) was in place when the genocide began. The *génocidaires* began their mission by first killing ten Belgian peace-keepers guarding the Prime Minister. As they had anticipated, the response from Belgium, and ultimately the UN, was to order the withdrawal of most of the peace-keepers then in Rwanda. Even before this withdrawal began, the first priority for foreign governments, the UN and foreign companies once the genocide in that country began was to evacuate foreign workers, putting the lives of Rwandans at risk in the process. While in some cases members of UNAMIR did provide protection to civilians during massacres, there are also infamous instances

---

[49] Elaine Scarry, *The Body in Pain: the Making and Unmaking of the World* (New York, 1985).

[50] David Campbell, 'Violence, Justice, and Identity in the Bosnian Conflict' in Jenny Edkins, Nalini Persram and Véronique Pin-Fat (eds.), *Sovereignty and Subjectivity* (Boulder, 1999), pp. 21–37 at p. 23.

in which they failed to do so. Perhaps the most striking example of this is the incident at the Ecole Technique Officielle at Kicukiro, where UNAMIR troops were stationed.[51] During the early days of the genocide about 2,000 Rwandans had gathered there under the protection of about ninety Belgian soldiers. About a fifth of those seeking protection were children, and many of the Rwandans were suffering machete wounds. The school was surrounded by Rwandan militia and government forces. On 11 April, UNAMIR troops 'were ordered to regroup at the airport to aid the evacuation of European civilians' and obeyed.[52] In so doing, they knowingly abandoned the thousands of refugees who were left behind 'at the mercy of the waiting forces of the Interahamwe'.[53] Samantha Power notes:

Knowing they were trapped, several Rwandans pursued the jeeps, shouting, 'Do not abandon us!' The UN soldiers shooed them away from their vehicles and fired warning shots over their heads. When the peacekeepers had gone out through one gate, Hutu militiamen entered through another, firing machine guns and throwing grenades. Most of the 2,000 gathered were killed.[54]

As the Independent Inquiry Report recognises, this withdrawal 'caused pain to the Rwandan people' and damaged trust in the UN.[55] It was part of a broader pattern in which the US government and many European governments made evacuation of their nationals a priority. Perhaps most strikingly, France, Belgium and Italy sent soldiers to secure Kigali Airport just long enough to allow their personnel to evacuate by air. Those troops were withdrawn immediately after the evacuation was complete. As General Romeo Dallaire, the Canadian commander of UNAMIR, notes, 'Mass slaughter was happening, and suddenly there in Kigali we had the forces that we needed to contain it, and maybe even to stop it...Yet they picked up their people and walked away.'[56] Indeed, the UN Department of Peacekeeping Operations also ordered Dallaire to make evacuation of foreigners his priority.[57] The overall effect, as Power notes, was that 'in the three days during which some 4,000 foreigners were evacuated, about 20,000 Rwandans were killed'.[58]

---

[51] Independent Inquiry Report, p. 29.
[52] Samantha Power, 'Bystanders to Genocide: Why the United States Let the Rwandan Tragedy Happen', *The Atlantic Online*, September 2001,
http://www.theatlantic.com/issues/2001/09/power.htm, accessed 4 April 2002, 10.
[53] Independent Inquiry Report, p. 29.   [54] Power, 'Bystanders', 10.
[55] Independent Inquiry Report, p. 29.   [56] Power, 'Bystanders', 10.   [57] *Ibid.*, 9.
[58] *Ibid.*, 10.

The UN as an organisation in turn distinguished between protecting its 'international civilian staff' and abandoning 'national staff'. The Independent Inquiry found:

When the international civilian staff of the United Nations were evacuated, national staff were left behind. There is considerable bitterness among the [surviving] national staff about what is perceived as a double standard within the United Nations as to the safety of different groups of staff members...The United Nations regulations at the time precluded the evacuation of national staff. While the decisions taken at the time may have been in conformity with United Nations regulations, there can be no doubt of the damage caused by these rules to the trust between members of staff.[59]

The Independent Inquiry found that in Rwanda 'United Nations staff members may have been at greater risk than others as a result of their employment with the organization.'[60] This failure by the UN to protect its national staff was further exacerbated by the '*mistaken perception among national staff members in Rwanda that the United Nations would and could protect them*'.[61] As a result, the Independent Inquiry concluded:

The United Nations must be aware that its presence in conflict areas also raises among...civilians an expectation of protection which must be borne in mind when analyzing the means necessary to conduct an operation. Whether or not an obligation to protect civilians is explicit in the mandate of a peacekeeping operation, the Rwandan genocide shows that the United Nations must be prepared to respond to the perception and the expectation of protection created by its very presence.[62]

The fall of Srebrenica offers a similar story of the ways in which the narrative of humanitarian intervention can prove destructive for those who believe that military intervention promises a rescue mission rather than a spectacle. The UN sought to respond to the Serbian 'ethnic cleansing' during the war in Bosnia by, *inter alia,* establishing 'safe havens'. The concept of 'safe havens', 'security zones', protected areas or protected zones was one that emerged during the search for compromise between Member States as to the appropriate mandate for UNPROFOR.[63] Some of the more powerful states on the Security Council, such as France and the UK, did not want to expand the UNPROFOR mandate to allow direct military confrontation with Bosnian Serb troops, while other Member States sought to expand the mandate and to use force to resist Serb aggression. The 'safe haven' concept was proposed by humanitarian organisations

[59] Independent Inquiry Report, p. 30.   [60] *Ibid.*   [61] *Ibid.*, emphasis in original.
[62] *Ibid.*, p. 33.   [63] Srebrenica report, para 45.

such as the International Committee for the Red Cross, and was designed to 'protect threatened communities in their places of residence'.[64]

Srebrenica was to become such a 'protected zone'. On 13 March 1993, the UNPROFOR Commander in Bosnia and Herzegovina visited Srebrenica, then under siege from Bosnian Serb troops. He told local inhabitants that 'they were under United Nations protection and he would not abandon them'.[65] Security Council Resolution 819 (1993) adopted on 16 April demanded that 'all parties and others treat Srebrenica and its surroundings as a safe area which should be free from any armed attack or any other hostile act'. By Resolution 824 (1993), the Security Council acting under Chapter VII declared that 'Sarajevo and other such threatened areas, in particular the towns of Tuzla, Zepa, Gorazde, Bihac, and their surroundings should be treated as safe areas by all the parties concerned, and should be free from armed attacks and from any other hostile act' (para 3). In each case, UNPROFOR stated that it could not implement the resolution without agreement between the parties or resources to enforce the resolutions. To be successful, the policy of creating safe havens required either that the warring parties agreed to the creation of demilitarised zones where civilians could be protected, or that the UN had in place a military force that could defend these havens. Neither condition was in place.[66] On 11 July 1995, the Bosnian Serbs overran the safe area of Srebrenica. Over 4,000 refugees sought protection in the compound of the UN peace-keepers at Potocari – another 15,000 to 20,000 refugees were prevented from entering the compound but remained in its immediate vicinity. The majority of the men and boys of Srebrenica attempted to escape on foot to Bosnian-controlled territory. The UN peace-keepers were not able to protect the refugees or maintain control over the town. Over the next few days, the Bosnian Serbs deported women, children and the elderly from the UN compound to Bosnian-held territory. During the same period, they executed and

---

[64] *Ibid.*   [65] *Ibid.*, para 38.

[66] Security Council Resolution 836 (1993) appeared to remedy this to an extent. There the Security Council acting under Chapter VII extended the mandate of UNPROFOR to enable it 'to deter attacks against the safe areas' and 'to occupy some key points on the ground' (para 5) and authorised UNPROFOR to use force in self-defence 'in reply to bombardments against the safe areas by any of the parties or to armed incursion into them' (para 9). The Secretary-General has suggested that the absence of the words 'protect' or 'defend' in that resolution should be treated as 'essential' to understanding the scope of UNPROFOR's mandate in this respect. (Srebrenica report, para 79). Needless to say it is unlikely that the import of this semantic distinction was appreciated by those relying on UNPROFOR protection in the safe havens.

buried thousands of men and boys, while the UN negotiated with their military leaders.[67]

Those people in Srebrenica and Rwanda who sought sanctuary with the UN, only to find themselves abandoned to murderers and militias, had faith in the international community as saviours. Similarly, those East Timorese who in 1999 believed the UN assurances and posters promising 'UNAMET will stay after the vote' soon found that the UN as an institution had limited resolve to ensure their security in the face of violence.[68] It was only the commitment of individual UN staffers in Dili who refused to obey the instructions from headquarters to evacuate that prevented yet another situation of 'international staff' abandoning 'national' civilians sheltering in the UN compound. While civilians in Srebrenica and Rwanda who relied on the promise (or perception) of international protection may in any case have been slaughtered, it is possible that without these assurances of security and sanctuary they could have hidden elsewhere or taken other steps to escape. Thus in some ways the promise of humanitarian intervention may be more damaging to 'human rights victims' than grounding intervention on security or national interest. Both protectors and protected suffer when they believe that international intervention is a mission of salvation. As the UN Secretary-General states in his report on the fall of Srebrenica:

When the international community makes a solemn promise to safeguard and protect innocent civilians from massacre, then it must be willing to back its promise with the necessary means. Otherwise, it is surely better not to raise hopes and expectations in the first place, and not to impede whatever capability they may be able to muster in their own defence.[69]

These cultural and material effects suggest that much of the revolutionary potential of human rights was contained through the performance of humanitarian intervention in the 1990s. The practice of military intervention and of post-conflict reconstruction limited the opportunities to make use of the radical potential of human rights to subvert the established order of things. In this sense, we are not now at the end of the human rights era. A commitment to human rights has long ceased to be the foundation of the work of the UN and other international organisations,

---

[67] Srebrenica report, paras 239–393.

[68] UN posters are displayed at http://www.un.org/peace/etimor99/POSTERS/posters_bottom.htm, accessed 24 July 2002.

[69] Srebrenica report, para 504.

if it ever was.[70] Human rights activists and scholars were aware well before 11 September 2001 that human rights and self-determination were
not the priorities of powerful states.[71] Indeed, some commentators suggest that the growing acceptance of humanitarian intervention was itself the end of a process by which the politicisation of human rights
had transformed the humanitarian impulse which 'started out as an expression of empathy with common humanity...into a lever for strategic
aims drawn up and acted upon by external agencies'.[72] Following this
trend, even the recent 'war against terrorism' has to some extent been
characterised as humanitarian, with the United States government raising the human rights abuses of women and girls in Afghanistan as one
factor legitimising its military action.[73] According to Secretary of State
Colin Powell, 'the recovery of Afghanistan must entail the restoration of
the rights of Afghan women...The rights of the women of Afghanistan
will not be negotiable.'[74]

This institutionalised commitment to a narrow range of civil and political rights as the end of military and monetary intervention has shut
out other opportunities for dissenting from the established order or
achieving emancipatory ends. As Shelley Wright argues, 'in some ways
there is now *less* room for critique and analysis than there was in 1989
despite the powerful new voice that human rights have gained since
the end of the Cold War'.[75] Yet it would be simplistic for me to suggest
that we have not lost some possibilities for achieving justice with the
shift to the new wars against terror in the post-September 11 world. In
the next part, I want to explore the possibilities for justice and bases

[70] Philip Alston, 'The Myopia of the Handmaidens: International Lawyers and
Globalization' (1997) 8 *European Journal of International Law* 435.

[71] In this sense, Ignatieff's portrayal of the end of the human rights era following
11 September 2001 resembles Fukuyama's belated sense of the end of history. Derrida
notes that the loss of faith in a certain institutionalised Marxism faced many
Europeans in the 1950s, long before Fukuyama's experience of an 'end of history' with
the break-up of the Soviet Union in 1989. See Derrida, *Specters*, p. 15.

[72] David Campbell, 'The Road of Military Humanitarianism: How the Human Rights
NGOs Shaped the New Humanitarian Agenda' (2001) 23 *Human Rights Quarterly* 678 at
700.

[73] See US Department of State, *Report on the Taliban's War against Women*, 17 November
2001, http://www.state.gov/g/drl/rls/c4804.htm (accessed 27 February 2002); Laura Bush,
First Lady, Radio Address to the Nation, *The Taliban's War against Women*, 17 November
2001, http://www.state.gov/g/drl/rls/rm/2001/6206.htm (accessed 27 February 2002).

[74] Secretary Colin L. Powell, *Afghan Women*, Remarks at the Eisenhower Executive Office
Building, Washington, 19 November 2001, http://www.state.gov/secretary/rm/2001/
6229.htm (accessed 27 February 2002).

[75] Shelly Wright, *International Human Rights, Decolonisation and Globalisation: Becoming
Human* (London, 2001), p. 212.

for resistance that were offered by the legal narratives of humanitarian intervention.

The haunting of humanitarian intervention

As I argued in Chapter 3, humanitarian intervention narratives work to reassure the international community that there is a differentiated other, and to locate this other 'somewhere else, outside'.[76] The call made in response to images of suffering in distant lands is not to admit those who have suffered abuses as refugees, but rather to intervene militarily and prevent exodus.[77] The notion that the suffering or chaotic other is located elsewhere is reinforced through the act of intervention – we use force to maintain 'safe havens' or to protect (local) civilians at home, while at the same time evacuating foreigners perceived to be out of place in these crisis situations. The effect of military intervention is to keep a distance between those we wish to save and our own community – through intervention we seek to locate the other elsewhere.

This space of humanitarian intervention can be imagined as the kind of 'collective day-dream' that Edward Said saw reflected in the texts of Orientalism.[78] If we follow this suggestion that colonial texts evoke a dream-space, we find that the cartography produced by texts which attempt to map the boundaries between us and them, here and there, seems far less stable. Geographer Steve Pile suggests we explore further this 'analogy between the production of dream-space and the production of space as dream-like' through Sigmund Freud's writing about the work of dreams.[79] For Freud, the space of dreams is dynamic.[80] If we follow Freud's lead along the royal road, the space of a dream is not a screen upon which images are projected. Rather, dreams exist in dynamic networks of meaning.[81] In dreams, trains of thought and images move back and forth across paths within the unconscious, changing direction and appearance without warning. Pile argues that we should thus not treat the images in the daydream of colonialism as fixed, as if the space of the dream were a screen upon which the coloniser could project his fantasies of the colonised. Rather, these dream images are uncontrollable and unstable exchanges.

---

[76] Pile, 'Freud', p. 233.

[77] See the discussion in James C. Hathaway, 'The Single Superpower and the Future of International Law' (2000) 94 *American Society of International Law Proceedings* 67–9.

[78] Edward W. Said, *Orientalism* (London, 1991), p. 52, citing V. G. Kiernan, *Lords of Human Kind*, p. 131.

[79] Pile, 'Freud', p. 207.   [80] *Ibid.*, pp. 208–21.   [81] *Ibid.*, p. 220.

In order for the Orient to become the blank screen-space onto which Western fantasies can be projected, the West needs to establish connections, extending networks of meaning and power into worlds interior and exterior. However, these networks ruin the screen; the Orient cannot simply be the West's other, nor merely the result of the West's fantasies and internal conflicts.[82]

Similarly, in order to manage, exploit, govern, save or reconstruct the states subjected to humanitarian intervention, the international community has had to have a physical presence in such locations – as observers, as peace-keepers, as technical development assistants, as aid workers. This then creates a dynamic, two-way process – the traffic along the royal road between us and them, here and there, moves both ways. We have to avoid knowing this to preserve the sense of ourselves as coherent, unified, valuable. Yet this denial of intimacy, this attempt to localise the other, fails. As we will see, the other always leaves a trace, and returns to unsettle those communities that it founds.

The narratives of humanitarian intervention also attempt to achieve stability and security in a second way, through trying to fix the identity of those states that make up the 'international community'. As we saw in the cases of Bosnia-Herzegovina, Rwanda and East Timor, the involvement of the international community through military intervention or post-intervention reconstruction is represented as a response to local problems of violence, incapacity for self-government or tribalism. At stake in any representation of humanitarian crises and mass suffering is the self-image of the Western state, and now the international community, as sovereign, civilised, autonomous, powerful and humane. This self-constitution depends upon establishing a narrative in which the chaotic other is separate from the heroic self.

Both the cartographic and the narrative attempts to fix or determine the boundaries between self and other are disturbed by the human rights victim. The response to this figure is at the heart of what is unsettling, and thus productive, about humanitarian intervention narratives. The figure of the human rights victim occupies an uneasy place in intervention texts – at once other and same, object both of our pity and of our military strategies, whether suffering directly at the hands of our bombing or sanctions, or at the hands of the local men of violence while in internationally protected 'safe havens'. In particular, it is the human rights victims who do not stay in place who threaten to unsettle the imaginative geography of intervention. These errant victims

[82] *Ibid.*, p. 225.

make insistent claims upon the international community. While humanitarian intervention represents a response to the suffering of others through violence, I want to suggest that the haunting presence of these figures might operate less as a call to arms than as a plea for refuge or sanctuary.

One group of human rights victims who have refused to stay in place are those who have responded to the implicit or explicit promise of protection offered by the presence of UN peace-keepers at times of crisis. As we saw, the people of Srebrenica had faith in the promise that the international community would protect them. Rwandans sought sanctuary with UN peace-keepers, only to be abandoned to militias. Rwandans who worked for the UN sought protection from their employer, only to be told that UN regulations dictated that only foreign employees could be evacuated. In these instances, 'nationals' believed in the story that the international community was there to protect them. They demanded that these foreign troops rise to the occasion. Yet as General Dallaire commented of the goals of the US administration in the aftermath of the Rwandan genocide: 'My mission was to save Rwandans. Their mission was to put on a show at no risk.'[83]

As this comment suggests, even if humanitarian intervention is merely a spectacle, it nonetheless has to be performed by human beings. For those human beings it is not easy to walk away from the victims or the place of genocide. The example of Belgian troops shredding their blue berets on the tarmac of Kigali airport as they were evacuated attests to the ways in which expectations engender a response in those who find themselves asked to perform (or betray) the advertised role of international protector. In some cases, such as that of the UN officials who disobeyed the instructions to leave the UN compound in Dili and abandon the East Timorese sheltering there, the claims of those who seek sanctuary from human rights abuses cannot be denied.

A second group of errant human rights victims are the spectres who haunt those involved in performing (or failing to perform) the role of international humanitarian. One such person is Romeo Dallaire, a major general in the Canadian army when he was sent in 1993 to command UNAMIR. Dallaire, a man 'who believed wholeheartedly in the promise of humanitarian action' and in the UN as the embodiment of 'soldiering, service and sacrifice', fought hard to retain enough peace-keepers and resources to prevent the genocide occurring.[84] Instead, as

[83] Power, 'Bystanders', 18.   [84] Ibid., 3.

I discussed above, Dallaire's troops were re-deployed to protect the airport to allow the evacuation of foreigners, leaving Rwandans sheltering with UNAMIR soldiers to be massacred. He was left in Rwanda during the genocide with a force of only 270 troops.[85] Samantha Power explores the effect of this experience on Dallaire, in her powerful examination of the reasons why the USA and the UN did so little to respond to the Rwandan genocide once it began.[86] Dallaire became highly distressed upon his return to Canada after completing his mission in Rwanda. He found himself haunted by the images of bodies piled up, carried a machete around, and found sleeping difficult. His symptoms worsened when he was called to testify before the Rwandan war crimes tribunal. Dallaire's superiors told him that 'he would have to choose between leaving the "Rwanda business" behind him or leaving his beloved armed forces'.[87] Dallaire chose the latter, and was discharged from the Canadian military suffering 'post-traumatic stress disorder'. Power writes:

Dallaire had always said, "The day I take my uniform off will be the day that I will also respond to my soul." But since becoming a civilian he has realized that his soul is not readily retrievable. "My soul is in Rwanda", he says. "It has never, ever come back, and I'm not sure it ever will." He carries the guilt of the genocide with him, and he feels that the eyes and the spirits of those killed are constantly watching him.[88]

'This spectral *someone other looks at us*, we feel ourselves being looked at by it' – for Derrida, it is this feature of the spectre which so disturbs us.[89] It is this which gives the spectre of the human rights victim its power to unsettle our identity. As Bhabha comments:

In the objectification of the scopic drive there is always the threatened return of the look; in the identification of the Imaginary relation there is always the alienating other (or mirror) which crucially returns its image to the subject; and in that form of substitution and fixation that is fetishism there is always the trace of loss, absence.[90]

This inability to keep the spirits of Rwandan victims in their place, and the unbearable nature of the reproach posed by the victim's look, is a striking theme of the stories of many Americans involved in the failure to respond to that genocide. For example, Prudence Bushnell, the US Deputy Assistant Secretary of State, had just returned from Rwanda

---

[85] See the detailed discussion in Chapter 3 above.
[86] Power, 'Bystanders', 23.   [87] *Ibid.*   [88] *Ibid.*   [89] Derrida, *Specters*, p. 7.
[90] Homi K. Bhabha, *The Location of Culture* (London, 1994), p. 81.

when the genocide began, and was unable to persuade her colleagues in the US Administration to take the necessary action to respond to the genocide.[91] She in turn remains haunted both by the ghosts of the Rwandan dead and by accusing eyes.

Prudence Bushnell will carry Rwanda with her permanently. During the genocide, when she went walking in the woods near her home in Reston, Virginia, she would see Rwandan mothers cowering with their children behind the trees, or stacked in neat piles along the bike path. After the genocide, when the new President of Rwanda visited Washington and met Bushnell and others, he leaned across the table toward her, eyes blazing, and said, 'You, madame, are partially responsible for the genocide, because we told you what was going to happen and you did nothing.'[92]

For a long time, Bushnell was 'haunted by these memories and admonitions'.[93] Similarly, during the Rwandan genocide the image of African children became too much to bear for Donald Steinberg, the National Security Council staffer who managed the Africa directorate. '[Steinberg] had tacked the photos of two six-year-old African girls he had sponsored above his desk at the White House. But when he began seeing the bodies clogging the Kagera River, he had to take the photos down, unable to bear the reminder of innocent lives being extinguished every minute.'[94]

These haunting stories of regret and shame are testimony to the damage caused to the souls of those who betrayed the humanitarian promise of international law and institutions. For if the Orient was the daydream of Europe, so too Europe was the dream of its others. And in that process of creation of images and stories, those whom we misrecognise as our doubles do not always offer us back the reflection of ourselves that we wish to see. As Slavenka Drakulic wrote of Europe after the Bosnian genocide:

It seems to me that a part of the tragedy of the Bosnians lies in their belief that Europe is what it is not. Europe did not intervene, it did not save them, because there was no Europe to intervene. They saw a ghost. It was us, the Eastern Europeans, who invented 'Europe', constructed it, dreamed about it, called upon it. This Europe is a myth created by us, not only Bosnians, but other Eastern Europeans, too... Should we not ask, must we not ask, then, what is Europe after Bosnia?[95]

---

[91] Power, 'Bystanders', 7.   [92] Ibid., 23.   [93] Ibid.   [94] Ibid., 22.
[95] Slavenka Drakulic, 'Bosnia, or What Europe Means to Us' in Marjorie Agosin, A Map of Hope: Women's Writing on Human Rights (London, 1999), pp. 223–9 at pp. 228–9.

Yet these ghost stories also suggest that the human rights victim is the figure that can hold the international community to the promise of human rights. This figure is haunting precisely because it embodies a memory of the trauma of what was done to the other to secure a self for the West. As Derrida shows us, the return of such spectres gives us the opportunity to learn from them about justice.

If he loves justice at least, the 'scholar' of the future, the 'intellectual' of tomorrow should learn it and from the ghost. He should learn to live by learning not how to make conversation with the ghost but how to talk with him, with her, how to let them speak or how to give them back speech, even if it is in oneself, in the other, in the other in oneself: they are always *there*, specters, even if they do not exist, even if they are no longer, even if they are not yet. They give us to rethink the 'there' as soon as we open our mouths.[96]

According to Derrida, we can exorcise the threat that such spectres represent, not 'in order to chase away the ghosts', but rather so that they may 'come back alive, as *revenants* who would no longer be *revenants*, but as other *arrivants* to whom a hospitable memory or promise must offer welcome'.[97] It is just such an *arrivant* – the refugee – who most insistently refuses to stay in place. It is the figure of the refugee that most clearly unsettles the comforting separation between us and them, here and there, that humanitarian intervention tries to maintain. Many instances in which humanitarian intervention has been invoked have been explicitly described in terms of the need to avert the threat of refugee 'flows'. Indeed, the desire to avert refugee 'flows' has been explicitly treated by the Security Council as one factor contributing to the perception of a threat to the peace and justifying the use of force in cases of internal conflict and humanitarian crisis. The feminine imagery of fluidity evokes well the threat that refugees are imagined as posing to the project of forming bounded, solid, stable nation-states.[98]

For example, in Security Council Resolution 688 (1991) responding to the repression of the Kurds in Northern Iraq, the Security Council expressed its grave concern at 'the repression of the Iraqi civilian population in many parts of Iraq, including most recently in Kurdish-populated areas, which led to a massive flow of refugees towards and across international frontiers and to cross-border incursions which threaten

---

[96] Derrida, *Specters*, p. 176.   [97] *Ibid.*, p. 175.
[98] On the feminine property of fluids, see further Luce Irigaray, *This Sex Which Is Not One* (trans. Catherine Porter, Ithaca, 1985), p. 118.

international peace and security in the region'. As Simon Chesterman observes, it is the flow of refugees and cross-border incursions that are perceived as posing a threat to peace and security.[99] The preamble of Security Council Resolution 918 (1994) establishing secure humanitarian areas in Rwanda also refers to the Council's deep concern at 'the massive exodus of refugees to neighbouring countries'. Security Council Resolution 841 (1993) establishing an economic and weapons embargo against Haiti lists the 'unique and exceptional circumstances' that had led the Security Council to conclude that the situation in Haiti posed a threat to peace and security, including the creation of 'a climate of fear of persecution and economic dislocation which could increase the number of Haitians seeking refuge in neighbouring Member States'.[100] The preamble of Security Council Resolution 940 (1994) authorising the establishment of a multinational force to restore the legitimately elected President and authorities of the Government of Haiti also expressed the Security Council's grave concern at the 'desperate plight of Haitian refugees'. These Haitian refugees arriving by boat in the USA posed a political threat for the US administration, and certainly motivated the actions taken by the US government in supporting and leading the multinational force.[101] Finally, Simon Chesterman suggests that 'concern about a refugee crisis' was a factor in Australia's decision to push for a multinational force to restore peace and security in East Timor in 1999.[102] As these Security Council resolutions make clear, refugee flows are now themselves characterised as a threat to peace and security.

Some refugee lawyers see the new enthusiasm for humanitarian intervention as linked to the decline in the commitment to international refugee law on the part of industrialised states.[103] Opposition to accepting refugees has grown throughout Europe, and in the United States and Australia. In the post-Cold War era, industrialised states have emphasised the need to address the causes of involuntary migration. International policy has in turn begun to focus on protection of those at risk within the state. Even the Office of the UN High Commissioner for Refugees (UNHCR), the international agency whose role it is to oversee

---

[99] Simon Chesterman, *Just War or Just Peace? Humanitarian Intervention and International Law* (Oxford, 2001), p. 132. As Chesterman notes there, this is also emphasised in the statements of most states voting for the resolution stressing that the flow of refugees into neighbouring countries was the key security issue posed by the situation.

[100] Security Council Resolution 918 (1994), preamble.

[101] Chesterman, *Just War*, pp. 152–5.   [102] *Ibid.*, p. 150.

[103] Hathaway, 'The Single Superpower', 67.

the implementation of international refugee law, has now been 'repositioned'. States have put 'pressure on UNHCR to condone premature refugee repatriation, predicated on the potential for the delivery of internal "protection".'[104] Related to this latter development is the link to intervention as a means of responding to displacement of peoples. If we think about intervention at least partly in the context of post-Cold War refugee politics, then part of what is at stake is the need to avoid being confronted by the 'refugee'.[105] We prefer to contain these endangered foreigners, these distant strangers with whom we nonetheless feel intimate due to the televised images of their suffering, in 'safe' havens. We return them to war zones prematurely, because, we argue, they will be 'protected' there by the international community. There are some situations in which there may be security or humanitarian reasons to seek to prevent mass exodus. For instance, this seems to have been the view of members of the Security Council in supporting the notion of 'safe havens' in Bosnia and Herzegovina, where the aim of the Serbs was precisely to 'depopulate' areas or ethnically cleanse territories in order to resettle them. In such situations, the international community may be reluctant to support these practices of ethnic cleansing or depopulation by encouraging victims of abuses to seek refuge outside the territory in question. Yet I want to suggest that the perception of refugees as a threat to peace and security is also a response to the failure of these human rights victims to know their place.

The refugee faces us as a reminder that the place of the other is not 'out there' but very much 'in here', central to the way in which the image of ourselves is constituted. We exclude the refugee, the stranger, from our nation because we want to protect a stable, unitary sense of identity. Yet this foreigner is always already a part of that very identity. In modernity, the subject's identity is structured through its relations to the nation-state, and one of the 'others' against whom the nation is formed is that of the foreigner, the stranger. Thus the subject as citizen has as one of its doubles the alien, or the refugee. For the law, the refugee represents this stranger in its most threatening form, because the refugee seeks to be recognised by the law, and thus to remind the law, and through it the subject, of the repressed otherness at the foundation of identity. As Giorgio Agamben suggests, 'the refugee represents such a disquieting element in the order of the nation-state

---

[104] *Ibid.*, 68.   [105] *Ibid.*, 67.

...primarily because...it brings the originary fiction of sovereignty to crisis'.[106] Through the claims or demands of these refugees from violence, we are confronted with the spectre of a suffering other who does not stay at home, who unsettles our sense of safety and separateness. Their arrival at the borders of the nation-state

is experienced as the symptom of the trauma, as the return of the repressed, the sign of the lack in the heart of the citizen. The exclusion of foreigners is...constitutive of national identity [and] human subjectivity. In asking to be recognised, refugees bring back the exclusion and repression at law's foundation, and demand of us to accept the difficulty we have to live with the other in us, to live as an other.[107]

The law 'uses a number of strategies of disavowal and denial in an attempt to shelter subjectivity and community from the recognition of [this] constitutive trauma'.[108] Through mechanisms that include humanitarian intervention, the law avoids facing or acknowledging refugees and their claims, and thus 'denies the traumatic object facing it'.[109] The more violent and irrational aspects of humanitarian intervention are a response to this sense of threat. Narratives of humanitarian intervention resolve anxieties produced by the threatening sense of closeness to the other that is the effect of images of suffering. We are presented with images of these neighbours whose suffering we 'know' intimately through the visions on our television screens, but the logic of intervention does not require us to welcome them into our 'home' as a sanctuary. The violence of intervention operates as a strategy for ensuring that the otherness which these strangers represent is kept in its place. Intervention ensures that the refugee is prevented from even presenting herself to the law. As soon as the potential for exodus is recognised, the refugee-to-be is prevented from leaving and is then 'protected', at least in theory, by humanitarian intervention. We refuse to recognise the part that such acts of violent exclusion play in constituting our identities as modern subjects of Western states, by seeking to avoid coming face to face with this stranger. Through intervention, the other is restored to an external location – boundaries are shored up, it is safe to feel compassion again. How might international law respond to the claims of the human rights

---

[106] Giorgio Agamben, *Means without End: Notes on Politics* (trans. Vincenzo Binetti and Cesare Casarino, Minneapolis, 2000), p. 21.

[107] Douzinas, *The End of Human Rights*, p. 357.   [108] *Ibid.*, p. 357.   [109] *Ibid.*, p. 364.

victim if it were not engaged in this frantic attempt to secure identity against 'otherness', to repress our loss of the (m)other?

The space of human rights

I have suggested throughout this book that the discourse of humanitarian intervention is grounded in the Imaginary. In particular, the fantasy of human rights institutes 'a psychical scene in which *all* bodies are invested with rights'.[110] As William MacNeil has shown, the 'universality' of human rights 'solicits a sense of One-ness among the many, in which corporeal boundaries are blurred and bodily borders dissolved. Thus, this fantasy promotes, not difference (as some other scenes do), but sameness: specifically, a shared identity among all rights-bearers, each having the same claim to the procedural safeguards and substantive entitlements which rights grant.'[111] As with the 'oceanic feeling' that Freud explores in his discussion of religion, the promised universality of human rights creates the feeling 'as of something limitless, unbounded'.[112] It is this sense of an identity merged in unity or wholeness which gives human rights its energy.

The figure of the victim of human rights abuses is a representative of the universal rights-holder. In this sense we recognise ourselves in this figure – our sense of 'One-ness among the many' is premised upon a shared identity which invokes our affection or compassion when confronted with the image of the suffering victim. Yet as I argued in Chapter 5, the fetishised nature of the human rights victim also potentially invokes difference – here is a subject that is alien, external, foreign and threatening. The dependence on this figure of the human rights victim about whom we feel so ambivalent gives the discourse of humanitarian intervention its productivity for those who identify with the heroic subject of the international community. The human rights victim as fetish refers back 'through displacements of the signifier, to vulnerable or highly charged areas in the social fantasy that produced [this figure]'.[113] Because the narrative of humanitarian intervention not only disavows the trauma of loss, but also commemorates

---

[110] William MacNeil, 'Law's *Corpus Delicti*: the Fantasmatic Body of Rights Discourse' (1998) 9 *Law and Critique* 37 at 48.

[111] *Ibid.*, 49.

[112] Sigmund Freud, 'Civilization and its Discontents' in James Strachey (ed.), *The Standard Edition of the Complete Psychological Works of Sigmund Freud*, Volume XXI (London, 1961), pp. 64–145 at p. 64.

[113] Laura Mulvey, *Fetishism and Curiosity* (London, 1996), p. 10.

or mourns that thing which is thought to be missing, it 'stays in touch with its original traumatic real and retains a potential access to its own historical story'.[114]

Is it possible to make a different use of this 'potential access' to the 'original traumatic real' that is offered by the narrative of humanitarian intervention? How might we rewrite the demands of justice in the era of globalisation in a way that builds on the acceptance and mourning of the loss or lack memorialised in the body of the human rights victim? My approach to thinking about this draws on the work of Jeanne Schroeder. For Schroeder, (hetero)sexuality represents two positions that we can take to respond to loss.[115] 'We are masculine when we try to deny castration and feminine when we accept castration.'[116] More specifically, the masculine subject attempts to deny that loss or castration ever occurred.[117] One strategy involves telling himself the story: 'Castration has occurred, but (thank God) it was not me who was castrated but someone else. I still possess the phallus. It must be the feminine who lost it.'[118]

This strategy gives rise to 'the fear of having to confront one's own castration, or even worse, the fear that one will not be able to keep up appearances so that other men will learn that [one] is castrated'.[119] This requires that the feminine be exiled. 'If she represents the castration that men try to deny, she must be put out of sight.'[120] It is this response which I would argue is performed in the violent rejection of refugees, and in those versions of humanitarian intervention which are premised upon keeping potential refugees in their 'safe' havens, out of our way. This hostile response targets human rights victims because they are a reminder of the trauma of difference, and of the inherent vulnerability of the Western subject and the international community.

In Schroeder's schema, the response of the feminine to loss is quite different. 'If we are masculine when we try to deny castration, we are feminine when we accept castration, loss and negativity...The feminine acceptance of castration is the understanding that we are no longer and can never again be self-sufficient, complete, and whole by ourselves.'[121]

While this can lead to depression, it also offers a way out of the vicious circle of violence and rejection instituted by the denial and fear of loss.

[114] *Ibid.*, p. 5.
[115] Jeanne Lorraine Schroeder, 'Juno Moneta: on the Erotics of the Marketplace' (1997) 54 *Washington and Lee Law Review* 995 at 1009.
[116] *Ibid.*   [117] *Ibid.*, 1012.   [118] *Ibid.*   [119] *Ibid.*, 1019.   [120] *Ibid.*, 1020.
[121] *Ibid.*, 1015.

The symbolic order tries to abject the feminine object by exiling her. But by being located at least partly in the real, the feminine opens up the possibility of escape from the symbolic order (i.e., freedom). It is true that the feminine, as the acceptance of castration, can be the position of inertia – depression. But as Freud taught, it is the acceptance of loss which enables us to mourn. And it is only mourning which allows us to bury the dead, and move on.[122]

I want to suggest that human rights discourse offers resources for attempting to create a universalist ethic that is not premised upon a denial of difference or a nostalgia for a lost, imagined wholeness.[123] Human rights has the potential to found an international law that is not limited to supporting the fantasy life of nations and the international community through recreating the violent exclusion of the alien or the foreign. Instead, as William MacNeil argues, 'rights actually give us something (the symptomatic identic support of a 'lack') rather than nothing (psychosis' lack of a lack) with which to image and reimagine the body', and thus the body politic.[124] In this sense, rights discourse can offer us a way to start the work of mourning, of moving on. However, this requires us to be able to accept the 'lack, gap and non-identity' which human rights memorialises.[125] In thinking about how we might do so, and thus respond differently to the claims of law's others, Costas Douzinas takes as a starting point Freud's dictum, 'if we detect foreignness in ourselves, we will not hound it outside of us'.[126] Rather than act out our desire to exclude that which threatens our perceived political unity, we can recognise the 'foreignness in ourselves'.

The refugee is within me, we are all refugees from another place, the unconscious for psychoanalysis…, which is not a *patria*, the place of the father, but a *matria*.[127]

Can we recognise this without feeling compelled to expel that other who reminds us of the violence of our exile from the motherland? For Michael Dillon, this is the key question for 'an international relations

---

[122] *Ibid.*, 1020.

[123] My development of a response to loss based on this 'feminine' position is a departure from Schroeder, who argues that neither the masculine nor the feminine response is to be valorised over the other – masculinity and femininity are simply two modes of failure: *ibid.* 1015. See also Salecl, *The Spoils of Freedom*, p. 116 ("'Masculine" and "feminine" are not the two species of the genus Man but rather two modes of the subject's *failure* to achieve the full identity of Man. "Man" and "woman" together do not form a whole, since each of them is already in itself a failed whole').

[124] MacNeil, 'Laws *Corpus Delicti*', 56.   [125] *Ibid.*

[126] Douzinas, *The End of Human Rights*, p. 365.   [127] *Ibid.*

that takes the "inter" or betweenness seriously' – how to develop communities that can respond to the 'call for the inherent Otherness of human being to be made welcome politically'.[128] For Dillon, this 'duty of hospitality' requires us to say 'not only how the stranger is to be received but also how the strangeness that haunts us as human beings is itself to be welcomed, or not'.[129] To suggest what this might mean for the dream of human rights, I want to finish with three images of mothers and children that appear in texts about war. In these texts we can trace a movement from action to stillness, from the wild violent refusal to face the fear of (and desire for) separation to the 'feminine' position of living with loss. We might also read this movement as one from the position of the male child to the position of mother; from the distance of vision to the intimacy of touch.

The first such image, one with which I opened this book, was broadcast in Australia in the terrible days following the announcement on 4 September 1999 that an overwhelming majority of East Timorese people had voted for independence from Indonesia in the UN-sponsored referendum. Australians watched images of Dili burning on their television screens, and read of women and children trying to seek refuge with the UN. One image shown repeatedly was particularly horrific. The scene was filmed at night, along the line of a barbed wire fence enclosing the UN compound in Dili. The image was one of desperate parents throwing their children over the barbed wire into the compound, trying to make sure that their children reached sanctuary. The bodies of some of the children caught on the barbed wire and hung there, while workers in the compound tried to help them down. This violent separation of children and parents was one of the images that provided the energy for hundreds of thousands of Australians to take to the streets, marching under banners proclaiming 'Indonesia out, peacekeepers in'.

The second image is from an article by *Guardian* newspaper war correspondent Maggie O'Kane.[130] The article explores the changes that came over O'Kane's perception and experience of war reporting after she had her first child. The story she relates, told by Vjolica Berisha, is of the aftermath of a massacre of women and children by two armed men that took place in the small town of Suva Reka, Kosovo, the day that NATO started its bombing campaign. Vjolica and her sister survived the

---

[128] Michael Dillon, 'The Sovereign and the Stranger' in Jenny Edkins, Nalini Persram and Véronique Pin-Fat, *Sovereignty and Subjectivity* (Boulder, 1999), pp. 117–40 at p. 135.

[129] *Ibid.*, pp. 134–5.

[130] Maggie O'Kane, 'I Feel the Madness More', *The Guardian Weekly*, 2–8 March 2000, p. 21.

cre, although between them they lost seven children, all murdered
their eyes. The two bereaved sisters were thrown onto a truck full
of corpses, the murderers thinking them dead. Vjolica tells of her sister's
grief at the death of her baby, and of the physical nature of her sister's
response to that loss:

As the truck took off she looked across at her sister, Shyreta, who still had her
dead two-year-old baby cradled in her arms. 'It was like she couldn't bear to put
him down. She was holding on to him until the very last minute. Shyreta saw
I was alive as well and said, "I am going to jump. If I die jumping it doesn't
matter because I am dead already inside"'.

None of her four children had survived. Vjolica remembers watching her sister
gently lay down the body of her baby – a small corpse in a pile of grown-up
blood. Then they jumped.[131]

For Maggie O'Kane this is the image that haunts her the most after ten
years as a war correspondent – 'a mother clinging for those last seconds
to the body of her two-year-old. The agony of watching your child die
and not being able to protect it.'[132] O'Kane, writing from the position
of mother, does not make of this a reason for military intervention,
although she recounts the welcome she as a foreign European received
that day, as if she had personally liberated Kosovo. Instead, she weaves
it into a story about treasuring the small moments of joy with her own
son – 'The joy of being alive on an icy Belfast day by the River Lagan,
and still having a child to hold.'[133]

This second image of mothers and children in war does not stage the
separation of mother and child as something that is linked to the need
for violent intervention. Rather, it stages that separation from the position of the mother, and thus I think does something slightly different
with it. The meanings made of the images of the children in East Timor
involved dealing with the haunting nature of separation by calling for
action. Here, O'Kane sits with a mother, calls up her grief, and does not
allow us to escape through action. Her story reminds us of the joys of
living, of the ways in which we are forever linked to the bodies of our
children. There is no final separation here in the way feared and desired
in the texts of the law.

The third image is a passage from the novel *Anil's Ghost*.[134] Michael
Ondaatje here eloquently speaks the desire for a reconciliation with our
lost mother. It is written in the voice of Gamini, a surgeon caught up

[131] *Ibid.*   [132] *Ibid.*   [133] *Ibid.*
[134] Michael Ondaatje, *Anil's Ghost* (London, 2001).

in the civil war in Sri Lanka, who spends his days and nights repairing the bodies that the war has torn apart.

When Gamini finished surgery in the middle of the night, he walked through the compound into the east buildings, where the sick children were. The mothers were always there. Sitting on stools, they rested their upper torso and head on their child's bed and slept holding the small hands. There were not too many fathers around then. He watched the children, who were unaware of their parents' arms. Fifty yards away in Emergency he had heard grown men scream for their mothers as they were dying. 'Wait for me!' 'I know you are here!' This was when he stopped believing in man's rule on earth. He turned away from every person who stood up for a war. Or the principle of one's land, or pride of ownership, or even personal rights. All of those motives ended up somehow in the arms of careless power. One was no worse and no better than the enemy. He believed only in the mothers sleeping against their children, the great sexuality of spirit in them, the sexuality of care, so the children would be confident and safe during the night.[135]

Ondaatje's poetic vision suggests a different way to approach the task of grieving or mourning the (necessary?) separation between the bodies of mothers and children. He constrasts the sexuality of care represented by the arc of the bodies of mothers sleeping against their sick children and holding their small hands, to 'man's rule on earth' and 'every person who stood up for a war...or even personal rights'. It seems to me that Ondaatje is showing us that there is a kind of quiet 'action' that exists outside the violent world of muscular humanitarian heroes. In intervention narratives, the suffering of children is mobilised as yet another prop for 'careless power', and to do something as a Western television spectator or aerial bombardier means to watch bombs falling from the position of a God-like observer. In contrast, both O'Kane and Ondaatje show us that doing something can also mean holding, soothing, touching, immediately creating a political response to suffering that is outside the relentless privileging of vision in postmodern war. The presence of mothers trying to endure their children's illness, holding their small hands, in order to help those children feel that the strange night of an emergency ward is a safe place seems to me to offer a rebuke to the adolescent fantasies of masculinity represented by those tales of heroism. This feminine imaginary is not a call to arms. It suggests a different mode of responding to the loss of our mother's bodies in a way that avoids re-enacting the violence of our exile from the motherland.

[135] *Ibid.*, p. 119.

Let me then end with this suggestion. I have attempted to explore the post-Cold War narrative of humanitarian intervention, in order to 'investigate where possibilities exist for reading it differently'.[136] The story of humanitarian intervention is one in which the bodies of massacred women, children and men are made to function as a call to arms. These texts ask us to create a certain kind of community in the name of humanity, and particularly in the name of those who have been slaughtered in places such as Rwanda and the former Yugoslavia. As Nathaniel Berman reminds us, international law's 'foundational celebrations always seem to take place in the shadow of some slaughterhouse'.[137] Yet the meanings of bodies are not fixed – the ways in which people mourn and remember their dead or honour their survivors exceed the capacity of international organisations and states to contain them. Here I have tried to make those bodies tell a different story, make a different set of demands of the international community in the name of justice.[138]

I opened this book with the terrible vision of small children being thrown by their parents over the barbed wire fences separating the sanctuary of the UN compound in Dili from the murderous militias terrorising the East Timorese. That image and other such images of suffering children and the parents determined and desperate to protect them haunt me when I think and write about humanitarian intervention. My being is so bound up with that of my young children, one of whom lies beside me purring in his sleep while I write, that I imagine the threat of their death like the fear of a wound to my own body. The resulting compassion I feel for these children and their parents seems to require of me my support for the use of violence in their name. Yet in Ondaatje's beautiful meditation on the responses of a doctor dealing with the casualties of civil war in Sri Lanka, there is an alternative reaction to the images of children suffering. I take from his poetic writing a point from which to start to think about another ethics of intervention, one not grounded quite so brutally in a politics of violence and exclusion.

---

[136] Judith Grbich, 'The Scent of Colonialism: *Mabo, Eucalyptus* and Excursions within Legal Racism' (2001) 15 *Australian Feminist Law Journal* 121 at 135.

[137] Nathaniel Berman, 'In the Wake of Empire' (1999) 14 *American University International Law Review* 1521 at 1524.

[138] For an exploration of the ways in which dead bodies are made to speak in the texts of law and literature, see Nina Puren and Peter Rush, 'Fatal (F)laws', *Law & Critique* (forthcoming).

If we attempt to build a body politic based on the recognition of difference and the desire to grant rights to the other, then a different set of demands is made of us in the name of humanitarian intervention. Our world order is currently built on a movement towards severe restrictions on asylum, strict controls over immigration, ruthless economic exploitation and an unjust international division of labour. It is these policies that should be put under challenge by an internationalism that is not founded upon fear of the other, but rather on an attempt to imagine new forms of universalism. Human rights may provide one basis for articulating the terms on which this new internationalism might be imagined. Yet this must be a version of human rights that is able to welcome rather than fear those 'curious guardians' at the margins who 'haunt what we start and get done' – the refugee, the mother cradling her child, the woman labouring in a reconstructed East Timor or Rwanda or Bosnia to produce the wealth of the industrialised world.[139] It is those figures who face us as a reminder of the demands of justice in an age dominated by internationalist narratives, whether of globalisation and harmonisation, or of high-tech wars on terror and for humanity. Perhaps then, while international lawyers should remain committed to the ideal that lies behind the notion of humanitarian intervention, what is required today is to put 'into question again...the very concept of the said ideal'.[140] To do so will reveal that measures other than increased military intervention are demanded of the international community in the name of humanitarian action in the post-Cold War era.

[139] On the curious guardians at the margins, see Gayatri Chakravorty Spivak, *A Critique of Postcolonial Reason: Toward a History of the Vanishing Present* (Cambridge, 1999), p. 175.
[140] Derrida, *Specters*, p. 87.

Bibliography

Abbott, Frederick, 'Remarks' (2000) 94 *American Society of International Law Proceedings* 219–20

Aditjondro, George, 'From Colony to Global Prize' (2000) 47 *Arena Magazine* 22–32

'Mapping the Political Terrain' (2000) 46 *Arena Magazine* 27–36

Agamben, Giorgio, *Means without End: Notes on Politics* (trans. Vincenzo Binetti and Cesare Casarino, Minneapolis, 2000)

Ahmad, Aijaz, 'The Politics of Literary Postcoloniality' (1995) 36 *Race and Class* 1–21

In Theory: Classes, Nations, Literatures (Oxford, 1992)

Aidwatch Briefing Note: the World Bank in East Timor, June 2001, http://www.aidwatch.org.au/timor/wb_et.html (accessed 20 February 2002)

Albright, Ambassador Madeleine K., 'International Law Approaches the Twenty-First Century: a US Perspective on Enforcement' (1995) 18 *Fordham Journal of International Law* 1595–1606

Alston, Philip, 'Reform of Treaty-Making Processes: Form over Substance?' in Philip Alston and Madelaine Chiam (eds.), *Treaty-Making and Australia: Globalisation versus Sovereignty?* (Canberra, 1995), pp. 1–26

'The Myopia of the Handmaidens: International Lawyers and Globalization' (1997) 8 *European Journal of International Law* 435–48

'The Security Council and Human Rights: Lessons to Be Learned from the Iraq–Kuwait Crisis and its Aftermath' (1992) 13 *Australian Year Book of International Law* 107–4

Althusser, Louis, *Lenin and Philosophy and Other Essays* (trans. Ben Brewster, 1971)

Alvarez, José E., 'Crimes of States/Crimes of Hate: Lessons from Rwanda' (1999) 24 *Yale Journal of International Law* 365–483

'Judging the Security Council' (1996) 90 *American Journal of International Law* 1–39

Amnesty International, *'Collateral Damage' or Unlawful Killings? Violations of the Laws of War by NATO during Operation Allied Force* (2000)

Anderson, Benedict, *Imagined Communities* (London, 1991)
  The Spectre of Comparisons: Nationalism, Southeast Asia and the World (London, 1998)
Anghie, Antony, 'Finding the Peripheries: Sovereignty and Colonialism in Nineteenth-Century International Law' (1999) 40 *Harvard International Law Journal* 1–80
  'Francisco de Vitoria and the Colonial Origins of International Law' (1996) 5 *Social and Legal Studies* 321–36
  'Time Present and Time Past: Globalization, International Financial Institutions, and the Third World' (2000) 32 *New York University Journal of International Law and Politics* 243–90
Annan, Kofi, 'Two Concepts of Sovereignty', *The Economist*, 18 September 1999, p. 49
Ashdown, Paddy, 'Collateral Costs in Fighting a New Court', *The New York Times on the Web*, 2 July 2002, http://www.nytimes.com/2002/07/ 02/opinion/ 02ASHD.html?todaysheadlines=&page want (accessed 3 July 2002)
Austin, John, *The Province of Jurisprudence Determined and the Uses of the Study of Jurisprudence* (London, 1954)
Beard, Jennifer, 'The Art of Development: Law and Ordering in the First World' (2002, unpublished doctoral thesis, copy on file with author)
Bellamy, Christopher, *Knights in White Armour: the New Art of War and Peace* (London, 1997)
Bello, Walden, 'Global Conspiracy or Capitalist Circus?', 'An All-American Show?', *Focus on Trade*, February 2000
Berger, John, *About Looking* (London, 1980)
Berman, Nathaniel, 'In the Wake of Empire' (1999) 14 *American University International Law Review* 1521–54
Bhabha, Homi K., *The Location of Culture* (London, 1994)
Blackburn, Robin, 'The Break-up of Yugoslavia' (1993) 45 *Labour Focus on Eastern Europe* 3–14
Blair, Tony, 'Doctrine of the International Community', Speech given to the Economic Club of Chicago, Chicago, 22 April 1999, http://www.fco.gov.uk/ news/speechtext.asp?2316 (accessed 2 May 2001)
  'Statement on the Suspension of NATO Air Strikes against Yugoslavia', London, 10 June 1999, http://www.fco.gov.uk/news/newstext.asp?2536 (accessed 2 May 2001)
Bloomfield, Lincoln P., 'Collective Security and US Interests' in Thomas G. Weiss (ed.), *Collective Security in a Changing World* (Boulder and London, 1993), pp. 3–18
Boose, Lynda, 'Techno-Muscularity and the "Boy Eternal": from the Quagmire to the Gulf' in Amy Kaplan and Donald E. Pease (eds.), *Cultures of United States Imperialism* (Durham and London, 1993), pp. 581–616
Boutros-Ghali, Boutros, *An Agenda for Peace* (New York, 1992)

Brada, Josef C., Hewett, Ed A. and Wolf, Thomas A. (eds), *Economic Adjustment and Reform in Eastern Europe and the Soviet Union* (Durham, 1988)

Brontë, Charlotte, *Jane Eyre* (New York, 1960)

Budhoo, D. L., *Enough Is Enough: Dear Mr Camdessus...Open Letter of Resignation to the Managing Director of the International Monetary Fund* (New York, 1990)

Bunce, Valerie, 'The Elusive Peace in the Former Yugoslavia' (1995) 28 *Cornell International Law Journal* 709–18

Bush, Laura, First Lady, Radio Address to the Nation, *The Taliban's War against Women*, 17 November 2001, http://www.state.gov/g/drl/ rls/rm/2001/6206.htm (accessed 27 February 2002)

Butler, Judith, *Bodies that Matter* (New York, 1993)

  Gender Trouble: Feminism and the Subversion of Identity (New York, 1990)

Byers, Michael, *Custom, Power and the Power of Rules: International Relations and Customary International Law* (Cambridge, 1999)

Cady, Jean-Christian, 'Building the New State of East Timor', lecture given at the Centre for International and Public Law, Australian National University, 18 May 2000

Campbell, David, 'Violence, Justice and Identity in the Bosnia Conflict' in Jenny Edkins, Nalim Persram and Véronique Pin-Fat (eds.), *Sovereignty and Subjectivity* (Boulder, 1999), pp. 21–37

  Writing Security: United States Foreign Policy and the Politics of Identity (Durham, 1992)

Caron, David D., 'Iraq and the Force of Law: Why Give a Shield of Immunity?' (1991) 85 *American Journal of International Law* 89–92

Cassese, Antonio, 'Ex Iniuria Ius Oritur: Are We Moving towards International Legitimation of Forcible Humanitarian Countermeasures in the World Community?' (1999) 10 *European Journal of International Law* 23–30

Catholic Institute for International Relations/International Platform of Jurists for East Timor, *International Law and the Question of East Timor* (London, 1995)

Chamberlain, Greg, 'Up by the Roots: Haitian History through 1987' in North American Congress on Latin America, *Haiti: Dangerous Crossroads* (Boston, 1995), pp. 13–28

Chandler, David, 'Bosnia: Prototype of a NATO Protectorate' in Tariq Ali (ed.), *Masters of the Universe? NATO's Balkan Crusade* (London, 2000), pp. 271–84

  Bosnia: Faking Democracy after Dayton (2nd edn, London, 2000)

  'The Road to Military Humanitarianism: How the Human Rights NGOs Shaped the New Humanitarian Agenda' (2001) 23 *Human Rights Quarterly* 678–700

Charlesworth, Hilary, 'Cries and Whispers: Responses to Feminist Scholarship in International Law' (1996) 65 *Nordic Journal of International Law* 557

  'Feminist Methods in International Law' (1999) 93 *American Journal of International Law* 379–94

Charlesworth, Hilary and Chinkin, Christine, *The Boundaries of International Law: a Feminist Analysis* (Manchester, 2000)

Charlesworth, Hilary and Wood, Mary, ' "Mainstreaming Gender" in International Peace and Security: the Case of East Timor' (2001) 26 *Yale Journal of International Law* 313–17

Charney, Jonathon I., 'Anticipatory Humanitarian Intervention in Kosovo' (1999) 93 *American Journal of International Law* 834–41

Chayes, Abram, 'The Use of Force in the Persian Gulf' in Lori F. Damrosch and David J. Scheffer (eds.), *Law and Force in the New International Order* (Boulder, 1991), p. 4

Chesterman, Simon, 'Law, Subject and Subjectivity in International Relations: International Law and the Postcolony' (1996) 20 *Melbourne University Law Review* 979–1022

'Never Again...and Again: Law, Order, and the Gender of War Crimes in Bosnia and beyond' (1997) 22 *Yale Journal of International Law* 299

Just War or Just Peace? Humanitarian Intervention and International Law (Oxford, 2001)

Chinkin, Christine M., 'Kosovo: a "Good" or "Bad" War?' (1999) 93 *American Journal of International Law* 841–7

Chinkin, Christine and Wright, Shelley, 'The Hunger Trap: Women, Food and Self-Determination' (1993) 14 *Michigan Journal of International Law* 262

Chomsky, Noam, *World Orders, Old and New* (London, 1994)

Chossudovsky, Michel, 'Dismantling Former Yugoslavia; Recolonising Bosnia', *Economic and Political Weekly*, 2 March 1996, 521

The Globalisation of Poverty: Impacts of IMF and World Bank Reforms (Penang, 1997)

Chow, Rey, 'Violence in the Other Country: China as Crisis, Spectacle and Woman' in Chandra Talpade Mohanty, Ann Russo and Lourdes Torres (eds.), *Third World Women and the Politics of Feminism* (Bloomington, 1991), pp. 81–100

Clark, Michael P., 'The Work of War after the Age of Mechanical Reproduction' in Michael Bibby, *The Vietnam War and Postmodernity* (Amherst, 1999), pp. 17–47

Cline, William R., *International Debt: Systemic Risk and Policy Response* (Washington, 1984)

Cohn, Carol, 'Sex and Death in the Rational World of Defense Intellectuals' (1987) 12 *Signs* 687–718

Cover, Robert M., 'Foreword: Nomos and Narrative' (1983) 97 *Harvard Law Review* 4–68

'Violence and the Word' in Martha Minow, Michael Ryan and Austin Sarat (eds.), *Narrative, Violence, and the Law: the Essays of Robert Cover* (Ann Arbor, 1992), pp. 203–38

Crawford, James, 'The Right of Self-Determination in International Law: its Development and Future' in Philip Alston (ed.), *Peoples' Rights* (Oxford, 2001), pp. 7–67

D'Amato, Anthony, 'Book Review: Rebecca Cook (ed.), *Human Rights of Women: National and International Perspectives*' (1995) 89 *American Journal of International Law* 840–4

  'Is International Law Really "Law"?' (1985) 79 *Northwestern University Law Review* 1293–1314

Davies, Margaret, 'The Heterosexual Economy' (1995) 5 *Australian Feminist Law Journal* 27–46

Deleuze, Gilles and Guattari, Félix, *Anti-Oedipus: Capitalism and Schizophrenia*, (trans. Robert Hurley, Mark Seem and Helen R. Lane, Minneapolis, 1983)

Denton, Jenny, 'Whose Agendas? East Timor Suffers under Weight of World Plans', *Canberra Times*, 14 April 2001

Derrida, Jacques, 'Force of Law: the "Mystical Foundation of Authority"' in Drucilla Cornell, Michel Rosenfeld and David Gray Carlson (eds.), *Deconstruction and the Possibility of Justice* (London, 1992), pp. 3–67

  Specters of Marx: the State of the Debt, the Work of Mourning, and the New International (New York, 1992)

Dillon, Michael, 'The Sovereign and the Stranger' in Jenny Edkins, Nalini Persram and Véronique Pin-Fat, *Sovereignty and Subjectivity* (Boulder, 1999), pp. 117–40.

Dirlik, Arif, 'The Postcolonial Aura: Third World Criticism in the Age of Global Capitalism' (1994) 20 *Critical Inquiry* 328

Douzinas, Costas, *The End of Human Rights* (Oxford, 2000)

Drahos, Peter, 'Global Property Rights in Information: the story of TRIPS at the GATT' (1995) *Prometheus* 6–19

Drakulic, Slavenka, 'Bosnia, or What Europe Means to Us' in Marjorie Agosin, *A Map of Hope: Women's Writing on Human Rights* (London, 1999), pp. 223–9

Drew, Catriona, 'The East Timor Story: International Law on Trial' (2001) 12 *European Journal of International Law* 651–84

Duncanson, Ian, 'Scripting Empire: the "Englishman" and Playing for Safety in Law and History' (2000) 24 *Melbourne University Law Review* 952–64

Dupuy, Alex, *Haiti in the New World Order* (Colorado, 1997)

Eagleton, Terry, 'Ideology and its Vicissitudes in Western Marxism' in Slavoj Zizek (ed.), *Mapping Ideology* (London, 1994), pp. 179–226

Eckstaedt, Anita, 'Two Complementary Cases of Identification Involving "Third Reich" Fathers' (1986) 67 *International Journal of Psycho-Analysis* 317–27

Elliott, Anthony, 'Symptoms of Globalization: or, Mapping Reflexivity in the Postmodern Age' in Joseph Camilleri, Anthony Jarvis and Albert Paolini (eds.), *The State in Transition: Reimagining Political Space* (Boulder, 1995), pp. 157–72

Enloe, Cynthia, *The Morning after: Sexual Politics at the End of the Cold War* (Berkeley, 1993)

Escobar, Arturo, *Encountering Development: the Making and Unmaking of the Third World* (Princeton, 1995)

Falk, Richard, 'The Haiti Intervention: a Dangerous World Order Precedent for the United Nations' (1995) 36 *Harvard International Law Journal* 341–58

Fanon, Frantz, *Black Skin, White Masks* (New York, 1967)

Farer, Tom J., 'Intervention in Unnatural Humanitarian Emergencies: Lessons of the First Phase' (1996) 18 *Human Rights Quarterly* 1–22

'A Paradigm of Legitimate Intervention' in Lori Fisler Damrosch, *Enforcing Restraint: Collective Intervention in Internal Conflicts* (New York, 1993), p. 316

Fenrick, W. J., 'Targeting and Proportionality during the NATO Bombing Campaign against Yugoslavia' (2001) 12 *European Journal of International Law* 489–502

Fitzpatrick, Daniel, 'Land Claims in East Timor: a Preliminary Assessment' (2001) 3 *Australian Journal of Asian Law* 135–66

Foucault, Michel, 'Two Lectures' in Colin Gordon (ed.), *Power-Knowledge: Selected Interviews and Other Writings 1972–1977* (trans. Colin Gordon, Leo Marshall, John Mepham and Kate Soper, New York, 1980), pp. 78–108

The History of Sexuality: an Introduction (trans. Robert Hurley, 3 vols., London, 1980), vol. I

Franck, Thomas M., 'Terrorism and the Right of Self-Defense' (2001) 95 *American Journal of International Law* 839–43

'The Emerging Right to Democratic Governance' (1992) 86 *American Journal of International Law* 46–91

Freud, Sigmund, ' "A Child Is Being Beaten": a Contribution to the Study of the Origin of Sexual Perversions' in *The Standard Edition of the Complete Psychological Works of Sigmund Freud* (trans. James Strachey, Anna Freud, Alix Strachey and Alan Tyson, 24 vols., London, 1955), vol. XVII, pp. 179–204

'Civilization and its Discontents' in James Strachey (ed.), *The Standard Edition of the Complete Psychological Works of Sigmund Freud*, Volume XXI (London, 1961), pp. 64–145

'Fetishism' in James Strachey (ed.), *The Standard Edition of the Complete Psychological Works of Sigmund Freud*, Volume XXI (London, 1961), pp. 152–7

Frow, John, 'Information as Gift and Commodity' (1996) Sept/Oct *New Left Review* 89–108

Fuss, Diana, *Identification Papers* (New York, 1995)

Gandhi, Leela, *Postcolonial Theory: a Critical Introduction* (St Leonards, 1998)

'The Dialectics of Globalisation' in Christopher Palmer and Iain Topliss (eds.), *Globalising Australia* (Melbourne, 2000), pp. 133–9

Gardam, Judith Gail, 'Proportionality and Force in International Law' (1993) 87 *American Journal of International Law* 391–413

Gatens, Moira, *Imaginary Bodies: Ethics, Power and Corporeality* (London, 1996)

Gathii, James Thuo, 'Neoliberalism, Colonialism and International Governance: Decentering the International Law of Governmental Legitimacy' (2000) 98 *Michigan Law Review* 1996–2055

Gavlak, Dale, 'Still Suffering Nonsuffrage in "Liberated" Kuwait' 3 *Ms.* 14

George, Jim, 'Quo Vadis Australia? Framing the Defence and Security Debate beyond the Cold War' in Graeme Cheeseman and Robert Bruce (eds.), *Discourses of Danger & Dread Frontiers: Australian Defence and Security Thinking after the Cold War* (St Leonards, 1996), pp. 10–48

Gerson, Allan, 'Peace Building: the Private Sector's Role' (2001) 95 *American Journal of International Law* 102–19

Gibson-Graham, J. K., *The End of Capitalism (As We Knew It): a Feminist Critique of Political Economy* (Cambridge, 1996)

Giddens, Anthony, *Runaway World: How Globalisation Is Reshaping our Lives* (London, 1999)

Glennon, Michael J., 'The New Interventionism: the Search for a Just International Law' (1999) 78 *Foreign Affairs* 2–7

Gordenker, Leon and Weiss, Thomas G., 'The Collective Security Idea and Changing World Politics' in Thomas G. Weiss (ed.), *Collective Security in a Changing World* (Boulder and London, 1993)

Gourevitch, Philip, *We Wish to Inform You that Tomorrow We Will Be Killed with our Families* (London, 1999)

Gowan, Peter, 'Neo-Liberal Theory and Practice for Eastern Europe' (1995) 213 *New Left Review* 3–60

'The NATO Powers and the Balkan Tragedy' (1999) 234 *New Left Review* 83–105

Grbich, Judith, 'Taxation Narratives of Economic Gain: Reading Bodies Transgressively' (1997) 5 *Feminist Legal Studies* 131–7

'The Body in Legal Theory' in Martha Fineman and Nancy Thomadsen (eds.), *At the Boundaries of Law: Feminism and Legal Theory* (New York, 1991), pp. 61–76

'The Scent of Colonialism: *Mabo, Eucalyptus* and Excursions within Legal Racism' (2001) 15 *Australian Feminist Law Journal* 121–48

Griffin, Susan, *A Chorus of Stones: the Private Life of War* (New York, 1992)

Grosz, Elizabeth, *Jacques Lacan: a Feminist Introduction* (Sydney, 1990)

Guest, Krysti Justine, 'Exploitation under Erasure: Economic, Social and Cultural Rights Engage Economic Globalisation' (1997) 19 *Adelaide Law Review* 73–93

Halperin, Morton H. and Scheffer, David J. with Small, Patricia L., *Self-Determination in the New World Order* (Washington, 1992)

Haraway, Donna J., *Modest_Witness@Second_Millenium* (New York, 1997)

Primate Visions: Gender, Race, and Nature in the World of Modern Science (New York, 1989)

Hathaway, James C., 'The Single Superpower and the Future of International Law' (2000) 94 *American Society of International Law Proceedings* 67–9

Henkin, Louis, 'Kosovo and the Law of "Humanitarian Intervention"' (1999) 93 *American Journal of International Law* 824–8

Hippler, Jochen, 'Democratisation of the Third World after the End of the Cold War' in Jochen Hippler (ed.), *The Democratisation of Disempowerment: the Problem of Democracy in the Third World* (London, 1995), pp. 1–31

Howland, Todd, 'Mirage, Magic, or Mixed Bag? The United Nations High Commissioner for Human Rights' Field Operation in Rwanda' (1999) 21 *Human Rights Quarterly* 1–55

Howse, Robert, 'From Politics to Technocracy – and Back Again: the Fate of the Multilateral Trading Regime' (2002) 96 *American Journal of International Law* 94–117

Human Rights Watch, *Civilian Deaths in the NATO Air Campaign* (2000) *World Report 2000*

Hyland, Tom and Murdoch, Lindsay, 'The Future Begins Here', *The Age*, 18 May 2002, Insight, p. 3

Ignatieff, Michael, 'Is the Human Rights Era Ending?', *The New York Times*, 5 February 2002

Virtual War: Kosovo and beyond (London, 2001)

IMF, Donors' Meeting on East Timor, Staff Statement by Stephen Schwartz, Deputy Division Chief, IMF Asia and Pacific Department, Dili, 14–15 May 2002, http://www.imf.org/external/np/dm/2002/ 051402.htm (accessed 28 June 2002)

Donors' Meeting on East Timor, Statement by Stephen Schwartz, Deputy Division Chief, IMF Asia and Pacific Department, Oslo, 11–12 December 2001

Irigaray, Luce, *This Sex Which Is Not One* (trans. Catherine Porter, Ithaca, 1985)

Jeffords, Susan, *Hard Bodies: Hollywood Masculinity in the Reagan Era* (New Brunswick, 1994)

Jopson, Debra, Mann, Simon and Seccombe, Mike, 'Ministers Tell UN Lobbyists: Stop Meddling', *Sydney Morning Herald*, 21 July 2000

Kampelman, Max M., 'Foreword' in Lori Fisler Damrosch, *Enforcing Restraint: Collective Intervention in Internal Conflicts* (New York, 1993), p. vii

Kaplan, E. Ann, *Looking for the Other: Feminism, Film and the Imperial Gaze* (New York, 1997)

Kennedy, David, 'A New World Order: Yesterday, Today and Tomorrow' (1994) 4 *Transnational Law and Contemporary Problems* 329–75

'Images of Religion in International Legal Theory' in Mark Janis (ed.), *The Influence of Religion on the Development of International Law* (Dordrecht, 1991), p. 137

'Receiving the International: What's the Public/Private Distinction Got to Do with It?', paper presented at the New York University Institute for Law and Society, 3 March 1995

'Spring Break' (1985) 63 *Texas Law Review* 1377–1423

'The Disciplines of International Law and Policy' (1999) 12 *Leiden Journal of International Law* 9

'The International Style in Postwar Law and Policy' (1994) 1 *Utah Law Review* 7–103

'When Renewal Repeats: Thinking against the Box' (2000) 32 *New York University Journal of International Law and Policy* 335–500

Kennedy, Roseanne, 'Global Mourning, Local Politics' in Re:Public (ed.), *Planet Diana: Cultural Studies and Global Mourning* (Nepean, 1997), pp. 49–53

Knightley, Philip, 'Fighting Dirty', *Guardian Weekly*, March 30–April 5, 2000, p. 23

Korhonen, Outi, *International Law Situated: an Analysis of the Lawyer's Stance towards Culture, History and Community* (The Hague, 2000)

Koskenniemi, Martti, 'National Self-Determination Today: Problems of Legal Theory and Practice' (1994) 43 *International and Comparative Law Quarterly* 241–69

'The Police in the Temple. Order, Justice and the United Nations: a Dialectical View' (1995) 6 *European Journal of International Law* 325–48

From Apology to Utopia: the Structure of International Legal Argument (Helsinki, 1989)

La'o Hamutuk, 'LH Editorial: Charity or Justice?', 1(2) *The La'o Hamutuk Bulletin*, July 2000, http://www.etan.org/lh/bulletin02.html (accessed 20 February 2002)

'The International Monetary Fund in East Timor', 2(3) *The La'o Hamutuk Bulletin*, June 2001, http://www.etan.org/lh/bulletinv2n3.html (accessed 20 February 2002)

'The World Bank in East Timor', 1(4) *The La'o Hamutuk Bulletin*, December 2000, http://www.etan.org/lh/bulletin04.html (accessed 20 February 2002)

Lacan, Jacque, *Ecrits: a Selection* (trans. Alan Sheridan, London, 1977)

Laursen, Andreas, 'NATO, the War over Kosovo, and the ICTY Investigation' (2002) 17 *American University International Law Review* 765–814

Lawrence, Thomas, *The Principles of International Law* (London, 1895)

Lindqvist, Sven, *A History of Bombing* (London, 2001)

Lobel, Jules, 'The Benefits of Legal Restraint' (2000) 94 *American Society of International Law Proceedings* 304–6

Locke, John, *Second Treatise of Government* (Cambridge, 1970)

Macaulay, Thomas Babington, 'Speeches in the House of Commons, dated 2 February, 1835' in G. W. Young (ed.), *Speeches* (Oxford, 1935), pp. 153–4

MacNeil, William, 'Law's *Corpus Delicti*: the Fantasmatic Body of Rights Discourse' (1998) 9 *Law and Critique* 37–57

Malcolm, Noel, *Bosnia: a Short History* (London, 1996)

Mandel, Michael, 'Politics and Human Rights in International Criminal Law: Our Case against NATO and the Lessons to Be Learned from it' (2001) 25 *Fordham International Law Journal* 95–128

Marx, Karl, 'On the Jewish Question' in Jeremy Waldron (ed.), *Nonsense upon Stilts: Bentham, Burke and Marx on the Rights of Man* (London, 1987)

Matheson, Michael J., 'Justification for the NATO Air Campaign in Kosovo' (2000) 94 *American Society of International Law Proceedings* 301

McClintock, Anne, *Imperial Leather: Race, Gender and Sexuality in the Colonial Conquest* (New York, 1995)

Melvern, L. R., *A People Betrayed: the Role of the West in Rwanda's Genocide* (London, 2000)

Metzl, Jamie Frederic, 'Rwandan Genocide and the International Law of Radio Jamming' (1997) 91 *American Journal of International Law* 628–51

Middle East Watch, *Needless Deaths in the Gulf War: Civilian Casualties during the Air Campaign and Violations of the Laws of War* (New York, 1991)

Mikesell, Raymond F., 'Appraising IMF Conditionality: Too Loose, Too Tight, Or Just Right?' in John Williamson (ed.), *IMF Conditionality* (Washington, 1983), pp. 47–62

Milivojevic, Marko, *The Debt Rescheduling Process* (London, 1985)

Minear, Larry and Guillot, Philippe, *Soldiers to the Rescue: Humanitarian Lessons from Rwanda* (Paris, 1996)

Minh-ha, Trinh T., *When the Moon Waxes Red: Representation, Gender and Cultural Politics* (New York, 1991)

Moore, Mike, Statement to the 11th International Military Chiefs of Chaplains Conference, 9 February 2000, reprinted at http://www.wto.org/wto/speeches/mm22.htm, accessed 1 April 2000

Morrison, Toni, *Playing in the Dark: Whiteness and the Literary Imagination* (London, 1992)

Mulvey, Laura, *Fetishism and Curiosity* (London, 1996)
Visual and Other Pleasures (Bloomington, 1989)

Murphy, Sean D., 'The Security Council, Legitimacy, and the Concept of Collective Security after the Cold War (1994) 32 *Columbia Journal of Transnational Law* 201–88

Nanda, Ved P., Muther, Jr, Thomas F., and Eckert, Amy E., 'Tragedies in Somalia, Yugoslavia, Haiti, Rwanda and Liberia – Revisiting the Validity of Humanitarian Intervention under International Law – Part II' (1998) 26 *Denver Journal of International Law and Policy* 827–70

Norris, Margot, 'Military Censorship and the Body Count in the Persian Gulf War' (1991) *Cultural Critique* 223–45

Nowrot, Karsten and Schabacker, Emily W., 'The Use of Force to Restore Democracy: International Legal Implications of the ECOWAS Intervention in Sierra Leone' (1998) 14 *American University International Law Review* 321–412

O'Kane, Maggie, 'I Feel the Madness More', *The Guardian Weekly*, 2–8 March 2000, p. 21

Oloka-Onyango, J., 'Heretical Reflections on the Right to Self-Determination: Prospects and Problems for a Democratic Global Future in the New Millennium' (1999) 15 *American University International Law Review* 151–208

Ondaatje, Michael, *Anil's Ghost* (London, 2001)

Orford, Anne, 'Contesting Globalization: a Feminist Perspective on the Future of Human Rights' (1998) 8 *Transnational Law and Contemporary Problems* 171–98

    'Globalisation and the Right to Development' in Philip Alston (ed.), *Peoples' Rights* (Oxford, 2001), pp. 127–84

    'Locating the International: Military and Monetary Interventions after the Cold War' (1997) 38 *Harvard International Law Journal* 443–85

    'Muscular Humanitarianism: Reading the Narratives of the New Interventionism' (1999) 10 *European Journal of International Law* 679–711

    'The Politics of Collective Security' (1996) 17 *Michigan Journal of International Law* 373–411

    'The Subject of Globalization: Economics, Identity and Human Rights' (2000) 94 *American Society of International Law Proceedings* 146–8

    'The Uses of Sovereignty in the New Imperial Order' (1996) 6 *Australian Feminist Law Journal* 63–86

Orford, Anne and Beard, Jennifer, 'Making the State Safe for the Market: the World Bank's *World Development Report 1997*' (1998) 22 *Melbourne University Law Review* 196–216

Otto, Dianne, 'Everything Is Dangerous: Some Post-Structural Tools for Rethinking the Universal Knowledge Claims of Human Rights Law' (1999) 5 *Australian Journal of Human Rights* 17–47

Peacock, Dorinda Lea, ' "It Happened and It Can Happen Again": the International Response to Genocide in Rwanda' (1997) 22 *North Carolina Journal of International Law and Commercial Regulation* 899–941

Persram, Nalini, 'Coda: Sovereignty, Subjectivity, Strategy' in Jenny Edkins, Nalim Persram and Véronique Pin-Fat (eds.), *Sovereignty and Subjectivity* (Boulder, 1999), pp. 163–75

Petersmann, Ernst-Ulrich, 'The WTO Constitution and Human Rights' (2000) 3 *Journal of International Economic Law* 19–25

Peterson, V. Spike, 'The Politics of Identity and Gendered Nationalism' in Laura Neack, Patrick J. Haney and Jeanne A. K. Hey (eds.), *Foreign Policy Analysis in Its Second Generation: Continuity and Change* (New Jersey, 1995), pp. 167–86

Petras, J. and Vieux, S., 'Bosnia and the Revival of US Hegemony' (1996) 218 *New Left Review* 3–25

Pile, Steve, 'Freud, Dreams and Imaginative Geographies' in Anthony Elliott (ed.), *Freud 2000* (Victoria, 1998), pp. 204–34

Powell, Secretary Colin L., *Afghan Women*, Remarks at the Eisenhower Executive
    Office Building, Washington, 19 November 2001, http://www.state.gov/
    secretary/rm/2001/6229.htm (accessed 27 February 2002)
Power, Samantha, 'Bystanders to Genocide: Why the United States Let the
    Rwandan Tragedy Happen', *The Atlantic Online*, September 2001,
    http://www.theatlantic.com/issues/2001/09/power.htm, accessed 4 April 2002
Provost, René, 'Starvation as a Weapon: Legal Implications of the United
    Nations Food Blockade against Iraq and Kuwait' (1992) 30 *Columbia Journal
    of Transnational Law* 577–639
Prunier, Gérard, *The Rwanda Crisis: History of a Genocide* (New York, 1995)
Puren, Nina and Rush, Peter, 'Fatal (F)laws', *Law & Critique* (forthcoming)
Puren, Nina and Young, Alison, 'Signifying Justice: Law, Culture and the
    Questions of Feminism' (1999) 13 *Australian Feminist Law Journal* 3–12
Race, Kane, 'The Beast with Two Backs: Bodies/Selves/Integrity' (1997) 9
    Australian Feminist Law Journal 24–44
Reisman, W. Michael, 'In Defense of World Public Order' (2001) 95 *American
    Journal of International Law* 833–35
    'Some Lessons from Iraq: International Law and Democratic Politics' (1991) 16
    Yale Journal of International Law 203–15
    'The Constitutional Crisis in the United Nations' (1993) 87 *American Journal of
    International Law* 83–100
Rhodes-Little, Andrea, 'Review Essay: Who Do We Think "We" Are' (1997) 8
    Australian Feminist Law Journal 149–61
Rhys, Jean, *Wide Sargasso Sea* (London, 1968)
Richardson III, Henry J., 'The Gulf Crisis and African-American Interests under
    International Law' (1993) 87 *American Journal of International Law* 42–82
Riles, Annelise, 'Global Designs: the Aesthetics of International Legal Practice'
    (1993) 93 *American Society of International Law Proceedings* 28–34
Robertson, Geoffrey, *Crimes against Humanity: The Struggle for Global Justice*
    (Ringwood, 1999)
Rogin, Michael, ' "Make My Day!": Spectacle as Amnesia in Imperial Politics
    [and] the Sequel' in Amy Kaplan and Donald E. Pease (eds.), *Cultures of
    United States Imperialism* (1993), p. 499
Rose, Jacqueline, *States of Fantasy* (Oxford, 1996)
    The Haunting of Sylvia Plath (London, 1992)
Ross, Kristin, *Fast Cars, Clean Bodies: Decolonization and the Reordering of French
    Culture* (Cambridge, 1996)
Roth, Brad R., 'Governmental Illegitimacy and Neocolonialism: Response to
    Review by James Thuo Gathii' (2000) 98 *Michigan Law Review* 2056–71
Ruffert, Matthias, 'The Administration of Kosovo and East Timor by the
    International Community' (2001) 50 *International and Comparative Law
    Quarterly* 613–31
Sachs, Jeffrey, 'What Is to Be done?' *The Economist*, 13 January 1990, p. 19

Said, Edward W., *Culture and Imperialism* (London, 1993)
  Orientalism (London, 1978)
  'Protecting the Kosovars?' (1999) 234 *New Left Review* 73–5
Salecl, Renata, *The Spoils of Freedom: Psychoanalysis and Feminism after the Fall of Socialism* (London, 1994)
Samary, Catherine, 'Behind the Breakup of Yugoslavia' (1993) 45 *Labour Focus on Eastern Europe* 27–30
Santner, Eric L., *My Own Private Germany: Daniel Paul Schreber's Secret History of Modernity* (Princeton, 1996)
Sartre, Jean-Paul, *Existentialism and Humanism* (trans. Philip Mairet, New York, 1948)
Scarry, Elaine, *The Body in Pain: the Making and Unmaking of the World* (New York, 1985)
Schachter, Oscar, 'United Nations Law in the Gulf Conflict' (1991) 85 *American Journal of International Law* 452–73
  International Law in Theory and Practice (Dordrecht, 1991)
Schroeder, Jeanne Lorraine, 'Juno Moneta: on the Erotics of the Marketplace' (1997) 54 *Washington and Lee Law Review* 995
Sedgwick, Eve, *Tendencies* (Durham, 1993)
Sforza, Julie M., 'The Timor Gap Dispute: the Validity of the Timor Gap Treaty, Self-Determination, and Decolonization' (1999) 22 *Suffolk Transnational Law Review* 481–528
Shiva, Vandana, 'The Greening of the Global Reach' in Wolfgang Sachs (ed.), *Global Ecology: a New Arena of Political Conflict* (London, 1993), pp. 149–56
Silverman, Kaja, *The Subject of Semiotics* (New York, 1983)
Simma, Bruno, 'NATO, the UN and the Use of Force: Legal Aspects' (1999) 10 *European Journal of International Law* 1–22
Simma, Bruno and Paulus, Andreas L., 'The Responsibility of Individuals for Human Rights Abuses in Internal Conflicts: a Positivist View' (1999) 93 *American Journal of International Law* 302–16
Simpson, Gerry, 'The Diffusion of Sovereignty: Self-Determination in the Post-Colonial Age' (1996) 32 *Stanford Journal of International Law* 255–86
  'Out of Law' in *International Legal Challenges for the Twenty-First Century: Proceedings of a Joint Meeting of the Australian and New Zealand Society of International Law and the American Society of International Law* (Canberra, 2000)
  'The Situation on the International Legal Theory Front: the Power of Rules and the Rule of Power' (2000) 11 *European Journal of International Law* 439–64
Sinclair, Scott and Grieshaber-Otto, Jim, *Facing the Facts: a Guide to the GATS Debate* (Canada, 2002)
Spivak, Gayatri Chakravorty, *A Critique of Postcolonial Reason: toward a History of the Vanishing Present* (Cambridge, 1999)
  In Other Worlds (New York, 1988)

The Postcolonial Critic: Interviews, Strategies, Dialogues (ed. Sarah Harasym, New York, 1990)

Stanič, Ana, 'Financial Aspects of State Succession: the Case of Yugoslavia' (2001) 12 *European Journal of International Law* 751–79

Steele, Jonathon, 'Aid Workers Protest at Nato's Role', *Guardian Weekly*, 6 June 1999, p. 23

Steinberg, James B., 'International Involvement in the Yugoslavia Conflict' in Lori Fisler Damrosch, *Enforcing Restraint: Collective Intervention in Internal Conflicts* (New York, 1993), p. 27

Stopford, Michael, 'Locating the Balance: the United Nations and the New World Disorder' (1994) 34 *Virginia Journal of International Law* 685–99

Talpade Mohanty, Chandra, 'Under Western Eyes: Feminist Scholarship and Colonial Discourses' in Chandra Talpade Mohanty, Ann Russo and Lourdes Torres (eds.), *Third World Women and the Politics of Feminism* (Bloomington, 1991), pp. 51–80

Taylor, Diana, 'Spectacular Bodies: Gender, Terror and Argentina's "Dirty War"' in Miriam Cooke and Angela Woollacott (eds.), *Gendering War Talk* (Princeton, 1993), pp. 20–40

Tesón, Fernando R., 'Collective Humanitarian Intervention' (1996) 17 *Michigan Journal of International Law* 323–71

Tharoor, Shashi, 'The Changing Face of Peace-Keeping and Peace-Enforcement' (1995) 19 *Fordham International Law Journal* 408–26

Threadgold, Terry, 'Book Review: *Law and Literature: Revised and Enlarged Edition* by Richard Posner' (1999) 23 *Melbourne University Law Review* 830–43

'Introduction' in Terry Threadgold and Anne Cranny-Francis (eds.), *Feminine, Masculine and Representation* (Sydney, 1990), pp. 1–35

Tickner, J. Ann, 'Inadequate Providers? A Gendered Analysis of States and Security' in Joseph A. Camilleri, Anthony P. Jarvis and Albert J. Paolini (eds.), *The State in Transition: Reimagining Political Space* (Boulder, 1995), pp. 125–37

Trindade Neves de Camoes, Jorge, 'East Timor Today: Perspectives from the Grassroots', paper presented at a seminar on *UNAMET, INTERFET, UNTAET, International NGOs, World Bank, and 'Paraquedistas': Are They Helping or Obstructing the Nation-Building Process in East Timor?*, The Australian National University, 2 March 2000

Urquhart, Brian, 'Learning from the Gulf' in Mara R. Bustelo and Philip Alston (eds.), *Whose New World Order? What Role for the United Nations?* (Leichhardt, 1991), p. 11

US Department of State, *Report on the Taliban's War against Women*, 17 November 2001, http://www.state.gov/g/drl/rls/c4804.htm (accessed 27 February 2002)

Uvin, Peter, *Aiding Violence: the Development Enterprise in Rwanda* (Connecticut, 1998)

Weedon, Chris, *Feminist Practice and Poststructuralist Theory* (Cambridge, 1987)

Weiler, J. H. H., 'The Rule of Lawyers and the Ethos of Diplomats' (2001) 35 *Journal of World Trade* 191–207

'Balancing National Regulatory Sovereignty with the Discipline of Free Trade', The Sir Kenneth Bailey Memorial Lecture, University of Melbourne, 15 August 2001

Weiss, Thomas G., 'On the Brink of a New Era? Humanitarian Interventions, 1991–94' in Donald C. F. Daniel and Bradd C. Hayes (eds.), *Beyond Traditional Peacekeeping* (New York, 1995), pp. 3–19

Wensley, Penny, Ambassador and Permanent Representative of Australia to the United Nations, *Statement at the Open Meeting on Women and Peace and Security of the United Nations Security Council*, 24 October 2000, www.un.int/australia/Statements/PS_Statements.htm (accessed 23 August 2001)

Westlake, John, *Chapters on the Principles of International Law* (Cambridge, 1894)

Wilde, Ralph, 'From Bosnia to Kosovo and East Timor: the Changing Role of the United Nations in the Administration of Territory' (2000) 6 *ILSA Journal of International and Comparative Law* 467–71

Williams, Andrew, 'Economic Intervention by International Economic Organizations in Central and Eastern Europe: Will it Lead to More or Less "Security" for the Region?' in Pal Dunay, Gabor Kardos and Andrew J. Williams (eds.), *New Forms of Security, Views from Central, Eastern and Western Europe* (Aldershot, 1995), pp. 103–16

Williams, Patricia J., 'Law and Everyday Life' in Austin Sarat and Thomas R. Kearns (eds.), *Law in Everyday Life* (Ann Arbor, 1993), pp. 171–90

The Rooster's Egg: on the Persistence of Prejudice (Cambridge, 1995)

Woodward, Susan L., *Balkan Tragedy: Chaos and Dissolution after the Cold War* (Washington, 1995)

World Bank East Asia and Pacific Region, *Background Paper Prepared for the Information Meeting on East Timor*, 29 September 1999

World Bank Group, 'World Bank Freezes All New Loans to Indonesia', *Development News*, 23 September 1999.

World Bank, East Timor: Donors Applaud East Timor's National Development Plan, Dili, 15 May 2002, http://web.worldbank.org/WBSITE/EXTERNAL/NEWS/O,contentMDK:20045490~menuPK:34466~pagePK:34370~piPK:34424~theSitePK:4607,00.html (accessed 28 June 2002)

World Bank, Donors' Meeting on East Timor, Staff Statement by Stephen Schwartz, Deputy Division Chief, IMF Asia and Pacific Department, Dili, 14–15 May 2002, http://www.imf.org/external/np/dm/2002/051402.htm (accessed 28 June 2002)

Indonesia: Country Assistance Strategy – Progress Report, 16 February 1999

Report of the Joint Assessment Mission to East Timor, 8 December 1999

Wright, Shelley, 'The Horizon of Becoming: Culture, Gender and History after
    September 11' (2002) *Nordic Journal of International Law* (forthcoming)
    International Human Rights, Decolonisation and Globalisation: Becoming Human
    (London, 2001)
Young, Alison, *Femininity in Dissent* (London, 1990)
Žižek, Slavoj, *Tarrying with the Negative: Kant, Hegel and the Critique of Ideology*
    (Durham, 1993)

Index

Printed in the United Kingdom
by Lightning Source UK Ltd.
106498UKS00001B/58-84